Youth Activism in the Radical Right of Brazil and Germany

Beatriz Besen

Youth Activism in the Radical Right of Brazil and Germany

On the Thresholds of Politics

Springer

Beatriz Besen
Center for the Study of Violence (NEV/USP)
University of São Paulo
São Paulo, São Paulo, Brazil

ISBN 978-3-031-87634-9 ISBN 978-3-031-87635-6 (eBook)
https://doi.org/10.1007/978-3-031-87635-6

This Springer imprint is published by the registered company Springer Nature Switzerland AG
The registered company address is: Gewerbestrasse 11, 6330 Cham, Switzerland

I dedicate this book to the youth of the past, who, through their political activism and daily actions, forged a democratic horizon for Brazil and Germany.

To the youth of the present, who continue to believe in and fight for a world free from poverty.

And to the youth of the future, to whom I wish the necessary breath to (re)create forms of politics and cultivate hope in social justice.

Foreword

The rise of the far-right and the participation of young people in radical right movements in the global political scene, as well as the adherence of sectors of the Brazilian population to hate speech and authoritarian proposals, constitute a phenomenon that has demanded a deep and urgent analysis! Beatriz Besen's book is the result of original research work, which culminated in her doctoral thesis, defended in 2023, and which I had the privilege of supervising. *Youth Activism in the Radical Right of Brazil and Germany: On the Thresholds of Politics* invites us to a profound reflection on the trajectories, identities, and meanings of young people's political participation in radical right movements. With academic rigour and sensitivity, the author conducted a comparative study between Brazil and Germany and, with her expertise as a political psychologist, reconstructed the biographies, experiences, and identities of young activists from both countries. Her unprecedented and complex analysis challenges preconceived notions about these movements and has the merit of expanding the field of research in political psychology, treating this form of youth engagement as an experience of political participation. For decades, studies in the area predominantly focused on progressive movements, leaving a gap regarding the right-wing. In this sense, by analysing the phenomenon, the author paves the way for an increasingly relevant and current field, deepening the intersection between **political participation** and **activism in radical right movements**.

Throughout the book, we are provoked by questions such as: what psychopolitical factors lead young people to engage in right-wing movements? How are political identities constructed in the context of right-wing activism? What discourses, narratives, and practices mobilize right-wing activists? How are these discourses constructed and disseminated? What emotions and affects motivate participation in these movements? How does political socialization within families, schools, and peer groups influence adherence to right-wing ideologies?

These questions permeate the entire book of the researcher who, with her critical and rigorous perspective, meticulously analyses the discourses and power strategies that sustain these movements. Her analysis sheds light on the psychopolitical microfoundations of youth participation in radical right groups, significantly contributing to the understanding of social conservatism and its implications for democracy.

By combining biographical reconstruction with narrative analysis in thematic categories, the research allows for an unprecedented exploration of the complex dynamics that drive youth engagement in radical right movements. By reconstructing the biographies of young activists, identified through in-depth interviews, the author reveals the role of conservative discourses and neoliberalism in constructing the identities and political agendas of these young people. Her analysis shows that activists strategically use the discourses of social conservatism (traditional values, family, religion) and neoliberalism (free market, individualism, social justice as a means of coercion) to construct their ideas and political actions. These discourses are not merely adopted passively but are actively and intentionally used to achieve specific objectives, justifying and legitimizing their agendas in the public sphere.

Using an interdisciplinary and post-structuralist approach, the author analyses right-wing youth activism as an experience of "liminal participation". This innovative perspective allows for understanding how these young people navigate between practices and agendas interpreted as both democratic and anti-democratic. By participating in grassroots movements, organizing demonstrations, and studying politics, these young people demonstrate a commitment to civic participation. At the same time, their agendas often rely on discourses of hate, exclusion, and attacks on minorities, challenging the democratic pact through counter-publicity strategies. This ambivalence demonstrates the tensions present in contemporary political participation.

With this analysis, the author leads the reader to reflect on the systems of representation that sustain the discourses of young people, the discursive positions they occupy, and the ways they negotiate their identities. By highlighting the complexity and dynamics of these constructions, her approach significantly contributes to understanding the mobilization strategies and how hate discourses articulate with democratic practices, challenging traditional notions of political participation.

With this original and compelling study, Beatriz Besen stands out as an extraordinary researcher, whose work enriches the existing scientific literature. For its scientific and social relevance, her research was recognized with honourable mentions in prestigious awards (Dissertation Awards of the International Society of Political Psychology (ISPP) and the Outstanding Thesis Award of the University of São Paulo—13th Edition), demonstrating that the work represents an important contribution to the field of political psychology in Brazil and Latin America.

The book *Youth Activism in the Radical Right of Brazil and Germany: On the Thresholds of Politics* with a pleasant, accessible, and engaging language is not limited to the academic audience, but to all those interested in understanding the growing youth engagement in radical right-wing movements and its implications in the current political and social landscape. It is an invitation for new reflections, new research, and a more in-depth debate on the causes and consequences of political radicalism, strategies to combat the spread of hate and intolerance, and ways to strengthen democracy.

Graduate Program in Social Change
and Political Participation - School of Arts,
Sciences and Humanities
University of São Paulo
São Paulo, Brazil
November 2, 2024

Soraia Ansara

Foreword

It is with great pleasure that I introduce *Youth Activism in the Radical Right of Brazil and Germany: On the Thresholds of Politics,* an important new work by Beatriz Besen. This book offers an insightful and deeply nuanced analysis of youth engagement within Radical Right movements across two distinct sociopolitical contexts.

My first encounter with Beatriz was relatively recent, when her dissertation was submitted for the International Society of Political Psychology's (ISPP) dissertation award. Serving on the selection committee, I read her work with great interest. What struck me immediately was her ability to navigate a politically charged and deeply complex topic with both methodological precision and a critical sensitivity that brought out its full complexity. Her dissertation earned an honourable mention—an accolade that speaks to its considerable impact on Political Psychology and the broader social sciences. I believe this work will add greatly to Political Psychology as a field.

What makes Besen's work especially compelling is her dedication to a transnational perspective that transcends surface-level comparisons. Through extensive multi-year investigation in Brazil and Germany, she not only examines the sociopolitical dynamics of these nations but also delves into the individual lives of young activists. This dual focus brings to light the ways local histories, political structures, and cultural climates intersect to shape political identities. By doing so, her research challenges us to think beyond static or siloed understandings of political subjectivity. It underscores the critical importance of attending to the macro-level forces that shape individual trajectories, offering insights that are essential for anyone seeking to understand the complexities of youth political engagement today.

A particularly remarkable aspect of Besen's work is her ability to humanize a group that is often caricatured or vilified rather than reducing young Radical Right activists to one-dimensional ideological categories, she unpacks their narratives with care, revealing a spectrum of motivations, frustrations, and identities. Her use of a post-structuralist framework allows her to expose the underlying power structures and discursive practices that shape these individuals' political choices. For scholars of Political Psychology, this approach provides an invaluable model for studying political identities as fluid and multifaceted, rather than fixed or reductive.

The methodological and ethical rigor in Besen's work is equally impressive. During the ISPP selection process, I was particularly struck by her transparency in addressing her positionality and reflexivity. As a Brazilian researcher working across both her home country and Germany, she navigates these political and cultural landscapes with critical awareness of her own biases and influences. This reflexive approach not only enhances the integrity of her findings but also serves as an important reminder of the ethical responsibility researchers have when working with politically sensitive topics. Her commitment to reflexivity is especially relevant for Political Psychology, a field deeply engaged with the nuanced interplay of identity and ideology. Research in this area often grapples with the complexity of individuals' lived experiences and their alignment—or misalignment—with broader political structures. By critically examining her own positionality and the influences shaping her analysis, Besen exemplifies the kind of thoughtful, reflective approach necessary to navigate these intricacies. This reflexivity not only enhances the depth and reliability of her findings but also serves as a methodological touchstone for scholars working on politically sensitive or polarizing topics.

Besen's work sheds light on themes that resonate deeply within Radical Right movements, including the emphasis on family values, the construction of "the Other", and the role of neoliberal and conservative discourses in shaping youth identities. Her nuanced attention to how gender, race, and religion intersect within these narratives is particularly valuable. Furthermore, her exploration of the performative dimensions of political identity—especially in digital spaces—offers timely insights into the ways young people articulate and display their ideological commitments in today's interconnected world.

Possibly one of my favourite contributions of this book lies in its engagement with the concept of liminality. Besen uses this framework to explore the "in-between" spaces that young people occupy within Radical Right movements—spaces where belonging and exclusion, recognition, and marginalization coexist. This lens challenges binary understandings of political identity, such as right versus left or deviant versus normative, and instead allows for understanding the fluid and dynamic nature of political subjectivities. This perspective is invaluable for Political Psychology, as it highlights the conditions that shape political participation and the potential for ideological shifts, especially among youth navigating prolonged experiences of disillusionment or marginalization.

Finally, Besen's work makes an important call for creating more inclusive public spheres where young people can engage with their political identities in ways that foster dialogue rather than deepen division. Her focus on breaking down ideological polarization is both timely and essential. This vision aligns closely with the goals of Political Psychology: to understand and facilitate constructive political engagement in ways that are informed by empathy, nuance, and a commitment to inclusion.

This book is a testament to the power of rigorous and empathetic research to illuminate the complexities of youth political engagement within ideologically charged spaces. By bridging two distinct political contexts and adopting a transnational perspective, Besen provides a model for how we might approach questions of political identity and participation with both depth and care. For scholars, practitioners, and anyone invested in the future of democratic participation, this book offers not only a wealth of insights but also a hopeful reminder of the importance of understanding and engaging with the political lives of young people.

As you engage with this book, I invite you to approach it with curiosity and openness—reflect on its challenges, absorb its insights, and consider its implications for shaping a more inclusive and empathetic understanding of political identity and youth engagement. I hope you find the journey through its pages as thought-provoking and rewarding as I did, and that it inspires new perspectives and meaningful conversations.

School of Psychology and Neuroscience
University of St Andrews
St Andrews, Scotland
November 14, 2024

Yasemin Gülsüm Acar

Preface

In many of the works I have developed to date, Eduardo Galeano's "Celebration of Contradictions/2" has occupied a central place. Based on the understanding that "identity is not a museum piece, quietly in the showcase, but the always astonishing synthesis of our daily contradictions" (Galeano, 1995, p. 123), the writer sought to reconstruct the trajectory of Latin America's formation, revealing the coexistence of a marvellous and horrific reality. Johann Wolfgang von Goethe, positioned in what we now call the global North, also highlighted contradiction as inherent to the human being: "The spirit of contradiction and the desire for paradox are in all of us" (Goethe, 1811/2017, p. 421). According to theologian Rudolf Herrmann (1976), Goethe (1811/2017) was inspired by Gottfried Arnold's book (1688) *Unpartheyische Kirchen- und Ketzer-Historie*, translated as *The Impartial History of the Church and the Heretics*. The book questioned the idea that "heresies" consisted of errors, nonsense, or madness, arguing that it was precisely the heretics who promoted the search for truth within the Church. In a complex way for their time, Arnold and Goethe understood that contradictions were revealing and endowed with power, as they combated Manichaeism and the idea of a static world. Arnold was one of the first to denounce the creation of heresy as a form of control by religious authorities—a mechanism of power that said more about the institutions than about the supposed heretics.

Admitting and exploring contradiction is also a fundamental trait of some areas of social and human sciences with which I identify and with which I have engaged since my undergraduate studies. It was the openness and interest in contradictions and conflict that led me to the studies of Psychoanalysis, back in 2010, and that later led me to Critical Theory, memory studies, and finally, post-structuralism. Pursuing and analysing contradiction were the driving forces behind my return to academia after years of coordinating and analysing projects aimed at social development. Starting with this acknowledgment is a way to bring readers into the theoretical universe in which this book is inscribed, but also a desire to highlight my "South", that is, my orientation and positioning in the world. As a psychologist and situating my work within the field of Political Psychology, I deeply believe in interdisciplinarity, that is, in the dialogue between different disciplines, which will be present throughout the chapters. However, I share, in essence, with the human sciences, the perception that no research is neutral, that is, that our position in the world influences our choices, as well as the paths we choose during the research process. Thus, the structure of this book reflects the belief that scientific production is only shareable on the condition that everyone on board understands the paths taken and not just the results achieved.

In this sense, and returning to the point of origin, I would like to share that the investigation on which the book is based was born from the search for displacement from known places and a renewed curiosity—which, as Michel Foucault mentions, is one of the central methods of scientific research. It was still in 2019 that I reconnected with a question that had pursued me since the time I worked as a project coordinator in a favela in the city of São Paulo (2015-2017). How did young people, who initially did not engage or mention politics among their topics of interest, come to be involved in movements whose main agendas are conservative and persecute minority rights? Even in then, it was possible to observe that the media and specialized literature formed a consensus about the international dimension of the phenomenon of the far-right expansion, mainly due to the election, in Europe and the United States, of leaders aligned with these agendas. However, it was also possible to observe the existence of preconceptions and rigid and Manichaean conceptions about the activists of such movements, as well as regarding the voters of such candidates.

As I conducted a review of the literature in Brazil, I noticed that activism in this "new right"—a nickname given to such movements in the country—was excluded from studies of political participation, with rare exceptions. The new "activists"—who should under no circumstances be confused with militants—seemed to gain the position of heretics, with whom "one cannot talk". They were labelled in informal spaces as "crazy" or "ignorant", and in academic research, they were commonly investigated through theories that reinforced stigmatization.

By expanding the literature review outside Brazil, I noticed the existence of a research tradition that had been consolidating for 30 years in the European context and that, more recently, was gaining some uniformity through the use of the concept of "radical right". This designation had expanded through the studies of the political scientist Cas Mudde, which originally referred to an emerging "party family" in Europe from the 1980s. Mudde established a differentiation between the extreme right and the radical right. In relation to the extreme right, the radical right would be differentiated by its partial acceptance of democratic principles, such as popular sovereignty and majority rule, although it shares with the extreme right the denial of aspects of liberal democracy, such as constitutional protections for minorities (ethnic, political, religious), the separation of powers, and the rule of law.

The European study of radical right began in the 1990s and resulted in a vast amount of publications and research projects. Within this tradition, I was able to identify also a body of recent research that focused specifically on youth activism and sought to highlight the heterogeneity of young people attracted to or engaged in the radical right. Through new qualitative research methodologies, these researchers pointed to a diversity of emerging movements and actors that translated into a complex and porous mosaic of identifications. Breaking with the tradition of electoral behaviour analysis, there was an encouragement to use qualitative methods, such as interviews and ethnographic observation, to grasp the particularities, inserting such participation into the field of social movement studies.

Relating to this literature, I was able to reflect that the frequent exclusion of radical right activism in investigations about youth and their political participation reflected a neglected relationship between analytical and normative perspectives, which limited the possibility of visualizing the trajectories of young people, as well as identifying the meanings attributed to political participation. Thus, keeping youth as the centre, my doctoral research became a study of youth activism among young people in Brazil and Germany. Through a DAAD scholarship, I was able to spend two years in Germany, where I attended the research group on political participation of Prof. Dr. Andreas Walther at the Goethe University of Frankfurt and the research group of Prof. Dr. Hanna Schwander, linked to the Department of Political Sociology at Humboldt University of Berlin.

This book is, therefore, an invitation to expand knowledge about youth activism in the radical right from this comparative study between Brazil and Germany, which reflected on the metamorphoses of political identities and transformations in modes of subjectivation. The research was situated within a post-structuralist analytical framework, from which it is understood that identities are discursive formations resulting from systems of signification, which organize and hierarchize social representations. With reference to Michel Foucault's studies, it is considered that discourse involves not only written or spoken communication but also narratives, symbols, the manner of addressing topics, as well as claims about knowledge and truth. Furthermore, discourse defines the existence of certain realities, which are understood as "true", while also silencing other possible "systems of representation". This means considering that discourse actively constructs the world as we know it and offers subjective positions that become more or less appealing in light of different modes of subjectivation.

The research was also guided by the horizon of social change and, therefore, considers the socio-historical influences of Cornelius Castoriadis, post-colonial influences of Homi K. Bhabha and Stuart Hall, as well as Brazilian studies on life narrative conducted by Antônio Ciampa. Castoriadis, an author who was long ignored in the psychoanalytic field, proposes a project of autonomy concerning the collective subject, which is subjected to the forces of institutionalization but can find, in politics, experiences of creation and imagination. Bhabha emphasizes that the conditions of resistance lie in overcoming binaries; along with Hall, he discusses that the oppositions *West and the Rest* defined a rigid and static world, also reflecting the very conditions of knowledge production in the social sciences. Finally, Ciampa discusses the fluidity of identities, observing that the metamorphoses that occur at the biographical level reflect and allow projecting transformations at the social level. Together, these authors serve as inspiration for the reflections constructed in terms of horizons of resistance, providing consideration of the subjects' capacity for self-reflection, as well as the emergence of forces of resistance situated at the borderline field.

Therefore, inserted in this structural and post-structuralist analytical framework and inspired by the research traditions listed above, the book presents and analyses biographies and narratives of young activists from the Radical Right in Brazil and Germany, which were captured and analysed through "life narrative interviews"—as they are known in the Brazilian context—or "biographical interviews"—as introduced by the german sociologist Fritz Schütze. Through the reconstruction of engagement trajectories, as well as the deconstruction of narratives and creation of thematic categories, similarities and differences were identified in the discourses, identities, and meanings of young people's political participation, taking into account the particular contexts of the two countries.

The current book is structured as follows: the first chapter is an introduction, in which I present and historically situate the central theme of this book, namely, the engagement of young people in the "radical right" in Brazil and Germany. The second chapter presents the phenomenon of the expansion of radical right in Brazil and Germany as a "tensioning" of liberal democracy. Through the review and articulation of the literature, the research sought to clarify the conceptual choices, also deepening the understanding of the tradition of studies on youth political participation and its normative limitation. Works addressing the theme of youth and political participation of young people in the far-right are revisited, emphasizing their contribution to the formulation of the research. Finally, I present what the modes of subjectivation are, based on a refinement of the concept of identities from post-structuralist studies. This allows, in the third chapter, the presentation of the research methodology, highlighting the path of choice and conducting life narrative interviews, as well as the methods of biographical reconstruction and critical thematic analysis of the transcripts. The challenges of positionality and reflexivity are also discussed, as well as the changes in course driven by contexts.

In the fourth chapter, 12 engagement trajectories of the interviewees are reconstructed, allowing visualization of the engagement processes. The turning-points of participation identified in the interviews are analysed, as well as the diversity of trajectories. This leads to reflection on liminality as a heuristic key for analysing the strategies, practices, and reflexivity of subjects who transition between recognized and unrecognized forms of democratic participation. The fifth chapter involves the thematic categories that, articulated with the literature, seek to reflect the discourses that sustain youth activism in radical right movements in Brazil and Germany. Through seven thematic categories, I discuss the signifiers "family", "culture", "freedom", "economy", "people", and "nation" that, together and in articulation, configure systems of representation, understood as systems of signification closely linked to power relations. I also seek to understand what the "discursive positions" are and, consequently, the "places" offered to such young people within the movements.

Finally, I present the gaps and fissures of resistance, located in what escapes this chain of signification and highlights the intersections and findings of power and oppression relations, related to the daily experiences of young people, as well as learning processes. Together, these chapters lead to the final considerations, in which I revisit the journey, synthesizing the findings and discussing the importance of expanding the public sphere for those who have not yet positioned themselves, creating the possibility of founding new places and projects that break and highlight the limits of binary and Manichean representations.

São Paulo, Brazil Beatriz Besen

Acknowledgments

To those who are my South,

To my husband and partner, Ramiro Neves da Silva Macedo, who often provided me with material bases—food and song—to get through the doctorate. But above all, who shared an incalculable amount of love, laughter, and dialogue. Our partnership and passion brought me one of life's greatest joys: nurturing Maya, who makes me more hopeful about the future.

To my mother and friend, Gina Rizpah Besen, who inspired me and gave me the foundations to face internal and external battles inherent in the complexity of being a woman in this world. Our complicity is my solid ground.

To my father, Roberto Alves de Oliveira, who passed on to me the ability to argue and a passion for debate. His confidence gives me the strength to fly higher.

To my stepfather, Pedro Roberto Jacobi, who gifted me with his unwavering affection and support.

To my sister Nina, who shared confidences and learnings and gave me the privilege of being an aunt to Paco and Benja.

To my brother, Murilo Gustavo Gírio, who was present even from a distance and reassured me that our partnership is for life.

To my sister, Cristina Silva Sacco de Oliveira, who gave me tight hugs and charmed me with her combination of tenderness and rebellion.

To my friends, Lenora, Olívia, Ticiana, Lucas, Luca, Flávia, Bianca, Maurício, Pedro, Marília, Gabriela, Yuri, Nina, Lívia, Mayra, Patrícia, Tiago, Beatriz, Ana, Matteo, Henrique, Breno, Julia. With you, I feel at home. Our connections and encounters bring brightness, joy, and lightness to life.

To my advisor, Soraia Ansara, who tirelessly showed me that generosity and exchange are still the foundations of education.

To the members of my doctoral committee, Vítor Ferreira, Benjamin Junge, Bruna Suruagy do Amaral, and Pablo Ortellado, for their attentive reading and generous arguments. To my advisors in Germany, Andreas Walther and Hanna Schwander, for providing me with an experience of displacement. To my reviewer Maurício Ayer, for the support in the editing and preparation process of this book.

To CAPES and DAAD, who funded and allowed me to carry out this project. And to FAPESP, which enabled me to pursue a research career and dedicate myself to the book's edition.

To Brazil, which is where I come from and where I always intend to return to.

Being Brazilian is an immense privilege. Living and growing in and with contradiction is both a pain and a delight.

Competing Interests The author has no competing interests to declare that are relevant to the content of this manuscript.

Contents

About the Author

Beatriz Besen is a psychologist and researcher, with an academic trajectory marked by an interdisciplinary approach and a focus on investigating contemporary social challenges. She holds a doctorate from the Graduate Program in Social Change and Political Participation at the University of São Paulo (USP), and two master's degrees: the first in Social Psychology from USP and the second in State, Government, and Public Policies from the Latin American Faculty of Social Sciences (Flacso). Currently, Beatriz is a postdoctoral researcher at the Center for the Study of Violence (NEV/USP), dedicating herself to the study of manifestations and representations of authoritarianism in Brazil. Her main research theme is youth political participation, offering insights into the connections between youth, local and global radical right and political discourses. Her international trajectory includes research stays at Goethe University in Frankfurt, Humboldt University in Berlin, and the Center for Discourse Studies in Barcelona, which enriched her critical perspective and expanded her contributions to the field of political psychology. Beatriz has been recognised by academic organizations, including honourable mentions received at the Dissertation Award of the International Society of Political Psychology (ISPP) and the 13th University of São Paulo Outstanding Thesis Award. With a deep commitment to scientific production and dissemination, she has contributed to and given interviews for Brazilian media outlets, seeking not only to analyse but also to communicate complex themes to diverse audiences.

List of Abbreviations

AfD	Alternative for Germany (*Alternative für Deutschland*)
AIB	Brazilian Integralist Action (*Ação Integralista Brasileira*)
CDU	Christian Democratic Union (*Christlich-Demokratische Union Deutschlands*)
DAAD	German Academic Exchange Service (*Deutscher Akademischer Austauschdienst*)
DP	German Party (*Deutsche Partei*)
DRP	German Reich Party (*Deutsche Reichspartei*)
DVU	German People's Union (*Deutsche Volksunion*)
FN	National Front (*Rassemblement/Front National*)
FPÖ	Freedom Party of Austria (*Freiheitliche Partei Österreichs*)
IPEC	Intelligence in Research and Strategic Consulting (*Inteligência em Pesquisa e Consultoria Estratégia*)
JA	Young Alternative (*Jung Alternative*)
NPD	National Democratic Party of Germany (*Nationaldemokratische Partei Deutschlands*)
ONU	United Nations Organization
PEGIDA	Patriotic Europeans Against the Islamization of the West (*Patriotische Europäer gegen die Islamisierung des Abendlandes*)
PT	Workers' Party (*Partido dos Trabalhadores*)
REP	Republicans (*Republikaner*)
SPD	Social Democratic Party (*Sozialdemokratische Partei Deutschlands*)
TFP	Brazilian Society for the Defense of Tradition, Family, and Property (*Sociedade Brasileira de Defesa da Tradição, Família e Propriedade*)

Chapter 1
Introduction

Year 2023 marked the 10-year anniversary of the June Journeys,[1] a series of mobilizations that brought millions of Brazilians to the streets. In the form of events and media reports, analyses of their meanings, developments, and relations with the current political scenario in Brazil were shared and revisited (Moliterno, 2023; Pericles, 2023; Stabile et al., 2023). The result was a diverse mosaic of impressions, ranging from divergent perspectives of researchers to a vast variety of individual experiences and accounts. These journeys are part of a larger context of global mobilizations, which share the similarity of having been exhaustively evaluated—in the political and intellectual world—and often function as *ground zero* or as a *source* of analysis for the changes observed in terms of the (re)configurations of the political and politics over the last decade. Two years ago, local and global media also analysed the 10-year anniversary of these other mobilizations, using the adjectives "contradictory", "ambiguous", and "polarized" to qualify both the events and the analyses developed. The reports refer to the *Occupy Wall Street* movement, characterized by protests whose *slogan*, "We are the 99%", also reflects dissonant voices. Some will say that the inspiration for the *slogan* was Joseph Stiglitz, an economist who popularized the distinction of the world's richest 1%, while others categorically claim it was the anthropologist and anarchist David Graeber (Anthony,

[1] Such manifestations began from a central agenda, "the right to the city", which was translated through the struggle against the increase in bus fares called by the Free Fare Movement, which declared itself "horizontal, autonomous, independent, and non-partisan, but not anti-partisan" (Scherer-Warren, 2014, p. 159). After violent police repression was broadcasted and publicized by the media, an increase in participation in the acts was seen and there was a proliferation of various agendas, including direct criticisms of the failures of representation in representative democracy. The demonstrations extended throughout the year and spread across the country. Initial analyses (Scherer-Warren, 2014; Bringel, 2013) pointed to an orientation towards social transformation and the search for new forms of political representation. However, more recent analyses (Rocha et al., 2021) identify these acts as the beginning of the occupation of the streets by counterpublics that would come to form the new right-wing movements.

B. Besen, *Youth Activism in the Radical Right of Brazil and Germany*,
https://doi.org/10.1007/978-3-031-87635-6_1

2021). The movement, which began in Manhattan's financial district in September 2011, gained global repercussion and reached other financial centres and world capitals, such as London, Paris, and Berlin.

Meanwhile, the occupations of Plaza Catalunya in Barcelona and Puerta del Sol in Madrid, also initiated in 2011, led Eduardo Galeano to declare: "this shitty world is pregnant with another!" Both movements did not deny the inspiration of the Arab Spring and the occupation of Tahrir Square in Egypt, which, due to their punctual victories, also served as a harbinger of a new decade of hope. In the same vein, it is impossible not to mention the *Euromaidan*, or the "Revolution of Dignity", which took place in 2014 in Ukraine but returned to the media spotlight after the start of the war against Russia, leading again to an ambiguous interpretation of the event. On one hand, some classify it as a revolution in search of dignity and the defence of liberal democracy—even declaring that "its greatest task was to lay the foundations for a stable liberal democracy" (Shveda & Park, 2016)—and on the other hand, some see it as a cauldron in which the main ingredient was the reactionism of neo-Nazi and anti-Semitic movements in the country (Aprile, 2023).

Considering the global context and extrapolating the particularities of each of these events, the idea of a geopolitics of indignation (Bringel, 2013) was highlighted at the time: a unanimous interpretation that there was dissatisfaction with the prevailing forms of political representation. The events were viewed as moments of collective catharsis, making evident the existence of an intense flow of emotions in politics, also signalling that the new century came accompanied by a great desire for experimentation and legitimation of new forms of political participation. And young people were seen at the heart of these new forms and as protagonists of such events. Some of these young people were not on the streets but were already relating to these events through social media, which gained centrality in communication and politics.

This view changed over the years, and the events that, during their emergence, were analysed as a source of hope came to be understood as a disruption and break with the "correct" forms of political participation, leading to the wear and tear of liberal democracy, now described as "precarious" (Jarrín et al., 2022). This transformation, in the Brazilian case, is mainly seen as having taken place after the election of Jair Bolsonaro in 2018—understood as a mark of the exhaustion of what was classified as a Pink Wave, a period where left-wing and progressive governments were in power in various Latin American countries at the beginning of the century.

In the European and North American cases, the election of leaders like Viktor Orbán, Donald Trump, and Giorgia Meloni, in addition to the growth of the representation of radical right-wing parties in countries like France, Switzerland, Sweden, and Germany, was also a series of events that strengthened the interpretation of a "democratic recession" (Carapanã, 2018) or a "de-democratization" (Lombardo et al., 2021; Pinheiro-Machado et al., 2019). Despite understanding the importance of temporal distance for the analysis of historical events, it seems important to me to revisit some of the initial analyses of these events and begin the present review with a rather basic question: What is understood by democracy? Only then do I believe it is possible to clarify whether the ideas of precariousness and recession are coherent with such a view.

To answer this question, I begin by listing some fundamental ideas of Foucault and Castoriadis, treating them as references that pointed out that democracy was not invented in a specific place and in a definitive way (Bringel & Echart, 2008). Castoriadis (2007) points out that, although its historical creation is attributed to the Greek-Western world, democracy is revived and constituted with new forms and categories in a post-revolutionary liberal context. This process of reinvention and establishment was predominantly conflictual. Thus, more than a "Greek model" of democracy—which excluded most of the population—the philosopher establishes as the greatest source of inspiration from the past the activities and struggles that took place around its institutions, that is, the historical instituting character of Greek democracy.

Castoriadis defines freedom as the opening of the social imaginary, resulting from the indeterminacy of ontological creation. In this way, freedom would be a philosophical precondition for individual and collective autonomy (Rendtorff, 2008). The philosopher and social theorist had a unique understanding of institutionalization as he saw institutions as social constructions that emerge from the collective imagination and the creative power of society. For him, institutions are not fixed or predetermined structures but dynamic creations in constant evolution of human activity, whose objective is also to provide stability and predictability through the establishment of rules, norms, and routines. Castoriadis recognizes that institutions can become rigid and oppressive, limiting the creative and transformative potential of individuals and society. The philosopher's theory establishes the existence of individual and collective agency, focusing on a socio-historical dimension of knowledge, with an emphasis on the continuous process of creation and interpretation.

Foucault (1980, 1991), on the other hand, reformulates two fundamental concepts involved in political philosophy: power and freedom. The philosopher understands that the forms of subjection and government instituted in modernity are traversed by disciplinary technologies, which are directed towards a political appropriation of bodies. Foucault's genealogy of power seeks to show that various historical moments, in which the idea of freedom was placed at the centre, also represented the creation of increasingly sophisticated strategies of subjection. Foucault actively questions the general theme of freedom and its centrality in various government projects (Orellana, 2012). For him, many discourses about freedom would be functional and would nurture an idea of human nature that is yet to come, that is, they would promote a concealment of the continuous dynamics of power relations. For the philosopher, power operates through institutions and discourses, shaping social practices. In a post-structuralist theoretical framework, Foucault challenges the idea of a fixed subject, emphasizing that power relations construct subjectivities and identities.

Despite the epistemological differences between the two social theorists, both contribute to the understanding that, for the establishment of what we understand today as liberal democracy, there were disputes and a series of interpretations were silenced and abandoned in the name of what was established as "truth and knowledge" and instituted as "Western liberalism". One of the main historical confrontations of the meaning of democratic politics—which still persists today—concerns the definition of democracy as a real popular power or a contribution of the majority to decision-making in a "representative" way. Another conflict also occurs in the understanding between a substantial definition and a procedural definition—a definition of what democracy actually is and a prescriptive plan that involves what it should be. Or, still, the definition of the difference between practices of liberation and practices of freedom—the contents that are attributed and define what would be the full realization of freedom and the ethical practices of freedom.

It is from these differentiations that the difference between the political and politics is positioned, that is, between the procedures and institutional functioning and the human projects and practices of negotiation and deliberation that aim at the construction of a societal project. These plans do not walk together, but there are moments when the boundaries and gaps between the different dimensions become deeper and more visible. Or rather, moments when the mechanisms of power (Foucault, 1991) are revealed, often through the articulation of popular forces and creative actions of resistance (Castoriadis, 1995, 2004).

This seems to be the case at the beginning of the twenty-first century, where social movements, based on social markers of difference, figured as the main actors of this denunciation. In the field of social movement studies, long before the June Journeys, there was already a diagnosis of the limitation of the incidence of popular power in democracy, even in the face of a certain "stabilization" of a Welfare State in Western Europe, and the expansion of affirmative and redistribution policies in the Latin American context. In the study of public policies, the Sociology of Public Action (Lascoumes & Le Galès, 2012) gained prominence, denouncing the growth of specialists and the constitution of an exclusionary management model. In Latin American studies, critical analyses gained strength, through participatory studies and ethnographic (Montero, 2006; Angrosino, 2009; Mattos & Castro, 2011) and oral history (Delgado, 2003; Lara & Antúnez, 2014), and highlighted the daily oppressions.

However, this scenario became more complex with the emergence of new movements and political actors during and after the previously mentioned global mobilizations. These actors also claimed to denounce and oppose the dominant forms of government, but they presented an agenda contrary to the expansion of minority rights and the strengthening of the state in combating inequalities. An example, in the Brazilian case, is the Conservative Movement—initially Right São Paulo—which emerged in 2016, "surfing" on the optimism of the movements that took to the streets for the impeachment of former President Dilma Rousseff, still in 2015.

The movement, from its inception, called on the "indignant" to continue demonstrating in the streets. One of these demonstrations gained national attention and involved burning a doll of the American philosopher Judith Butler during her visit to Brazil in 2017 (Cyfer, 2018). Its leaders declared that their intention was to eradicate the "gender ideology" from Brazil, presenting on their website an agenda defending the lives of military police officers, fighting for the repeal of the disarmament statute, and opposing abortion and the migration law (Conservative Movement, 2022). They gathered their members to study classic texts of conservative and libertarian theorists and began to promote affiliations, seeking to form nuclei in various parts of the country. They carried as one of their banners the need for the "right" to engage in grassroots militancy, occupy the streets, and form new leaders, including through systematic studies.

Among these young leaders was its founder Douglas Garcia, a young black man who declared himself gay and from the favelas[2] and was elected state deputy by the Brazilian Labor Party in the 2019 elections (Cruz, 2021). Douglas was involved in a series of controversies and faces various criminal proceedings. Even before his election, the young man created the "carnival group" called Porão do Dops (Department of Political and Social Order[3]), whose idea was to present itself as an anti-communist parade but clearly legitimized the violations of the Brazilian military dictatorship. Among the accusations are acts of misogyny and LGBTphobia, as well as the organization of the "anti-fascist dossier", in which personal data of 1000 people opposing the Bolsonaro government were disclosed (Lino, 2022).

Recently, the group declared on its social networks that its activities are suspended, but in 2022, on its website, it read: "those who know the Conservative Movement already realize that we were not born just to make noise on the internet, raise hashtags, and fight from the couch at home. No! We 'show our face' (literally, many times)!" (Conservative Movement, 2022). The comment about "showing the face" translated into the group's effort to differentiate itself from other movements, whose activities took place only in the digital environment, but it became especially interesting in light of the event on January 8, 2023, when a crowd invaded the Brazilian National Congress, the Supreme Federal Court, and the Planalto Palace buildings, seats of the Legislative, Judicial, and Executive powers in Brazil. During this episode, the individuals involved "showed their face" (literally!) and created content on Instagram while vandalizing the buildings and calling for military intervention in a democratic regime. Besides those directly involved in the attack, there

[2] Cruz (2021) analyses the growth of right-wing gay activism in Brazil and explains that Douglas Garcia's decision to make his sexual orientation public corresponded to a "strategy of 'upward defence': besides the imminence of a process in the Ethics Committee for breach of parliamentary decorum, the deputy had to face the pressure from some of his former colleagues who condemned his speech and now threatened to expose him in the press. Instantly, the focus of the debate shifted to Garcia's sexual orientation and the intersection with other social markers of difference that catapulted his political career. 'Gay, black, and from the slums. That's it, I'm the combo of Brazilian victimhood,' he said to the *Folha de São Paulo* a few days after coming out, without, however, renouncing the discriminatory positions that put him in the spotlight in the first place" (Cruz, 2021, p. 11).

[3] The DOPS, Department of Political and Social Order, was a Brazilian government agency active during the Estado Novo period (1937–1945) and the Brazilian civil-military dictatorship (1964–1985). During the military regime, DOPS also referred to the Political and Social Order Police Stations, which were state-level agencies. According to Sodré and Roncaglio (2017, p. 255), "its function was that of a political police force which, in the course of its activities, employed practices that violated human rights (such as torture and other violent methods) with the aim of obtaining information and repressing groups considered 'subversive'".

were also their supporters who broadcasted these actions on social media and legitimized them, using the slogan "Supreme is the people", focusing mainly on supporting the attack on the Supreme Federal Court (Moreira & Ramirez Bohorquez, 2022).

Although some journalists and communicators classified the invasion as the action of a group of radical "Bolsonarists", the scale of the event and the chosen targets raise an alert for the need to reflect on the processes of radicalization. Furthermore, the invasion can be connected to recent similar acts, such as the invasion of the Capitol in the United States in 2021 and the threat to the German parliament in 2020. These events highlight that new flows of emotions circulate today in politics, beyond Brazil, leading scholars to observe and analyse the global dimension of radical right movements and the election of their young leaders in various countries (Mudde, 2014, 2016; Varga & Buzogány, 2022).

A large part of these movements takes pride in displaying their conservative agenda, which, in the understanding of the progressive tradition of studies on social movements and political participation, does not contribute to a progressive construction of democracy, representing an anti-democratic and authoritarian turn. However, this realization leads us back to the analysis of what we understand as democracy and the questioning of whether there really is a linear progression in its construction and deepening. This question is fuelled by the Foucauldian tradition of studies but also gains strength with the my life experience in Germany, which allows one to observe that one of the elements sustaining the discourse of the superiority and political maturity of Western Europe compared to the rest of the world is the classification of other democracies, such as those in Latin America, as "immature" and "young", in addition to the constant use of "populism"[4] as an analytical key (Knight, 1998; Conniff, 2012).

Even with the supposed "democratic maturity", Germany, like most of Europe, has witnessed the growth of radical right-wing parties and movements (Arzheimer & Berning, 2019). In the same year that the June Journeys of 2013 were taking place in Brazil, the Alternative for Germany (*Alternative für Deutschland*, AfD) emerged. The party made headlines in June 2023, due to its strong performance in regional elections and the first victory of a party politician as a district chief in Thuringia. The event is being interpreted as a general warning about the breaking of the *cordon sanitaire,*[5] organized by traditional parties to keep the party isolated. The AfD was

[4] The metaconcept of "populism" will be constantly cited in this book because it is central to European analyses of the rise of the radical right. However, it is insufficient as it neglects the political, historical, and cultural specificities of Latin America—where there is considered to be a "broad and enduring variety of left and right-wing populism" (Wahl, 2020, p. 336). The definition centres on the construction of a "people" discourse that opposes political and economic elites—being sufficiently broad to be applied to both the current president Lula and former president Jair Bolsonaro. Jarrín et al. (2022) point to an analytical weakness, as well as a reiteration of the historically constructed notion of passivity of colonized peoples, who would be easily "deceived", "by the media, neoliberal capitalism, fake news, corrupt politicians, etc."—taken by feelings inherently "bad for democracy" (Jarrín et al., 2022, p. 21).

[5] Riera and Pastor (2022) explain that two strategies have been applied in the context of European parliamentarism to deal with what they call populist parties. On one hand, the "cordon sanitaire",

the first party identified as part of the German radical right and what would be interpreted, in the European context, as a "fourth wave" of the far-right (Mudde, 2016).

It emerges as a new party founded by Eurosceptic economists, advocating for the end of efforts to save the Euro and criticizing multiculturalism and the promotion of gender equity policies (Wahl, 2020). The party has been gaining ground in the federal legislative power and, as early as 2013, had accessed regional parliaments. In 2017, the AfD reached the national parliament with 12.6% of the votes. In the region corresponding to former East Germany, the party's success was much greater than in West Germany (Arzheimer, 2015). In early 2025, the AfD secured 20.8% of the votes, becoming the second-largest political force in the German Parliament and achieving its best historical performance.

AfD members include leaders of the Patriotic Europeans Against the Islamization of the West (PEGIDA; in German, *Patriotische Europäer gegen die Islamisierung des Abendlandes*) and the Identitarian Movement, both protagonists of demonstrations against the German government and what they call the "Islamization of the West". The PEGIDA group emerged in 2014 in the city of Dresden, Germany, starting through a Facebook group, and brought about 35,000 people to the streets in Dresden and more than 100,000 across Germany (Vorländer et al., 2016). The Identitarian Movement has been spreading throughout Europe since 2014 and holds lectures and meetings also in Germany. There, the group takes as its main agenda the fight against "Islamization", through the defence of "ethnopluralism" (Åsbrink, 2021). The movement's agenda is the protection of a European cultural and ethnic identity, which is said to be under threat. Under the *slogan* "Homeland, Freedom, and Tradition", the movement only accepts young people, setting as prerequisites for membership being under 30 years old and ensuring a "truly German" nationality and origin.

The AfD also created the *Jung Alternative* (JA) as a specific space for youth organizations in different regions of the country. The JA holds its own meetings and uses social media platforms, such as Facebook and Instagram, to express itself against what they call mainstream media. There, the discourse against political correctness is spread, accompanied by terms like "honour, loyalty, blood, and homeland" (Klikauer, 2019). During the pandemic, other right-wing movements emerged, presenting themselves as defenders of freedom. They joined the AfD in demonstrations to protest against the *lockdown* and other restrictive measures adopted by the German federal government (Rovira Kaltwasser & Taggart, 2024).

It is essential to emphasize that Brazil and Germany share a common pattern in the expansion of radical right after 2013 (Rocha et al., 2021; Schwander & Manow, 2017), but they are two nations with distinct political regimes, unique historical contexts, and different welfare regimes—factors that influence the policies shaping

---

used consistently in Germany, refers to an alliance between traditional parties to ensure that populist parties do not become part of coalitions. Another strategy is known as "tainted coalition", in which they invite these parties into the coalition, considering that this formation may lead to a deterioration of the subsequent electoral success of the parties and a "dilution" of extremist capacity.

the growth and development of young people. Germany is a conservative social state centred on employment that connects social rights to employment and family *status*. In this country, services and policies for youth are well structured but adhere to the principle of (selective) socialization of young people for defined (or occupational) positions within the normal course of life (Walther, 2022). In contrast, Brazil is sometimes classified as a social development state (Draibe, 2007) that combines infrastructure deficits and family dependency with a growing emphasis on individual responsibility. It has also been classified as a conservative-based welfare model, characteristic of countries that have undergone a recent democratic transition. Such classification considers that the country is moving towards the universalization of policies but has deep stratifications between those who consume private and public services (Benevides, 2011).

Regarding the political regime, Germany adopts parliamentarism, while Brazil's political organization has been defined as coalition presidentialism (Abranches, 2018). The main difference between the two systems lies in the separation of origin and survival between the Executive and Legislative powers. In "pure" presidentialism, whose paradigm has been the American model, the president is elected by direct vote and has autonomy to determine the composition of the government. His stability is based on the mandate and does not depend on legislative support. Coalition presidentialism, on the other hand, presents itself as an institutional variant that combines the hierarchical structure centred on the president with the formation of multiparty coalitions. In the case of parliamentarism, the government only survives as long as it maintains the support of the majority of the Legislature, and power is concentrated in the cabinet. When no party achieves a majority, a government is formed through a multiparty coalition, which is common in many European democracies, such as the German one (Batista, 2016).

Finally, there are also distinct historical contexts—with different temporal relations between periods of massive human rights violations in Germany and Latin America (Huhle, 2016). Latin American countries experienced long periods of dictatorial governments, in addition to having lived through long periods of colonization and, in the Brazilian case, slavery. Brazil was a Portuguese colony for 322 years (1500–1822), had a slave regime for 388 years (1500–1888), and for another 21 years (1964–1985) was under a civil-military dictatorial regime. Meanwhile, in Germany, the Nazi regime was defeated in 1945, after 12 years of the most brutal period of the Third Reich. Furthermore, the Cold War and the temporary division of the country between East and West, which lasted from 1945 to 1989, is also a relevant issue for understanding its political context (Schellenberg, 2013).

These differences highlight the potential of conducting a comparative study to analyse youth activism in radical right, as well as warn of the need for reflection on their influences on the phenomenon being studied. In the context of Political Psychology, comparative studies have been considered a very important tool, which can vary between a deductive, inductive, and mixed methodology, that is, ranging from a hypothesis test, an exploratory study, or a combination of both (van de Vijver, 2009). In the present study, an exploratory character prevails, in which the aim is to expand understandings of the phenomenon through the exploration of its developments in different contexts.

Still looking at the contexts of the countries, I find it important to mention their potential effects in terms of "positionality" (Massey, 1994). By this, I refer to the fact that social markers of differences (Collins, 2000; Crenshaw, 2002) can operate differently in Brazil and Germany. In Brazil, I am personally often identified as a white woman from an upper-middle-class background. In the case of Germany, I continue to be identified as a white woman but also as an immigrant without fluent command of the language. In both cases, my position at the university was an important legitimizing element, which served as an entry point to various spaces. These intersections will be analysed in detail in the second chapter of the thesis—in which I present the research methodology—which defined different practical and ethical challenges in the consolidation of the research, as well as in the construction of the analysis. In the Brazilian case, I managed to conduct 11 interviews with activists who identified as men and women. In the German case, there was greater difficulty in finding potential interviewees, resulting in a total universe of 5 interviewees who identified as men.

As a strategy for approaching and recruiting interviewees, I created a professional profile on Instagram to follow movements and actors of the radical right in both countries. As from 2020, I observed the movements and leaderships, noting a continuous expansion in the number of group profiles on Instagram, as well as the growth of the set of references, both in terms of public figures and in terms of an increasing production of digital and printed editorial content (da Silva, 2018). Initially, young people who identified as activists in their social media profiles or who were tagged in movement posts were invited to participate in the interviews. Subsequently, I employed the "snowball" method as a recognized strategy that allows for non-probabilistic sampling and is useful for studying certain hard-to-access groups (Vinuto, 2014). Complementarily, I sent invitations by email to youth movements and organizations of the parties in Germany.

Initially, face-to-face interviews were planned. However, the Covid-19 pandemic, regional distances, as well as security issues led me to opt for online interviews via video calls. The present research involved, therefore, a total universe of 16 interviews conducted between October 2021 and February 2023 with radical right activists from Brazil and Germany, which were carried out in Portuguese, German, or English. From the life trajectory interviews and the articulation and review of the literature, I selected[6] and conducted reconstructions (Rosenthal, 2004) of the engagement trajectories of 12 young people, analysing the particularities and similarities in terms of self-representation, as well as practices and strategies.

---

[6] The third chapter will address the methodology in detail, highlighting that the criterion for selecting the 12 interviews was the diversity of groups and movements in which the young people reported participating. All interviews were transcribed, and it was observed that some recurrences and discursive patterns were associated with sharing the same space of action. With the broader objective of analysing the discursive interpellations of radical right, I chose not to include the interviews obtained by the "snowball" method in the analyses and, consequently, in this book.

Subsequently, I conducted a critical thematic analysis (Braun & Clarke, 2006), seeking, through coding and recurrence research in the transcripts, to locate the narratives in thematic categories that reflected on the systems of representation and discourses that interpellate these young people. Thus, in the entirety of the research, I sought to work with dimensions that reflected the theoretical positioning of the present research, which defines that the subject is traversed and formed by discourses but also impacts vectors of resistance (Pineda & Cubides, 2012).

References

Abranches, S. (2018). *Presidencialismo de coalizão: raízes e evolução do modelo político brasileiro*. Companhia das Letras.

Angrosino, M. (2009). *Etnografia e observação participante*. Artmed.

Anthony, A. (2021). We showed it was possible to create a movement from almost nothing: Occupy Wall Street 10 years on. *The Guardian*. Retrieved December 2021, from https://www.theguardian.com/us-news/2021/sep/12/occupy-wall-street-10-years-on

Arzheimer, K. (2015). The AfD: Finally a successful right-wing populist Eurosceptic party for Germany? *West European Politics, 38*(3), 535–556.

Arzheimer, K., & Berning, C. C. (2019). How the alternative for Germany (AfD) and their voters veered to the radical right, 2013–2017. *Electoral Studies, 60*, 102040.

Åsbrink, E. (2021). When race was removed from racism: Per Engdahl, the networks that saved fascism and the making of the concept of ethnopluralism. *Journal of the History of Ideas, 82*(1), 133–151.

Batista, M. (2016). O Poder no Executivo: explicações no presidencialismo, parlamentarismo e presidencialismo de coalizão. *Revista de sociologia e política, 24*, 127–155.

Benevides, C. D. V. (2011). Um Estado de bem-estar social no Brasil. [Master's thesis, Universidade Federal Fluminense].

Braun, V., & Clarke, V. (2006). Using thematic analysis in psychology. *Qualitative Research in Psychology, 3*(2), 77–101. https://doi.org/10.1191/1478088706qp063oa

Bringel, B. (2013). O Brasil na geopolítica da indignação global. *Brasil de Fato*. Retrieved June 13, 2013, from https://www.academia.edu/download/31865346/O_Brasil_na_geopolitica_da_indignacao_global___Brasil_de_Fato.pdf

Bringel, B., & Echart, E. (2008). Movimentos sociais e democracia: os dois lados das "fronteiras". *Caderno CRH, 21*(54), 457–475. https://doi.org/10.1590/S0103-49792008000300004

Carapanã. (2018). A nova direita e a normalização do nazismo e fascismo. In E. Solano (Ed.), *O ódio como política*. Boitempo.

Castoriadis, C. (1995). *A instituição imaginária da sociedade*. Paz e Terra.

Castoriadis, C. (2004). *Figuras do pensável. As encruzilhadas do labirinto VI*. (E. Aguiar Trad.). Civilização Brasileira.

Castoriadis, C. (2007). *Democracia y relativismo. Debate con el MAUSS*. Trotta.

Collins, P. H. (2000). *Black feminist thought: Knowledge, consciousness, and the politics of empowerment* (2nd ed.). Routledge.

Conniff, M. L. (Ed.). (2012). *Populism in Latin America*. University of Alabama Press.

Crenshaw, K. (2002). Documento para o Encontro de Especialistas em aspectos da discriminação racial relativos ao gênero. *Estudos Feministas, 171*(1).

Cruz, R. (2021). "Sou gay e o movimento LGBTQI+ não me representa": mapeando a emergência de um ativismo gay à direita no Brasil. *Cahiers des Amériques latines, 98*, 43–66.

Cyfer, I. (2018). A bruxa está solta: os protestos contra a visita de Judith Butler ao Brasil à luz de sua reflexão sobre ética, política e vulnerabilidade. *Cadernos Pagu, 53*. https://doi.org/10.1590/18094449201800530003

da Silva, L. N. (2018). O mercado editorial e a Nova Direita brasileira. *Teoria e Cultura, 13*(2), 73–84.

da Silva Aprile, C. A. (2023). A reacionarização do Estado Ucraniano. *Revista Ibero-Americana de Humanidades, Ciências e Educação, 9*(2), 1036–1056. https://doi.org/10.51891/rease.v9i2.8604

del Valle Orellana, N. (2012). Entre poder y resistencia. Tras los rastros de la política en Foucault. *Revista Enfoques: Ciencia Política y Administración Pública, 10*(17), 147–168.

Delgado, L. D. A. N. (2003). História oral e narrativa: tempo, memória e identidades. *História Oral, 6*.

Draibe, S. M. (2007). Estado de bem-estar, desenvolvimento econômico e cidadania: algumas lições da literatura contemporânea. In G. Hochman et al. (Eds.), *Políticas públicas no Brasil*. Editora Fiocruz.

Foucault, M. (1980). *El orden del discurso*. Tusquets Editores.

Foucault, M. (1991). *El sujeto y el poder*. Carpe Diem.

Huhle, R. (2016). Human rights education and historical learning. In C. Lenz, S. Brattland, & L. Kvande (Eds.), *Crossing borders. Combining human rights education and history education* (pp. 209–225). LIT.

Jarrín, A., Junge, B., Mitchell, S., Cantero, L., & Biondi, K. (Eds.). (2022). *Democracia Precária: etnografias de esperança, desespero e resistência no Brasil*. Zouk.

Klikauer, T. (2019). German neo-nazis and a new party. *Jewish Political Studies Review, 30*(1/2), 243–252.

Knight, A. (1998). Populism and neo-populism in Latin America, especially Mexico. *Journal of Latin American Studies, 30*(2), 223–248.

Lara, P., & Antúnez, Á. (2014). La historia oral como alternativa metodológica para las ciencias sociales. *Revista de teoría y didáctica de las ciencias sociales, 20*, 45–62.

Lascoumes, P., & Le Galès, P. (2012). *Sociologia da Ação Pública*. Editora da Universidade Federal de Alagoas.

Lino, N. (2022, September 14). *Exaltação ao Dops, ataques e transfobia: o histórico de Douglas Garcia*. UOL. Retrieved from https://noticias.uol.com.br/eleicoes/2022/09/14/as-polemicas-de-douglas-garcia.html

Lombardo, E., Kantola, J., & Rubio-Marin, R. (2021). De-democratization and opposition to gender equality politics in Europe. *Social Politics: International Studies in Gender, State & Society, 28*(3), 521–531.

Massey, D. (1994). *Space, place and gender*. University of Minnesota Press.

Mattos, C. L. G. D., & Castro, P. A. D. (2011). *Etnografia e educação: conceitos e usos*. EDUEPB.

Moliterno, D. (2023, June 3). *Dez anos após protestos, política brasileira carrega marcas e consequências das jornadas de junho*. CNN Brasil. Retrieved from https://www.cnnbrasil.com.br/politica/dez-anos-apos-protestos-politica-brasileira-carrega-marcas-e-consequencias-das-jornadas-de-junho

Montero, M. (2006). *Hacer para transformar: el método en Psicología Comunitaria*. Paidós.

Moreira, T., & Ramirez Bohorquez, J. L. (2022). O povo quer democracia de verdade: como os apoiadores de Jair Bolsonaro veiculam noções associadas a palavra democracia no YouTube. *Revista Estudos Políticos, 12*(24), 96–129. https://doi.org/10.22409/rep.v12i24.51172

Movimento Conservador. (2022). *O Movimento*. Retrieved July 18, 2022, from https://movimentoconservador.com/o-movimento/

Mudde, C. (2014). Fighting the system? Populist radical right parties and party system change. *Party Politics, 20*(2), 217–226.

Mudde, C. (Ed.). (2016). *The populist radical right: A reader*. Routledge.

Pericles, L. (2023). Lições dos dez anos das Jornadas de Junho de 2013 — A Verdade. *Jornal A Verdade*. Retrieved July 14, 2023, from https://averdade.org.br/2023/07/licoes-dos-dez-anos-das-jornadas-de-junho-de-2013

Pineda, M. C. M., & Cubides, J. (2012). Sujeito e política: vínculos e modos de subjetivação. *Revista Colombiana de Educación, 63*, 67–88.

Pinheiro-Machado, R., et al. (2019). *Brasil em transe: Bolsonarismo, nova direita e desdemocratização*. Oficina Raquel.

Rendtorff, J. D. (2008). Castoriadis' concept of institution and democracy. *Nordicum-Mediterraneum, 3*(2). https://doi.org/10.33112/nm.3.2.7

Riera, P., & Pastor, M. (2022). Cordons sanitaires or tainted coalitions? The electoral consequences of populist participation in government. *Party Politics, 28*(5), 889–902.

Rocha, C., Solano, E., & Medeiros, J. (2021). *The Bolsonaro paradox. The public sphere and right-wing counterpublicity in contemporary Brazil*. Springer.

Rosenthal, G. (2004). Biographical research. In C. Seale et al. (Eds.), *Qualitative research practice* (pp. 48–64). Sage.

Rovira Kaltwasser, C., & Taggart, P. (2024). The populist radical right and the pandemic. *Government and Opposition, 59*(4), 977–997. https://doi.org/10.1017/gov.2022.46

Schellenberg, B. (2013). Developments within the radical right in Germany: Discourses, attitudes and actors. In R. Wodak, M. Khosravinik, & B. Mral (Eds.), *Right-wing populism in Europe: Politics and discourse* (pp. 149–162). Bloomsbury.

Scherer-Warren, I. (2014). Manifestações de rua no Brasil 2013: encontros e desencontros na política. *Caderno Crh, 27*, 417–429.

Schwander, H., & Manow, P. (2017). It's not the economy, stupid! Explaining the electoral success of the German right-wing populist AfD. CIS Working Paper 94, University of Zurich.

Shveda, Y., & Park, J. H. (2016). Ukraine's revolution of dignity: The dynamics of Euromaidan. *Journal of Eurasian Studies, 7*(1), 85–91.

Sodré, G. A., & Roncaglio, B. (2017). O caráter de prova dos documentos produzidos pelas DOPS. *Perspectivas em Ciência da Informação, 22*(3), 245–260. https://doi.org/10.1590/1981-5344/2623

Stabile, A., Castelo Branco, C., Paiva, D., Tito, F., & Franco, L. (2023). *VÍDEO: jornadas de junho 2013, 10 anos depois*. G1. Retrieved June 13, 2023, from https://g1.globo.com/sp/sao-paulo/noticia/2023/06/13/video-jornadas-de-junho-2013-10-anos-depois.ghtml

Van de Vijver, F. J. (2009). Types of comparative studies in cross-cultural psychology. *Online Readings in Psychology and Culture, 2*(2). https://doi.org/10.9707/2307-0919.1017

Varga, M., & Buzogány, A. (2022). The two faces of the "global right": Revolutionary conservatives and national-conservatives. *Critical Sociology, 48*(6), 1089–1107.

Vinuto, J. (2014). A amostragem em bola de neve na pesquisa qualitativa: um debate em aberto. *Temáticas, 22*(44), 203–220.

Vorländer, H., Herold, M., & Schäller, S. (2016). PEGIDA — eine rechtsextremistische Bewegung. *Extremismus in Sachsen: Eine kritische Bestandsaufnahme*, 109–118.

Wahl, K. (2020). *The radical right: Biopsychosocial roots and international variations*. Palgrave Macmillan.

Walther, A. (2022). Welfare states as transition regimes: Reconstruction from international comparisons of young people's transitions to work. In B. Stauber, A. Walther, & R. A. Settersten (Eds.), *Doing transitions in the life courses — Practices and processes* (pp. 37–55). Springer.

Chapter 2
(Re)Constructing the Knowledge About the Radical Right in Brazil and Germany

In the introduction to the book "Hatred as Politics: The Reinvention of the Right in Brazil" (2018), Esther Solano describes an encounter she had with a "young Bolsonaro supporter" who, in a critical tone, told her: "Professor, you academics study so much and it seems you still haven't understood many things. You treat us as if we were all stupid. We are not. You should listen more, because you don't know everything". This young man's confrontation mobilizes the researcher with regard to the necessity of understanding reality before combating it. In the case of the present book, however, it is considered that, before seeking to understand the reality studied, a central challenge is to highlight what *truths* and *knowledge* have already been constituted about it.

The cited book is part of a collection that includes works that sought to analyse the June Journeys and the pro-impeachment acts of former President Dilma Rousseff as triggers of a political crisis in Brazil. The title of the collection is *Red Ink*, in reference to a speech by Slavoj Zizek to the protesters of the *Occupy Wall Street* movement, in which he says: "We have all the freedom we want—the only thing missing is the 'red ink': We 'feel free' because we are deprived of the language to articulate our lack of freedom".[1]

Zizek draws attention to the power that language has to constitute realities—this same language that is often (re)invented and discussed in the academic field. In the case of the emergence of "new right" phenomena, there is a profound challenge in producing a theoretical consensus within the academic and activist fields. However, the dimension that this political phenomenon has acquired has led a significant number of researchers to turn their eyes and attention to it, employing a diverse and rich conceptual apparatus in the quest to understand it.

This chapter seeks to establish a dialogue with the literature, that is, to highlight what has already been addressed and constructed on the subject, explaining the reasons why I see the need to place certain concepts "under erasure", as Hall (2000) proposes. The act of placing concepts under erasure represents a dual movement: considering their importance and inevitability for studies but at the same time highlighting the need for re-significations. According to Hall (2000), by fixing meanings, a discursive closure action takes place that distances the movements of

[1] The full speech was published at https://www.recantodasletras.com.br/discursos/3273021.

B. Besen, *Youth Activism in the Radical Right of Brazil and Germany*,
https://doi.org/10.1007/978-3-031-87635-6_2

estrangement and defamiliarization, fundamental for scientific research and for the broadening of meanings.

The movements and groups that have challenged liberal democracy have been predominantly identified as "*novas direitas*" (a plural new right) in Latin America (Cepêda, 2018; Gentile, 2018, 2020; Rocha, 2019), as a "radical right" in Europe (Mudde, 2016), and, specifically in Brazil, with the label of "*extrema-direita bolsonarista*" (a Bolsonarist' far-right) (Fernandes & Machado, 2022). Despite the different nomenclatures, the field of study of the phenomenon has been expanding and advancing, requiring, however, that researchers take a stance regarding the conceptual choice, which often also reflects a theoretical position. Placing at the centre of the study the tensioning of liberal democracy—an idea that opposes that of de-democratization or regression—this chapter aims to clarify my decision to label these actors, movements, and parties as "radical right". This choice reflects the challenges of capturing the plural form in English while retaining the intended meaning. For this, I present a more general overview of the literature that has focused on the expansion of radical right in Brazil and Europe, providing an analysis and critical review of the literature on the phenomenon.

The second part of the chapter presents research on activism within radical right following an interpretative line from the tradition of studies on youth and youth political participation. With this itinerary, it was possible to bring to the discussion the concepts of subjectivation and political identities, highlighting the influence of post-structuralist studies and the analysis of neoliberalism as rationality. Such studies indicate that identities—no longer understood as rigid and stable essences—can be interpreted as discursive formations related to mechanisms of power and the pursuit of efficacy and institutional representation.

Overall, this chapter aims to introduce the readers to the main axes of the book, enabling them to enter the subsequent chapters with familiarity regarding the concepts used, as well as their genealogy within research traditions.

2.1 Ultraliberal and Authoritarian: Investigations into the New Right in Brazil

The new right[2] in Brazil attracted considerable interest with the election of Jair Bolsonaro as president of Brazil in 2018. Within academic discussions, a clear divergence was established between those who believed they were witnessing a new

[2] The term "new right" is used here to replace instances of the terms "*novas direitas*" and "*nova direita*" in Portuguese, as well as "*nueva derecha*" and "*nuevas derechas*" in Spanish. While it would be valuable to detail the distinct uses by various authors, the scope of this book focuses primarily on surveying the different interpretations of the phenomenon in Latin America – primarily Brazil – and Europe. In the North American context, a substantial body of research on the topic has also emerged, gaining momentum after Donald Trump's election in 2016. There, the conservative right has been differentiated from the alternative right (alt-right). More recently, in this frame-

phenomenon (Gentile, 2018; Rocha, 2019) and those who understood it as merely a resurgence of the traditional right with new guises (Miguel, 2018; Salles, 2017; Pereira, 2015). In this sense, there were also studies that sought to explore the phenomenon from the traits of authoritarianism and the authoritarian personality—as addressed within critical theory (González et al., 2021)—and others that understood neoliberalism as the main key of analysis, involving the foundation of new subjectivities (Dardot & Laval, 2016; Safatle et al., 2020). Many studies also focused on the expansion of neo-Pentecostalism (Dantas, 2013, Lopes & Dantas, 2017; Teixeira, 2019; Teixeira & Barbosa, 2022) and the intertwining of religion and politics. Finally, other studies focused on the study of counterpublics, emphasizing the transformations of the post-bourgeois public sphere (Rocha, 2019; Rocha et al., 2021). Faced with a complex and ongoing phenomenon, the existence of multiple perspectives is considered normal.

Pinheiro-Machado et al. (2019) state that the June 2013 demonstrations brought two major novelties to the Brazilian political scene. Firstly, they displaced the Workers' Party and the movements related to it from the position of protagonists in street occupations. Secondly, and in a related manner, they represented a "discovery" of the streets by the right, which began to occupy spaces that, since the period of the civil-military dictatorship (1964–1985), had been identified as loci of progressive forces and movements. The researchers state that, on the streets, there were extremist nationalist organizations, young people with the rhetoric of anti-politics and diffuse liberalism, skinhead groups, advocates of a new military coup in the country, conservative and fundamentalist religious groups, citizens with anti-communist discourse, and a generic anti-corruption struggle.

Regarding interpretations, the researchers identify two lines of analysis: The first is related to the global context of disillusionment with democracy of a liberal matrix and the failure of classical models of political representation, and the second concerns the exhaustion of the PT or Lula government model, which was based on redistributive policies and the increased role of the State, but did not mobilize structural reforms that would guarantee a radicalization of Brazilian democracy. After Dilma Rousseff's re-election in 2014, the failure to establish "governability" is identified, due to the internal dissatisfaction of the party's traditional bases and the left with austerity policies, combined with the deepening and continuity of Operation Car Wash,[3] which explored new allegations of bribes and other irregularities. This

work, the concept of alt-lite has also been proposed, which would address a "light" alternative right (alt-lite). Taylor (2020, p. 15) clarifies that the alt-right encompasses 'white nationalists,' 'racial realists,' neo-Nazis, far-right academics, esoteric antimodernists, and the misogynistic 'manosphere,'. This diversity is reflected in the division between the alt-right, which openly embraces white nationalism, fascism, or Nazism, and the alt-lite, which advocates for civic nationalism instead of white nationalism and welcomes the participation of Jews, gays, and people of colour. They would be united by the belief that "all men are created unequal" (Taylor, 2020, p. 15).

[3] Inspired by the Operation Clean Hands conducted in Italy, Operation Car Wash consisted of a set of investigations led by the Brazilian Federal Police (PF) starting in March 2014, spearheaded by federal judge Sérgio Moro with a task force concentrated in the Federal Public Ministry (MPF) of Curitiba. The operation was presented as an anti-corruption judicial initiative launched in light of

entire context would have led to the acts in favour of the president's impeachment, organized in 2015 and 2016, which would represent a form of "selective indignation" with the Workers' Party, stimulated by the "dissemination of narratives formulated by conservative-oriented columnists of the mainstream press and numerous conspiracy theories through social networks and WhatsApp groups" (Pinheiro-Machado et al., 2019, p. 13). Together with the growth of an economic crisis, the authors list the "politicization" of the judiciary, the Federal Public Ministry, and the Federal Police as a fundamental element to understand the process they identified as a "de-democratization in Brazil".

Miguel (2018, p. 17) addresses the phenomenon as a reemergence of Brazilian right, seeking to interpret the "growing visibility and relevance of groups that openly assume a conservative or reactionary discourse". According to the author, the new right, once again pointed out as plural, have a pragmatic convergence motivated by the perception of a common enemy. They would have emerged during the cycle of the PT governments, promoting a reframing of the public debate in Brazil through the use of new technological tools and the space achieved in traditional media. According to Miguel (2018), consensuses that would have been formed since the end of the military dictatorship and the establishment of the 1988 Constitution—such as the defence of democracy, respect for human rights, and the fight against social inequality—would have been destabilized by the new right. For the researcher, such groups combine "libertarianism", understood as an ideology descending from the Austrian economic school and influential in academic and activist circles in the United States; religious "fundamentalism", mainly represented by the expansion of neo-Pentecostalism; and the recycling of the "red scare", which revives anti-communism in the form of Bolivarianism. Libertarianism would be marked by the sacralization of the market as the ultimate regulator of social relations, reducing "all rights to the right of property", with an "aversion to any bond of social solidarity" (Miguel, 2018, p. 16). Among its spokespersons, the buzzword would be "freedom", radicalizing oppositions previously constituted by the liberals of the eighteenth century. According to the researcher, equality would be established as a threat to freedom, the State as a threat to the market, and politics to the economy.

Rocha et al. (2021) also state that the new right present particularities in relation to the traditional right, breaking with the democratic pact that had come into effect in the country from 1988 with the "Citizen Constitution". The new democratic order, named by Abranches (2018) as a "coalition presidentialism", would have broken with the political model of the military dictatorship and contributed to the gradual construction of a post-bourgeois public sphere that increasingly aimed to include socially subordinate groups. Moreover, the pact pushed new right-wing groups that were active during the military regime to try to adapt to their new restrictions. The authors state that, after redemocratization, openly identifying as

---

the "Petrolão" scandals and maintained as its main focus the pursuit of the Workers' Party. Recently, many convictions from the operation were annulled by the Supreme Federal Court (STF). For more details on the plot of the constitution of heroes and villains, see Bello, Capela, and Keller (2021).

right-wing had become uncomfortable, reproducing an Argentine phenomenon, known as the "ashamed right" (Power, 2000). This shame extended beyond politicians, also affecting supporters and voters, who would have begun to form a new alternative public sphere, at the height of lulismo,[4] between 2006 and 2010.

Such analysis is also part of the brilliant doctoral dissertation by Camila Rocha (2019)—"More Mises less Marx: a genesis of the New Right in Brazil"—in which the new right is introduced as a conservative ultraliberal amalgam, whose origin is related to the organization of "counterpublics" (alternative public spheres) in this period. Rocha points out that, in those years, there was a meeting and debate—through platforms like Orkut and later Facebook—among those who felt marginalized and unrepresented in the dominant public sphere and who began to contribute to the dissemination of ultraliberal writings and ideas. Her analysis traces back to the 1980s and the creation of think tanks and neoliberal institutes, as well as the expansion of neo-Pentecostal organizations that gained strength in institutional public spaces since the governments of Luiz Inácio Lula da Silva (2003–2010).

In this sense, Camila Rocha (2018) also analysed the militancy in the new right, indicating and contesting the current claim that such militancy was the result of private funding. The researcher demonstrates that the boom of the new right is concentrated mainly in the period after the cycle of pro-impeachment protests of Dilma Rousseff. Emerging from online groups and forums, the militancy would have been formed mainly from voluntary work by young people. Using counterpublicity as a strategy, such groups would be characterized by their disruptive behaviours in the public sphere. Many of these groups began to mobilize in person through protests, meetings, and training sessions (Bringel & Pleyers, 2019; Klüppel et al., 2021; Sousa et al., 2022). Furthermore, they have combined the defence of Christian morals and the "traditional" family with the abjection of feminist claims and struggles for the recognition (Honneth, 1995) of the LGBTQIA+ community (Codato et al., 2015). Religious groups, predominantly Catholic and evangelical Protestants, also seem to be related to this activism (Severo et al., 2021). The motto "God, Homeland, Family, and Freedom", widely adopted by the former Brazilian president, Jair Bolsonaro, and used with slight variations by the new right, also requires a look at the past and the Brazilian Integralist Action, which, with a similar motto and led in the past by journalist Plínio Salgado, mobilized a large part of the Brazilian population in the 1960s (Caldeira Neto & Gonçalves, 2020).

[4] "Lulismo" is a term coined in articles and books by André Singer, referring to the broad electoral support gained by Luiz Inácio Lula da Silva, starting in 2006. The current Brazilian president is considered a symbolic figure of the Workers' Party and the Brazilian left; however, Singer was concerned with analysing how the entry of an opposition party into the institutional order represented a shift in its mobilizing and ideological aspect (Singer, 2009). In more common usage, "lulismo" refers solely to the massive support for Lula, becoming a factor of criticism and forming what is called the "anti-PTism", or the creation of counterpublics that directly attacked the party and its leader.

The Brazilian Integralist Action (AIB) came into being inspired by European fascism[5] and became known for its aggressive rhetoric and paramilitary tactics. Along with the Society for the Defence of Tradition, Family, and Property, known as TFP, the AIB took part in the famous March for the Family with God for Freedom, a prominent and foundational act for the Brazilian military dictatorship. The two groups can be understood as exponents of Brazilian clerical fascism. The "two Plínios"—Plínio Salgado and Plínio Corrêa de Oliveira—are still referenced figures, and the traditions inaugurated by their groups provide elements and symbols adopted by the new right. Both are significantly influenced by Catholicism, also leading to the need to reflect on religious influence. However, beyond the religious aspect, it is also through Adolpho Lindbergh—currently president of the Instituto Plínio Corrêa de Oliveira (IPCO)—that the first works of neoliberalism were brought to Brazil. Rocha (2019) explains that the translation of Hayek's work "The Road to Serfdom", in 1946, was already an initiative to block the advance of the Catholic left and the agendas it carried, such as land reform.

In this sense, Pleyers (2020) points out the central importance of the neo-Pentecostal church, which would have reclaimed the spaces left in Brazilian favelas by liberation Christianity, which was strongly persecuted before and during Brazilian military dictatorship. He understands that Bolsonaro's electoral victory in 2018 is part of a process of profound transformation, initiated in the early 1980s and carried forward with continuity and intelligence over four decades by conservative religious actors. Dantas (2013) analyses that the boundaries that previously separated public and private spaces, as well as politics and religion, are undergoing changes. Politics would be invading the private sphere, while religion would be reaching the public space. In the neo-Pentecostal context, the Theology of Dominion and the Theology of Spiritual Warfare would play a fundamental role in understanding the political actions of the churches. Dantas points out that, in neo-Pentecostalism, the battle between good and evil occurs in the social and political realm, through voting, electronic media, and property acquisition. This battle seeks to conquer the political domain of society, which is achieved by obtaining elective positions, expanding parliamentary representation, and consolidating political power.

[5] Pollard (2007) defines the term "clerical fascism" as a way to encompass individuals, movements, and regimes, or simply moments of encounter between Christian religion and fascism, both in terms of its geographical spread and the Christian denominations involved. This means that it is not only about Catholicism but also different forms of Protestantism and other extremist churches. Some Brazilian groups that combine religion and extremism, such as the integralist lineage, as well as the heirs of the Society for the Defence of Tradition, Family, and Property, are still present in the form of groups like IPCO (Plínio Corrêa de Oliveira Institute), Arcy Lopes Estrella Civic Association, Revolutionary Integral Action, Brazilian Integral Front (FIB), and the Brazilian Linearist Integral Movement. With different levels of radicalization, these groups are institutional organizations; however, Integralism has served and still serves as inspiration for the emergence of neo-Nazi groups and cells, such as the Skinheads of the Suburb and ABC, in addition to groups related to *White Power*. Costa's work (1993) is a reference for understanding the complexities of the "skinheads", as well as the subsequent divisions. Meanwhile, the work of Caldeira Neto and Gonçalves (2020) focuses mainly on the Integralists, their history, and subsequent branches.

In summary, in the Brazilian context, the emergence of a new right is highlighted, characterized by central features of authoritarianism and the adoption of ultraliberal agendas. Furthermore, with the expansion of neo-Pentecostalism, religion has occupied a central place in analyses that contribute to constructing the image of a complex phenomenon. Condensing many of these perspectives, historian Daniel Aarão Reis summarizes this as:

> an unashamed, active, and proactive far-right, with significant public activism, frequently taking to the streets, exploiting the shortcomings and deficiencies of democratic regimes, instrumentalizing them when convenient, disfiguring them "from within," and intensely using the mechanisms of the digital revolution. (Aarão Reis, 2020, p. 3)

In the European context, other traits have been considered fundamental and explored more actively in recent literature. As we will see, concepts such as radicalization and populism are considered fundamental marks that have led to theories about the "normalization" or "*mainstreaming*" of radical right-wing discourses (Mudde, 2016).

2.2 Radical, Populist, and Illiberal: Investigations into the Radical Right in Europe

Mayer (2020) states that the main shifts within political science studies on the European far-right occurred in the transition from extremism to radicalism and populism, from demand-focused interpretation to supply, and from the predominant application of quantitative methods and electoral analysis to a progressive—though still inferior—use of qualitative methodologies. In Europe, it is common to observe the differentiation between studies that focus on demand elements and others on supply. On one hand, demand analysis consists of the factors that lead to a "disposition" towards far-right ideas and movements, while supply analysis concerns the actors and strategies that promote and disseminate ideas and opportunities. On the demand side, there is the examination of social, economic, political, and cultural factors that would lead people to seek and identify with extremist agendas, actors, and movements. On the supply side, interpretations include activist groups, leaders, traditional and alternative media, and social networks—seeking to understand their strategies and how they shape their narratives to mobilize and expand the influence of the groups.

Despite the differentiation, the lines become more blurred when we closely analyse this literature. It is possible to state that most studies on the far-right in Europe have concentrated on (1) socioeconomic explanations related to precariousness (Hernández & Kriesi, 2016; Stockemer et al., 2018). There are also (2) sociopolitical explanations associated with the alienation of political elites, which would be more distant, disconnected, or oblivious to popular needs (Zhirkov, 2014), and (3) sociocultural explanations related to cultural changes in late modern societies, specifically the conflict between fundamentalist and postmodern values, with a special focus on reactions to multiculturalism (Ignazi, 1992; Mrozowicki et al., 2019).

Additionally, (4) other analyses identify a decline in neoliberal democracy and the repressive hardening of political regimes chosen through democratic procedures (Castells, 2018; Runciman, 2018). There are also (5) interpretations that replicate theories used for the analysis of Nazism and fascism, including certain psychological and psychoanalytical explanations, in which the idea of right-wing extremism as a "common pathological condition" prevails, which could recur in times of crisis and anomie (Scheuch & Klingermann, 1967).

On the supply side, there are mainly (1) theories of mobilization and leadership, in which populism often appears as a key analysis tool, highlighting the existence of charismatic leaders and groups that appeal through discourses opposing the people to political and economic elites (Minkenberg, 1992, 2017). Other (2) theories have focused on political and party competition, demonstrating that this would create a "political opportunity structure" (POS) (Kitschelt & McGann, 1997).

One of the theories that gained most attention is Betz's (1994), which focused on the political consequences of social change, pointing out that urbanization, social mobility, and the decline of class and religion-based solidarity produced a more fluid and atomized society, weakening old party loyalties and favouring "resentment politics" or "anti-politics". In his theory, Betz (1994) discusses the "losers of modernization" and seeks to consider the globalization process and the production of losers and winners. These losers would be those who attribute job losses and other changes to migratory flows. Such groups would see multiculturalism, cosmopolitanism, and universal norms as threats to their identities.

Within the set of socioeconomic explanations, there is also a series of works that relate neoliberalism, described as an economic policy that produces precariousness and flexibility in labour relations, with the prioritization of the market as a mediator of social relations. Within this current, there are also theories interpreting the dualization of the labour market in capitalist societies. Generally, the works are inspired by Standing (2014), who introduced the term *precariat* as a common and dangerous class that could politically vary between the extremes of right and left, as well as being more susceptible to populist demagoguery. Populism has been interpreted as a "thin-ideology" in contrast to what would be understood as complete ideologies, such as liberalism, socialism, and conservatism. These would offer a system of thoughts with specific and practical political solutions, while populism would consist of a simplified approach to the political world that, therefore, could attach itself to these different ideologies (Stanley, 2008; Wahl, 2020).

In the German case, Mudde (2016) identifies this as a fourth wave of radical right in the country. According to him, the first three post-World War II waves (1950s–1960s, 1980s–1990s, and 2010) were characterized by distinct ideological elements and political strategies; this fourth wave would represent a more nuanced and adaptable form of radical right politics that combines elements of the previous ones. In Germany, due to the Nazi past, right-wing political parties were largely associated with National Socialism. After World War II, some parts of the far-right restructured and founded the German Reich Party (Deutsche Reichspartei, DRP) and the German Party (Deutsche Partei, DP). In the first general elections after the war, in 1949, the far-right won only five seats in West Germany. Since then, far-right parties have had little lasting representation in the national parliament (Bundestag) and have remained a marginal factor in German politics. The most successful far-right party was the National Democratic Party of Germany (Nationaldemokratische Partei Deutschlands, NPD), which gained some seats in various German states (Länder) in the 1960s, with a nationalist, racist, anti-immigrant, extremist, and partially anti-capitalist agenda, along with open hostility towards the ruling system (Wahl, 2020).

Other far-right parties include the Republicans (Republikaner, REP), who gained votes in some states in the 1980s and 1990s, and the German People's Union (Deutsche Volksunion, DVU), which was successful in the 1990s. Generally, the voters of these parties were young, male, and from lower social strata or the lower middle class. After German reunification in 1990, far-right parties also found success in some East German states, where radical right movements were not previously officially allowed. However, in some states, they achieved levels of success not seen since post-war Germany (Schellenberg, 2013). The historical differences between West and East Germany from World War II until reunification in 1990, along with subsequent economic, demographic, social, cultural, and political changes, are understood to be responsible for a new political culture in the eastern regions to this day. Authoritarian and anti-immigrant attitudes are understood to be more common in East Germany (Decker et al., 2016).

The Alternative for Germany (AfD) emerged in 2013, assuming its heritage from the tradition of the new German right, which originated in the 1970s. It was during this time that revolutionary conservatives began advocating for the intellectualization of the right and the struggle for the construction of cultural hegemony. Through the concept of ethnopluralism, the movements and radical right-wing parties in Germany seek to disconnect from the Nazi past and the National Socialist Party. The party's platform structure is built on the claim of ideological freedom. They present themselves as the party with *expertise* and economic competence, combining market fundamentalism with right-wing conservatism. Salzborn (2016) states that the main foundations are concentrated in different schools of thought of neoliberalism and conservatism. These foundations include support for market fundamentalism and opposition to state interventionism, along with anti-egalitarian positions and opposition to the welfare state.

The late development of fourth-wave far-right parties in the country is often associated with the country's political culture, with a persistent shadow of the Nazi past. The fundamental change is attributed to the process that began post 2015, when the German federal government decided to accept a large number of war refugees from the Middle East. The refugee influx, which already existed before and increased considerably after this decision, was accompanied by additional immigrants from Africa and Asia. This situation led to a polarization in Germany between a "welcoming culture", on one hand, and, on the other, xenophobic and Islamophobic movements, such as PEGIDA and AfD, which gained notable support and now seem to be stable elements of the system (Schwander & Manow, 2017). Some authors (Kováts, 2018; Lewicki, 2018) analyse that the growth of the radical right in Europe is deeply related to racialization and consequent Islamophobia, as well as confrontation with gender policies, also crystallized in the fight against the so-called "gender ideology".

Schwander and Manow (2017) agree that, compared to other European countries, Germany was late in seeing the return of far-right party representation. The authors also indicate that the tradition of studies on this topic was connected to Hanz George Hetz's theory of the "resistance of the losers of modernization". This thesis argues that the voters of far-right parties would be those who "lost" with modernization, therefore those who would wish to undo its recent effects. In general, analyses focus on socioeconomic losses, but the data collected by the authors do not corroborate this perspective. According to Schwander and Manow (2017, p. 19),

> the support for the AfD is rather independent from economic factors and particularly strong now at a moment in which the German economy is doing extremely well, (it) suggests that this new party is going to stay and to become a stable element in the party system. It will also not do to simply address economic grievances, when the main conflict line is of socio-cultural character.

Regarding the mentioned stabilization, Mudde (2019) has pointed out that the German populist far-right should be seen as a radical interpretation of *mainstream* values or even as a form of "pathological normality". This argument is supported by an empirical analysis of party ideologies and voter attitudes. This proposed paradigmatic change has profound implications for understanding the relationship between the far-right and Western democracy, as well as for studying the phenomenon itself. Notably, Mudde (2016) proposes considering the demand for populist far-right policies more as an assumption than a puzzle. The notion of "*normal pathology*" would challenge the idea that the populist far-right is a completely external and strange phenomenon to the political and social system, arguing that it reflects distorted or exaggerated aspects of existing social and political norms. This has also transformed perspectives regarding voters who, for a long time, were interpreted as emotional, irrational, and driven by revolt rather than by ideological convictions. Recent studies speak about rational choices showing how votes for the radical right in Germany can be "protest votes" (Mayer, 2020), demonstrating rejection of other parties.

Moving in the same direction, there is a recent trend of studies that has gained magnitude in recent years and presents the growth trajectory of such groups, movements, and parties as part of "illiberalism" (Laruelle, 2022). Illiberalism is an emerging concept in social sciences, considered by some as an ideology, but having as its main element its intrinsic dependence on liberalism. What is interesting in the more recent use of the concept is that it has led to a deeper analysis of liberalism itself and its *scripts*, inviting researchers to decentre the values and policies related to it as "intrinsically correct". Additionally, studies that centralize groups classified as "illiberal" as external and present their existence as a threat and representation of a setback to the liberal democratic script have also been questioned.

Through the concept, a black-and-white dichotomy between liberalism and illiberalism is avoided, conceptualizing illiberalism as a response or challenge to some of liberalism's scripts (political, economic, cultural, geopolitical, and colonial[6]). This means that the relationship between the two terms depends on the context and evolves according to changes in liberalism over time and space. Illiberalism, therefore, arises from and within liberalism, not as the existential opposite but rather as a denunciation of liberalism for failing to achieve its democratic objectives. Illiberalism presents itself, therefore, as post-liberal, competing with liberalism through the use of its own conceptual language. The most widespread definition is made by Laruelle (2022, p. 304), when stating that:

> 1/illiberalism is a new ideological universe that, even if doctrinally fluid and context-based, is to some degree coherent; 2/ it represents a backlash against today's liberalism in all its varied scripts—political, economic, cultural, geopolitical, civilizational—often in the name of democratic principles and thanks to them (by winning the popular vote); 3/ it proposes solutions that are majoritarian, nation-centric or sovereigntist, favouring traditional hierarchies and cultural homogeneity; and 4/it calls for a shift from politics to culture and is post-post-modern in its claims of rootedness in an age of globalisation.

The concept has not yet gained traction in the Brazilian and Latin American academic context, where, as we discussed earlier, issues such as the authoritarian past, religion, and colonialism hold critical importance in analyses. However, illiberalism stands out in the context of this book because it directly engages with understandings about the non-existence of an "inside" and "outside" of liberalism. Thus, the concept resonates with the discussion of activism within radical right-wing groups as part of the liberal democratic script, creating tension from within rather than eroding it from the outside. The notion of illiberalism, therefore, centralizes the idea of "tension", requiring researchers to delve into understanding the paths of constitution of the liberal democratic script within the contexts of countries. This also clarifies that actors, groups, and movements of the radical right will reference the conceptual language constructed within liberal democracy, disputing meanings and constituting new chains of signification.

2.3 The Radical Right: Plurality and Radicalization

Mudde (1996) states that between 1980 and 1995, there was a "war of words" to define the phenomenon of the emergence of a series of parties in Western Europe. This war involved 28 different definitions, based on 58 distinct ideological traits. One of the most used definitions initially was Ignazi's (1992), which addressed the existence of a "silent counter-revolution" in reaction to the spread of values he termed post-materialist. The author created a scale, differentiating spatial dimensions (positions within a right/left scale), an ideological criterion (e.g., with or without references to fascism), and finally, an attitudinal measure (pro- or anti-system, which meant pro- or anti-democracy). This scale was used to differentiate the new

[6] To understand the five *scripts* of liberalism and the threats related to it, see "Liberalism(s), illiberalism(s), and their inner tensions" in Laruelle (2022).

right from the old traditional right-wing parties in European countries. Heitmeyer (2003, p. 401), another fundamental name in these studies in Europe, began to list two central elements for the sociological concept of "right-wing extremism": "Ideologies of inequality on the one hand, such as exaggerated nationalism, racist denigration, and totalitarian views of the law, are associated with varying levels of acceptance of violence on the other".

It was in France, through Pierre-André Taguieff, as early as 1984, that the concept of populism began to be used to define European parties. Previously, the concept was fundamentally applied to the study of political processes in Latin America, where there is considered to be a "broad and enduring variety of left and right populisms" (Wahl, 2020, p. 336). The researcher was the first to interpret and label the ideology of the French National Front (FN) as national populist for using a mix of nationalism, xenophobia, and demagoguery in the name "of the people". In English-language literature, Betz (1994) established the main difference between the new parties and the traditional far-right as the fact that they did not reject democratic rules nor advocated violence. In relation to the centre, they differed because they favoured a radical transformation in the post-war democratic society consensus and, therefore, in the Welfare State and the acceptance of multicultural society. Finally, they were populists in their argumentation—declaring faith in common sense and the moral superiority of the common man, offering simple solutions to complex problems—and in their political strategy, articulating a "politics of resentment" to mobilize people against the political class and elites (Mayer, 2020).

Despite previous uses, it was Mudde and Kaltwasser (2017) who consolidated themselves as the main names in the dissemination of populism studies. "Radical right populism" was defined by Mudde (2016) as the core ideology of groups and parties that combine three main traits: nativism (as a combination of nationalism and xenophobia), authoritarianism (the belief in a strictly organized society), and populism (seeing the people as pure as opposed to the corrupt elites). The term radical right—derived from the use of "radicalism" to explore the phenomenon—began to be propagated in the mid-1990s in European studies, replacing the term extremism. The term quickly gained ground due to its lesser stigmatization and its supposed disconnection from fascism and Nazism. In the German case, left and right extremism in the post-war period were recognized as anti-democratic and unconstitutional. In this sense, parties and groups classified under this terminology were under surveillance and even banned. Radicals, who opposed certain principles of the Constitution, were understood as "less threatening" and were not subjected to such procedures.[7]

[7] The concept of "*militant democracy*" is used in the context of studies on democratic responses to political extremism. In the German case, there is a policy of proscription and banning of parties, as well as surveillance of movements. Decisions regarding movements and groups occur at the level of the Ministry of Interior Affairs and do not need to be taken for legislative analysis. Recent analyses discuss the effectiveness of these mechanisms in terms of controlling radicalization. In the context of this book, it is interesting to consider the existence of this law in the German context, which has differences in the Brazilian context. For a group or movement in Brazil to be investi-

Arzheimer (2019), in a recent article, dedicated himself to discussing the conceptual issues in the field in Western Europe. The author states that despite the different nomenclatures, the field of study of the phenomenon has been expanding and advancing, maintaining, however, a more recurrent use of "radical right" based on Mudde's studies (2016, 2019) to refer to the new manifestations of the "far right". Mudde establishes the broad existence of the "far-right"[8] and differentiates between "extreme-right" and "radical right". Regarding the extreme right, the radical right is differentiated by its partial acceptance of democratic principles, such as popular sovereignty and majority rule, although it shares the extreme right's denial of liberal democracy, especially concerning constitutional protections for minorities (ethnic, political, religious), the separation of powers, and the rule of law (Mudde, 2016).

Despite the importance of the differentiation constructed in the European context and its widespread use in the literature, the recent invasions—of the three branches of government in Brazil, the Capitol in the United States, as well as the threat to the German Parliament—challenge the assertion about the acceptance of popular sovereignty and majority rule. In this sense, it can be stated that Arzheimer (2019) offers an alternative by asserting that such movements present an ambiguous relationship with liberal democracy, where, on one hand, there is participation in democratic instances and the pursuit of legislative and executive positions, and on the other, there is a constant breach of democratic norms, either through the denial of the principle of equality or through the legitimization of political violence and radicalization.

In the Latin American context, researchers (Gentile, 2018; Stefanoni, 2021; Díaz, 2021) have pointed to the existence of diverse constellations within the new right. They highlight the coexistence of a myriad of political identities, whose main trait is the defence of a neoliberal and conservative agenda. As early as 1987, Pierucci commented on the foundations of what he called a new Brazilian right, stating that the central framework of these new groups was the feeling of threat in relation to the "others", these being criminals, northeastern migrants, certain immigrants, "liberated" women, and homosexuals. In a precise diagnosis, the author speaks of the existence of constellations within this new right characterized by diluted contours, undefined boundaries, and uncertain limits. The researcher observed that:

> the different positions or alignments we find in this cultural zone of far-right expansion are not pieces of a puzzle that could fit together as independent subsets, forming a harmonious and confined whole. They interpenetrate, react to one another, sometimes mix, always

---

gated, the decision occurs at the level of the Supreme Federal Court. When authorized, the investigation is conducted by the Federal Police, which has some specialized units. For more on the policy of proscription in Germany, see Bourne (2011) and Bertoa and Bourne (2017). In the Brazilian context, I have not found articles that directly discuss the topic.

[8] In Portuguese, the problem lies in the translation of the terms "*far-right*" and "*extreme-right*". Both have been translated as "*extrema-direita*". However, it can be understood that "*far-right*" refers to the idea of distant or far, referring to the position in the general political spectrum. Meanwhile, "*extreme*" can be understood as an interpretation of extremist practices and agendas.

> engulf each other, here they enrich, there they nullify, here they appear and there they hide, like stellar masses, distinct but no less nebulous. (Pierucci, 1987, p. 40)

Thus, Pierucci contributes to an understanding of the new right as constellations composed of a diversity of identities, which will not always "fit", potentially producing a nebulous effect for those observing them.

Gentile (2020), in "A 'plural' right: ideological configurations and political organizations of the contemporary Brazilian right", states that we are facing a new phenomenon, where authoritarian thought and the Brazilian dictatorial heritage are combined with the conservative-liberal theories of Hayek and the neoliberal doctrine of Milton Friedman. He highlights the existence of a plurality within the new right, or the contemporary Brazilian right, where groups organized around a "common ideological-political platform, ranging from anti-PTism to anti-Bolivarianism (…) passing through anti-politics and moral conservatism (…) to the traditional arguments of neoliberalism" (Gentile, 2020, p. 236). The use of the expression "new right" would be justified by a temporal issue and to differentiate from the mainstream or traditional right, also emphasizing the idea of plurality.

In this sense, Stefanoni (2021), in his recent book *La rebeldía se volvió de derecha* also sought to highlight the porous configurations of the new right and their ability to capitalize on social indignation, presenting themselves as a "challenge" to the system. These "*derechas*", also placed in the plural by the author, have had the ability to mobilize indignation in the face of reality, presenting proposals to transform it. Stefanoni advocates the use of "*derechas*" in the plural to emphasize the diversity and complexity within right-wing movements and ideologies. He highlights in his book that right-wing politics and movements encompass a wide range of perspectives, factions, and actors, recognizing that the right-wing spectrum is not a monolithic entity but rather a heterogeneous collection of political orientations. As examples, he indicates that it encompasses conservative, nationalist, populist, neoliberal, and authoritarian currents. Furthermore, the author is concerned with asserting that the right is not a fixed and static entity but rather subject to internal debates, contradictions, and changes over time.

Díaz (2021) argues that liberal democracy should not become the main point of reference for political analyses, pointing out that there is no substantial difference between what is understood and analysed in Latin America as the "*new right*" and what has been interpreted in Europe as "illiberal conservatism". Based on her ethnographic work and interviews in Brazil, the author advocates the notion of a "*plural right*", which encompasses various ideological expressions and takes into account the nature of the psychological motivations and identity crises that drive individuals towards radical right movements. The second tradition involves sociological approaches that examine the structural and cultural conditions fostering the rise of these movements, such as economic instability and social dislocation. These perspectives highlight the complex interplay between individual agency and broader societal factors in understanding the appeal and growth of radical right activism.

The researcher emphasizes the existence of neoliberalization processes combined with coercive processes, where there is an activation of movements and organizations to mobilize and fight for discursive and political hegemony. She also stresses that contemporary right-wing actors and phenomena are far from coherent as they present elements that do not fit into the constructed theoretical categorizations. From this perspective, the new right should not refer to specific political individuals or a well-defined set of characteristics but should serve as a heuristic category to explore enduring features and signs of renewal in contemporary right-wing projects.

In light of such contributions from Latin American and European literature on the subject, I have chosen for my doctoral dissertation the expression "*direitas radicais*", which could be translated as "radical rights" or a "plural radical right". This expression seeks to emphasize the issue of plurality—affirmed in the Latin American context—and to establish a differentiation from the traditional right through the adjective "*radicais*"—following the European tradition. "*Direitas radicais*" is proposed as a heuristic category encompassing actors, groups, movements, and parties that generate tensions within liberal democracy by attacking the constitutional protections afforded to minorities (ethnic, religious, and economic) and challenging the role of the state as a regulator of social and economic inequalities.

I highlight that the concept of radicalization—in the European and North American context—has been exhaustively used to understand the trajectories of actors related to Islamic religious extremism (Sedgwick, 2010; McCauley & Moskalenko, 2011; Hofmann, 2020). This also occurred in some Brazilian studies (Gonçalves, 2014; Begeres Bisneto, 2019) that focused on the "terrorist" category, expressing a valid concern but contributing to a stigmatization and reduction of the understanding of radicalization processes solely from the perspective of global jihadism and Islamic fundamentalism. More recent studies have contributed to defining radicalization as a multidimensional process, encompassing social, psychological, and cultural factors that lead to the legitimization of hate speech, conspiracy theories, and the justification or practice of political violence (Miller-Idriss, 2018a, 2018b; Adorno, 2022).

The use of the "plural" also involves understanding that such actors, groups, movements, and parties have particularities in different regions of the world, acquiring elements related to social contexts and national policies, as well as the historical past of each region or country. Despite the importance of emphasizing plurality, throughout this book and in the following chapters, I adopt the term "radical right". The expression "radical rights" is avoided because incorporating the plural does not convey the intended meaning. Similarly, "plural radical right" is set aside due to its lack of fluidity. The choice of "radical right", however, does not imply adherence to the concept as it is used in the European context but rather reflects a decision based on the best balance between translation and readability.

In the next section, I aim to gather research that has addressed the radical right in the Brazilian and German contexts, constituting a local state of the art on the subject. I emphasize, however, that for this review, I will use the terms and concepts most used in the context, also reproducing those chosen by the referenced authors. In this way, I seek to respect and enable the visualization of their theoretical choices.

As presented throughout this chapter, the conceptual trajectory has direct effects on the understanding of actors, groups, and movements, including defining which would be the valid sources for understanding the prevailing power mechanisms. Therefore, new interpretations and new concepts influence and are influenced by empirical studies. In the next section, I explore the traditions of empirical research on activism in the radical right, revealing how such studies have highlighted neglected dimensions of the phenomenon, also leading to conceptual revisions.

2.4 Exploring Youth Activism on the Radical Right

Despite the radical right movements explicitly trying to distance themselves from any correlation with the fascist past and not identifying with the term "radical", research has pointed out that their expansion has direct connections with racism, sexism, and the justification of violence against individuals and groups (Blee & Creasap, 2010; Quintão, 2017; Pettersson & Sakki, 2022). This has justified the analysis of participation in such movements as being different and external to democracy or similar to past fascism.[9] Additionally, radicalism on the left and right has received different lenses of observation, in the first case, with the use of mobilization theories while in the second, through breakdown theories (Caiani et al., 2012). Such analyses regarding engagement in the radical right have integrated some present investigation traditions; the first is based on psychological or psychoanalytic theories that bring to the centre of the discussion issues like personality disorders and traumatic experiences, including also analyses on "authoritarian personalities" (Wahl, 2020; Pucci, 2020; Monteiro, 2023; Heitmeyer, 2018). Within this set, there are also studies that seek to establish correlations between far-right political ideologies and aggressive tendencies to rationalizations of emotional problems, which would be related to childhood and family experiences (Wahl et al., 2013; Meier et al., 2022).

The second would be the explanations that connect extremism to job insecurity, inferior status quo, or social isolation. Many of them are based on the positioning of

[9] Sahd (2022) will explore the classificatory disputes involving the use of the concepts of fascism, neo-fascism, and post-fascism. The author revisits the works of Finchelstein (2017), Laqueur (1997), Stanley (2018), and Traverso (2019) to understand how the concept has been applied to the analysis of emerging movements, leaders, and parties since the 1980s. Despite understanding the validity of the reference to fascism, it is understood that many analyses ignore the particularities found through empirical investigations. There is an importance in developing typologies for the study of political manifestations; however, when shifted to research that focuses on the normative and discursive levels, the search is for the interpretation of emerging mechanisms. In this sense, Traverso's work (2019) is the one with which we find the greatest dialogue, as it emphasizes the plurality of the phenomenon, understood as "composite and heterogeneous". The author also highlights the influences of neoliberalism, in addition to pointing out the need to use the past to illuminate the present, seeking "analogies and differences" and not "homologies and repetitions" (Sahd, 2022, p. 116).

activists as "victims of the system" and, in the case of young people, emphasize exclusion and social inequalities as factors that make the transition to adult life later and more troubled (Buchholz et al., 2009; Giugni & Grasso, 2021). Others also emphasize the failures of democratic institutions in ensuring equal rights for all (Mouffe, 2018; Huke, 2021; Lorenzen et al., 2016). There is also the cognitive style approach, based on Rokeach (1960), which points to a "simplistic view", which would connect activism in such movements to a low level of education and a black-and-white worldview.

Individually, the research brings important elements for the analysis of the phenomenon, contributing to the understanding of possible influencing factors. However, when considered as research traditions, they contribute to the stigmatization and reproduction of a Manichean view of activists, sometimes presenting them as passive and victimized in the face of macrostructural conditions, sometimes presenting them as a homogeneous group marked by "deviation" or "pathology"—even if, ultimately, the pathology can be described as "normal" (Mudde, 2016).

This issue also expands to the terminological tradition for referring to the groups. There is reluctance to frame activism in the radical right within the studies of social movements. In this sense, it is possible to understand that the frequent exclusion of radical right activism in investigations about young people and their political participation reflects a neglected relationship between analytical and normative perspectives. The distinction between the "real" political participation of young people and participation in radical right movements neglects the distinction between politics and the political and between existing democratic orders and institutions and the principle of democracy, besides not taking into account the transformations arising from new normativities in political subjectivation (Dardot & Laval, 2016; Cooper, 2017). Moreover, it tends to stigmatize the young people involved in these movements, which limits the possibility of visualizing their trajectories, as well as identifying the meanings attributed to political participation (Besen & Walther, 2023).

Such traditions have been questioned by research that seeks to highlight the heterogeneity of activists attracted or engaged in radical right movements. This set of research (Schellenberg, 2013; Krasteva, 2017; Miller-Idriss, 2018a, 2018b; Mrozowicki et al., 2019; Pasieka, 2021, 2022) developed and applied new qualitative methodologies that allowed visualizing the diversity of emerging movements, as well as a complex and porous mosaic of identifications. These researchers abandoned the analysis of electoral behaviour to focus on interviews and ethnographic observation (Mayer, 2020), placing special emphasis on the possibility of analysing the actors similarly to others involved in "conventional" forms of participation. Thus, such research presents a view of these activists as rational and instrumental, who mobilize due to collective interests and identities.

The first large-scale research was conducted by Klandermans and Mayer (2005)[10] and involved 157 life trajectory interviews with members of radical right parties in

[10] Klandermans and Mayer (2005) were pioneers in looking at the trajectories and seeking to discuss such activism within the studies of social movements. Two results are highlighted, the first concerning the fact that these subjects do not come from contexts of prior marginalization. For this

5 European countries. Another large-scale research was developed by David Art[11] (2011) with 140 interviews with activists from 20 parties in 11 different countries. These studies have already challenged and questioned stereotypes that project onto activists the image of violent and extremist, whose origin dates back to analyses of members of neo-Nazi and neo-fascist groups. These studies highlighted, mainly, the importance of party agency and leadership, gender relations, the way the radical right recruit and train their members, as well as party structures and communication and alliance formation strategies. Moreover, they revealed that the activists formed a very diverse group, with different backgrounds, ages, and education, involving a majority of socially integrated and connected people.

More recent research (Miller-Idriss, 2018b; Pasieka, 2021; Krasteva, 2017; Klandermans, 2013, 2020) has extended this finding to young activists and assessed that this diversity is not only evidence of the broad appeal and success of mobilization of these movements but also a political "asset"—in the sense that having a variety of skills and attributes in their activists brings benefits to the groups. Furthermore, recent studies (Blee, 2017, Pilkington, 2016; Toscano, 2019; also inspired by Klandermans and Mayer (2005)) have stated that these groups "meet the criteria to be analysed as social movements, as they constitute a network of interactions between individuals who share an identity, are engaged in a political/cultural/social conflict, and use collective action to voice specific concerns and grievances" (Pasieka, 2021, p. 87).

Nilan (2021), in a recently published book, "Youth and Far Right", constructs one of the most comprehensive analyses on the subject, seeking to condense the literature to produce new categories of analysis for the "fourth wave" of extremism (Mudde, 2019) and its appeal to young people. The book was written amid the Covid-19 pandemic and sheds light on the issues faced by young people in terms of the mismatch between their youthful aspirations and the realities of contemporary

reason, they point out that exclusion cannot be identified as a cause, but often as a consequence of activism. Many families reproduce exclusion, with stigma being a factor that deepens engagement with the group and, therefore, a factor that hinders activists' exit. The authors also discuss that almost all interviewees were motivated mainly by an exclusive nationalism, a rejection of immigration, and an "anti-foreigner" stance, while anti-Semitism and the glorification of the Nazi past were not very present. Finally, they highlight that, when compared to activism on the far left, the similarities lie only in the willingness to act politically, with the central axes of their participation being quite conflicting elements. On one hand, within the far-right, there would be a defence of discipline and authority, while on the left, equality would establish itself as a fundamental axis.

[11] Art (2011) was interested in understanding how the profile of activists translated into conditions of party success or failure. With this purpose, he divides activists into moderates, extremists, and opportunists and, in a theoretical and practical manner, seeks to demonstrate how the distribution of these "types" within parties leads to different developments. Thus, his main focus is on the interrelation between parties and activists, pointing out that some parties have strategies that will work to attract activists with higher levels of education and experience, while others will only mobilize lower social classes without prior political experience. Embedded in the period it was produced, the study is important as it brings new focuses to the field; however, the stigmatization of activists remains present so that, despite the shift to trajectories and experiences, the work still seeks to understand and predict the electoral success of parties.

social and political life. The researcher states that young people from the far-right have a desire to be active agents in building their futures, but these are often idealized. Therefore, the main focus of the book is the far-right ideologies that would have the ability to identify or create a sense of injustice and inspire young people to imagine a better future, connecting such a future to an agenda of political action.

Nilan (2021) mentions the existence of "narratives of hope", such as Western ultranationalism. In the European context, this would function as a "tale of hope", projecting a utopian society free of immigration, miscegenation, and cultural diversity into the future. One of the main tools of the new far-right movements, groups, and parties would be to provide an empowered vision of oneself, a vision of heroic action equipped with the power to mitigate an imminent danger. In this way, the movements would not seek to present themselves as conservative but rather as spaces for radical political action.

The researcher asserts that it is essential to avoid stereotypes and understand that it is no longer the angry young neo-Nazi who dominates contemporary far-right movements but rather "ordinary" young people. Despite the interesting elements of the book, the main issue is precisely that "ordinary" men are characterized only as young white men, who would fight against amorphous feelings of anger and resentment as privileges traditionally granted to them are perceived as threatened or withdrawn (Smith, 2022). This issue is not ignored by the author, who even problematizes and points to exceptions. However, the choice permeates the book, which focuses mainly on the appeal to this group.

The author assumes that the emotional foundation transcends the explanatory power of the "white supremacy" ideology and seeks to think about elements of these young people's everyday lives that provide a basis for identification with the far-right. Thus, she analyses the playing of video games and points out that the lives of young men and boys are increasingly shaped by a militarized variant of youth culture, which comes through first-person shooter (FPS) games. She understands this environment, dominated by men, "with synchronous live chat functions and the player's subjective position in a 'killing space' during an epic battle for survival as conducive to socialization in far-right subcultural environments" (Nilan, 2021, p. 41).

In contrast to studies centred on the involvement of white men (Nilan, 2021) or the predominance of adherence among resentful lower classes (Betz, 2018), there are studies like those of Pasieka (2022), Krasteva (2017), and Miller-Idriss (2018b), which see young activists as a complex and diverse set of individuals, including "well-established middle-class citizens with dense networks of social ties who do not feel excluded in any way; as well as students, intellectuals, and entrepreneurs" (Pasieka, 2022, p. 174). Furthermore, these studies suggest avoiding the use of the term "radical right youth", as it indicates a fixed position or identity rather than a movement. Miller-Idriss (2018b) proposes thinking of identities as "fluid, complex and contradictory, with boundaries that are porous rather than fixed" (Miller-Idriss, 2018a, 2018b, p. 351). Additionally, such research has shown that young people's involvement with radical right is driven by a combination of structural conditions and subjective factors that mutually reinforce each other.

Krasteva (2016, 2017), combining ethnography and interviews with young leaders of European radical right movements, establishes three main problematic areas in the field of investigation: the theoretical understanding of far-right youth activism, the process of constructing activist figures in the radical right, and possible democratic responses to youth radicalization. Her analysis presents two theoretical perspectives: the concept of a lost generation and that of contestatory citizenship. In the case of the first concept, the author focuses on structural causes and factors for activism, pointing out that the economic crisis would have generated marginalization, and neoliberal globalization would have generated pressure and unemployment. According to Krasteva, the socioeconomic deficits and contradictions produced in this process would be an important basis for engagement.

The concept of contestatory citizenship seeks to highlight young people as actors in their political choices that involve energy and activism and thus open theoretical horizons in two lines: The first concerns theoretical sensitivity to data showing that the far-right attracts young people from different social classes and that the reasons for joining it may have less to do with socioeconomic marginalization than with identities and protests, and the second line is based on a conceptual apparatus, whose focus is not on society and its deficiencies but on the actors with their potential for action. Krasteva (2017) points to protest as a form of mobilization characteristic of societies in the face of an "expansion of conflict" in the political scene and indicates that there is still little research opting for this path, with a tradition contributing to the stigmatization of young people, hindering the construction of democratic solutions to radicalization. Through the process of articulating both analyses, she argues that "the activists themselves are situated in different positions across the wide spectrum of far-right agency, forming a bricolage of identities, images, imaginaries" (Krasteva, 2017, p. 152).

Pasieka (2021) conducted an ethnographic study on activists in Italy, Poland, Hungary, and Slovakia and identified that far-right movements provide young people with tools to be active and believe they will be agents of change. The activists develop an emotional bond with the transnational fostering community, identified by researchers in various European countries. Caiani et al. (2012) defined radical right movements as rational, intentional, and organized, relying on organizational resources, repertoires, and structures that reflect political opportunities. Additionally, they identified a complex discourse in radical right groups structured by frameworks that pay considerable attention to broad political issues and form the self-identity of right-wing activists. Similarly, Braun et al. (2009) state that right-wing extremism presents itself as a planned world of experiences, whose offerings are precisely tailored to the needs of a young and heterogeneous target group.

de Sousa et al. (2022) conducted an analysis of the new right positioned in the Brazilian political debate based on interviews with activists from a Brazilian university located in the northeast of Brazil. The objective was "to identify the different attributes of the right-wing identity formulated in narratives of right-wing activists in a Brazilian public university, the contradictions in the content of this identity, and the rhetorical-discursive resources mobilized in its construction" (de Sousa et al., 2022, p. 4). The researchers point out that, after 2013, there is the constitution of a militancy that not only begins to publicly assume its identity but also demands the occupation of public spaces. Thus, these groups develop direct actions to produce new subjectivities and political identities in the student environment, aligned with "right-wing thought". These activists mention three political groups as constituents of the right (the conservatives, the liberals, and the libertarians), but only two are used as self-identification categories: the conservatives and the libertarians.

Identity attributes, such as appreciation for truth, defence of freedom, distrust of abrupt changes, and the valuing of family and Christian religiosity, were observed as defining the identity of the right. Regarding the definition of the right, they affirm that students constructed distinct identity positions for right-wing militancy in universities, but the discrimination experienced within university spaces was one of the most recurring themes. The university was identified as a threatening environment for right-wing students, as left-wing groups in the university would be antagonistic and of authoritarian, hegemonic, oppressive nature, and incapable of dialogue. The right is, therefore, identified as a minority movement.

Díaz (2021, p. 3), in "Make (neo)liberalism Cool Again", uses the case of the Free Brazil Movement as an example of the "amalgamation of neoliberalism and conservatism that has consolidated as fertile ground for anti-leftism". Based on interviews and participant observation at events and protests, the researcher says that right-wing militancy has consolidated itself in everyday social spaces perceived as cool and countercultural. The researcher points out that central elements of the neoliberal script, such as the defence of meritocracy, would have aligned with the conservative discourse against "cultural Marxism" and "gender ideology". She reconstructs a path of encounter between the defence of entrepreneurship and opposition to "political correctness", which forge a right-wing political project combining ideological currents and symbols of humour, resulting in young and attractive political cultures.

Other academics in the field of youth studies have interpreted the rise of the radical right as an insurgency of a generation of young conservatives (Weller & Bassalo, 2020; Severo et al., 2021). Based on Mannheim (1982), these researchers argue that with each new generation, young people establish new ways of interpreting and understanding the world, resulting in a constant formation of new connections and social identities. These studies indicate that the worldview shared by this generation of young conservatives combines traditionalist values and customs with a liberal economic model, as reflected in the slogan "Liberal in the economy, conservative in customs" (Silva, 2021).

Severo et al. (2021) conducted research in Brazilian public high schools to analyse the political alignment of young people, finding that significant markers in the ideological formation of the right-wing political spectrum, such as the religious community and family, require more attention and the adoption of other qualitative research methods that can capture the specificities of these important social institutions. Weller and Bassalo (2020) analysed Facebook groups related to conservative movements and identified that the period from 2013 to 2016 stood out as the one with the most page launches, corresponding to 63% of the total. From observing Facebook pages of conservative groups, they sought to understand how groups of young people publicly announce and in a virtual environment a cultural heritage related to a conservative style of thought (Weller & Bassalo, 2020, p. 1).

On Facebook pages, the authors identified clear strategies of polarization with other groups and styles of thought and emphasize that these young people underwent an individual calling, primarily through online means. On Brazilian Facebook pages of groups identified as conservative, they identified various images of characters and figures that reference the armed forces, exalting the period when the military was in power as a counter-revolution against communism. This reinterpretation of violent actions during the military dictatorship as legitimate protective actions has been articulated with attacks on the current human rights policy (Teixeira & Barbosa, 2022).

Despite the contribution of research focused on networks, Weller and Bassalo (2020) criticize the still existing gap in studies on youth concerning the understanding of young people's engagement in radical right-wing movements, in particular because a significant part of the research on youth excludes radical right-wing activism from young people's participation. In this sense, I will seek, in the next sections, to explore what has been the tradition of studies on youth and youth political participation, aiming to introduce the theme of young activism in radical right-wing movements in this field of study.

2.4.1 *Traditions in Youth Studies*

Youth cannot be considered a recent and limited field of investigation. There is a vast universe of research, comparative studies, and reports from state and private institutions that have built definitions about youth, pointing out their issues, ways of acting, life trajectories, forms of grouping, and, finally, modes of "political participation". Youth is defined as a social, generational, and political category, centred and focused on sociological, psychological, and educational studies, as well as multidisciplinary ones. Conducting systematic reviews[12] allows us to see that the production of the youth category occurred through reiterated discourses and norms, beginning at the start of the last century in the form of the production of "youth as a social problem".

In the early twentieth century, theorists who turned to the study of youth had urban violence as their central concern. Many biological/genetic explanations defined dangerousness and delinquency as typically juvenile behaviours. The problems of "juvenile delinquency" and "youth gangs" were articulated as part of a

[12] Studies such as those by Foracchi (1972), Cardoso and Sampaio (1995), Sposito (2009), Santos (2011), Freire Filho (2005), Tavares (2012), Abramo (1997, 2005), Trancoso and Oliveira (2016), Sposito and Tarábola (2017), and Walther et al. (2020) proposed to establish a path for studies on youth, participation, and youth cultures, coining their own proposals for defining the category of youth and participation, as well as establishing forecasts and indications about studies on the topic in countries.

larger concern with the problems of city organization and urban life. The Chicago School, starting in 1920, inaugurated sociological interpretations on the subject, with Human Ecology as one of its main theories.[13]

Researchers established the city as their main "laboratory", focusing on research in urban areas considered "degraded". Authors like Thrasher (1927), Shaw (1966), and Whyte (2005) conducted their studies on American gangs. Almeida (2009, p. 122) explains that "from the understanding of 'ecological zones' and 'city territories', Chicago School researchers built links between 'social disorganization and violence, transition zone and crime, urban violence and youth'". Whyte (2005) was the first researcher to question the passivity attributed to youth collectives through ethnographic research conducted with migrant groups in Boston. The author highlighted the tensions, alliances, and active behaviours of young people both in terms of the variety of territories and in their movement between the legal and illegal fields. Whyte, along with Coleman and Parsons, form a group of researchers who began to analyse the existence of "youth cultures". Youth groupings began to be understood as transitional spaces between the private and parental world to public life, within which young people developed their identity aspects. From this framework, ideas began to emerge that youth is a reflection/image of current social and economic transformations and that their behaviours could be "reactive".

Cultural studies related to youth began in England in the post-war context. The Centre for Contemporary Cultural Studies (CCCS), under the rubric of the Birmingham School, is the space where a series of studies was developed, not only with the aim of redefining the meaning of culture but of inserting, within the scope of valid fields of interdisciplinary investigation, the experiences, lifestyles, and symbolic production within youth collectives. The centre was founded in 1964 by Richard Hoggart and was linked to the English Department of the University of Birmingham, constituting a postgraduate research centre of the same institution. "The relationships between contemporary culture and society, that is, its cultural forms, institutions, and cultural practices, as well as their relationships with society and social changes, compose its main research axis" (Escosteguy, 1998, p. 88).

Still in the 1960s, cultural studies were impacted by their research focused on everyday life, using Marxist assumptions to understand what they considered to conform to or not movements of resistance. Cultural studies traversed various paths and arrived with force in Brazil years later. Work of Freire Filho (2005), for example, established an extremely interesting path, addressing how cultural studies can articulate with the conception of resistance; *Reinventions of Youth Resistance* marks a trajectory from Anglo-American cultural studies to Brazilian ones. Freire Filho states that cultural studies sought to distance themselves from the functionalist views of the Chicago School, as well as from others that suggested there was a

[13] There are still authors who use Human Ecology theories to reflect on urban violence in Brazil within the legal field. Examples of this approach can be seen in "Respect for Urban Functions and the Prevention of Urban Crime: An Integrated Vision in Light of the Chicago School" (Farias, 2009) and "Youth and Crime from the Perspective of the Chicago School" (Catão & Pereira, 2015).

"homogeneous youth consumer culture—a solidly integrated social block (...) a harbinger of prosperity that would extend to all" (Freire Filho, 2005, p. 140).

In the post-war period, youth emerged as the main consumer, both due to their growing cultural interests and the purchasing power they acquired in European countries. Current analyses of the "youth issue", mainly from Anglo-American psychology, highlighted a pathologization of youth. Young consumers were seen as "hedonistic" and "irrational", and juvenile delinquency still figured as an image of deviant youth. Cohen (1997a) was one of the first to break with the criminalization of working-class youth, analysing "subcultures" and youth "behaviours" as practices with meaning and coherence, not just as a symptom. The function of the emerging subcultures was to deal with the contradictions arising from parental culture and the already emerging transformations in the world of work. The "*mods, skinheads, crombies*" are understood as attempts to produce social cohesion in a changing world.

Cohen (1997b) will use the term bricolage, taken from Lévi-Strauss's structuralism, to refer to how magical forms used by "primitive peoples" could be seen coherently, constituting a meaning. For the author, young people, even on an imaginary level, used a series of improvised combinations that, in contrast with other "cultural styles", produced shared meanings. Style would be an imagistic solution to issues arising in other sectors, such as family, school, and work; cultural styles were interpreted as reactions to global changes amid societies considered complex.

According to Tavares (2012), Paul Willis was the CCCS member who stood out by conducting an ethnography on the transition from school to the world of work among working-class youth. The author pointed out, in *Learning to Labour* (1977), that the reactions of young people were connected to their findings regarding social inequality, as well as to the low social mobility. For this entire first formation of cultural studies, Marxism was central, but, along with it, concepts like Gramsci's "hegemony" were also used to describe relations of domination. This led to a historiography of Marxist inspiration combined with cultural anthropology.

Youth began to be perceived in an interclass manner in relation to the dominant culture, where the emphasis was on age and generation. Hall and Jefferson (2006) mention that both working-class youths, like the *teds*, *mods*, and *skins*, and those inspired by the middle classes, like the *hippies* and *freaks*, were attempts to deal with the contradictions of parental culture. This parental culture would be responsible for the primary socialization that would significantly influence the personality formation of each group and, consequently, the worldview of young people (Tavares, 2012).

The new understanding of the CCCS regarding youth culture or "spectacular subcultures" brought new perspectives, indicating that there were creative forms of resistance to the dominant order. The CCCS's proposal became to dismantle and question the commercial concept of youth culture and, instead, develop a more detailed analysis of the social, economic, and cultural origins of various youth subcultures, also considering their connections with the structure of society and production relations. This focus did not ignore the particularities of the content and the age and generational position of these subcultures (Freire Filho, 2005, p. 141).

Cultural studies used different concepts to define the movements: subcultures, scenes, tribes, etc. After analysing the *punks*, *skinheads*, and *hippies*, an analysis of the powerful mix between the black movement and *hip hop* was also initiated, which would culminate in significant changes in the identities and political struggles of the twenty-first century. Post-subcultural studies have already begun to focus on analysing these movements, with Stuart Hall as a central figure. However, as Grossberg (2006) points out, the twenty-first century brought new elements to be analysed, requiring new energy to articulate identity, subjectivity, politics, and economy.

Freire Filho (2005) pointed out, in his book, a rigidity of meanings in the youth category: At times, new cultural youth movements were defined as mere reflections of consumption and the "society of the spectacle; at other times, they were seen as extremely transgressive and transformative. This dichotomy is still present in various works that attempt to answer questions about youth, sometimes placing young people in the position of manipulable victims of system changes, sometimes presenting their struggles and organizations as ruptures and transgressions of the prevailing order.

Under the influence of cultural studies, it will be Groppo who will produce, still in 2000, one of the main reference works for the construction of the concept of youth used today in Brazilian sociological studies, which sought to directly oppose the pathologization of youth. The author sets the goal of overcoming structural-functionalist views that had become consolidated in the trajectory of youth studies, showing how many age definitions of youth had eliminated from the horizon the defining character of social inequality related to social classes. The dialectical theory of youth (Groppo, 2016) seeks to highlight that pathologizing and discriminatory conceptions were constituted within and through the institutions to which these young people "should belong".

The "dialectic of youth" would operate through two opposing forces. On one hand, there is the action of institutions and socializing agencies, such as schools, youth groups controlled by adults, and the cultural industry. These institutions group individuals based on similar ages and seek to impose a specific meaning on the transition to adulthood. This perspective is the only one recognized by structural-functionalism. On the other hand, there are the youth subjects and groups who develop their own values, identities, and meanings in relation to youth, which may diverge from what is expected by the institutions (Groppo & Silveira, 2020).

This dialectical conception seeks to overcome discourses that correlate youth behaviours with pathologies, that is, that classify as deviations, dysfunctions, or anomalies the characteristics associated with the movements of young people in search of the constitution of identities, values, and sociabilities. The dialectical conception of youth values action and disruption, valuing the contingent and experimentation, also centralizing the relationship between age categories and class structures. Groppo emphasizes the importance of Karl Mannheim (1982) for the dialectical definition of youth.[14] He points out that through his analysis of the renewing character of youth, Mannheim managed to visualize dimensions previously ignored by sociologists. For Mannheim, youth would be connected to what he called "vital reserve", which would be like a reserve of latent resources that could be mobilized and used for various transformations in society. Youth would contain within itself a latent potential to contribute to social renewal. However, Groppo warns that Mannheim, at various points in his writings, proposes a structure of age categories that ignores the intersections of aspects such as class, gender, race, religion, sexual orientation, etc. The proposal presented is the adoption of a dialectical conception of youth that collaborates for the understanding that:

> there is no homogeneous youth in a given society or nation, but different ways of living the youthful condition according to numerous social variables. In this way, cultural studies help to build what will be known as intersectionality in social analysis. (Groppo & Silveira, 2020, p. 9)

Intersectionality today gains space in studies about youth and was one of the aspects considered in the construction of the Youth Statute in Brazil. The most recent studies on youth have described the heterogeneity and specificities of youth, raising different variables that affect their trajectories. Aspects such as gender, education, socioeconomic status, religion, nationality, employment structure, ethnicity, and race are crossed with the social category of youth to construct analyses on the subject.

One of the consequences of the dialectic of youth and the new interpretations regarding intersectionality is the recent prevalence of the use of "youths" in the plural. This usage occurs both in governmental documents and in academic studies and aims to produce a new meaning for the category, which would contain within itself the idea of plurality. Savegnado (2019) warns that such use does not necessarily reflect an escape from the production of normativities in relation to youth. She analyses the Latin American production on the subject and establishes five main axes on which social practices and discourses regarding young people focus: "youth as an ideal of life, youth understood as a moment of crisis, youth as a social problem, the association between youth and the future, and youth as a social moratorium" (Savegnado, 2019, p. 197–8).

---

[14] Karl Mannheim (1952), observing the effects of Nazifascism, highlighted that the "control" and "tutelage" of youth were essential for the conduct and maintenance of a totalitarian regime. He identifies youth as the engine of social reorganization but emphasizes its use as a social technique, that is, he also adopts a discourse that categorizes young people as possessing a "manipulable character", which would be easily maneuvered by hegemonic groups. Groppo will diverge from Mannheim (1982) regarding the issue of youth autonomy and how such a renewing potential is realized. Mannheim also identified a growing "anomie" in society as a factor that contributed to the rise of Nazifascism; however, his tendency was to see the solution to such anomie in attachment and return to traditions and in a proposal for reformist social democracy. Despite conservative elements present in his writings, Mannheim was fundamental for the generational understanding of youth. His studies were also referenced in the studies of Weller and Bassalo (2020), who interpreted youth participation in radical right movements in light of studies on generation and German conservatism.

Youth understood as the future can also be translated by the discourse about the "youth power" of social renewal. The youthful condition would be correlated with progress and social transformation. Two consequences are notable: the need for the presence of youth for the legitimation of political projects and the creation of institutional forms of political participation for youth. The main format of transformative youth participation is translated into the concept of "youth protagonism". I present below some research that questioned this perspective of participation and sought to broaden the meaning of youth and politics, reaching broader analyses of the normativity involved in the political participation of youth.

2.4.2 *Traditions in Studies on Youth Political Participation*

Historically, studies on youth have analysed the political participation of young people mainly through research that evaluated the attitudes, orientations, and behaviours of young people in relation to politics, democracy, or activities such as voting or participating in political organizations. Most studies associated participation with the student condition and analysed the socialization processes of "young students".[15] In Western societies, support and involvement with existing political institutions and procedures, such as elections, came to be widely equated with pro-democratic attitudes. These studies focused on the historical trends of increasing or declining participation and on differences according to social inequalities among social groups (Pollock et al., 2015; Giugni & Grasso, 2021; Ellison et al., 2020), also analysing intergenerational dimensions of youth political participation (Fuks, 2011).

For several decades, concerns have also been raised regarding an apparent decline in youth political participation, attributed, on one hand, to an increasingly individualized stance, weakening long-term commitments and affiliation to formal organizations. On the other hand, there was evidence of a decrease in individuals' trust, especially among the youth, in institutions, which was attributed to the biographization, fragmentation, and uncertainty of young people's transitions to adulthood (Perasović et al., 2022).

With the cultural turn in youth research, new interpretations and methodologies have gained prominence, including the analysis of everyday experiences and cultural practices of youth (cf. Pfaff, 2009). New biographical studies represented a

[15] When discussing the 1980s and 1990s in Brazil, there is also the proliferation of studies on youth political participation centred on the experiences of student movements resisting the military dictatorship, mainly recovering their historical character and investigating the trajectory of the movements (Silva, 1987; Andrade, 1994; Sanfelice, 2008). The set of new studies and new youth movements would have led the youth to a valid condition beyond the middle class and demanded the understanding of the existence of different youths, including in the public sphere. The youth that, for a long time, was a term associated with groups of students and university students who were part of parties, academic directories, and unions, from the 1990s onwards, undergoes expansion and displacement, resulting in new sociological studies that sought to overcome the association between youth, dangerousness, and tendencies towards misconduct.

shift towards interpreting political participation in terms of subjectivity and identities and how different forms of participation emerge in the growth process (Schwanenflügel et al., 2019). These studies indicate that engagement and participation arise from young people's search for belonging and recognition, leading them to step out of their familiar social contexts and traverse public spaces, not only intentionally but also out of necessity (cf. Renström et al., 2021). Starting from different biographical constellations and unequal access to specific participation contexts, previous experiences of (non)recognition in formal institutions, especially in school or youth assistance, are pointed out as having an influence on the choice between formal participation and informal youth culture configurations.

Walther (2012) and Walther et al. (2020), in their recent research, analyse that, even today, public and scientific discourses tend to measure "youth social and political participation" from a single dimension and according to formally institutionalized and recognized contents and forms of participation. That is, many studies attempt to define what would be a "true" youth participation. Walther explains that the concept of citizenship, deeply implicated in democracy, has come to include a set of rights and responsibilities that translate conceptions about the normality and legitimacy of individual and collective demands. He emphasizes that there is a great normative power in current discourses about active youth citizenship. Avoiding definitions about participation or non-participation, the author proposes conducting comparative studies that consider youth biographies, seeking to understand the new relationships established between identities, subjectivities, and participation.

The UP2YOUTH research adopted such a perspective and is an important example of a comparative study on the various forms and trajectories of youth participation in Europe (Walther et al., 2009). The research did not only seek to identify practices but also the discourses that configured what currently fits as democratic political participation. They highlight that youth was understood by governments, for much of the twentieth century, as a "social problem", but came to be considered, at the end of the twentieth century and the beginning of the twenty-first, as a "resource".

Walther (2012) analyses the construction of the "youth participation" category from discourses about youth made by governmental organizations. He gives the example of the speech by Pierre Mairesse, director of the Youth Office of the European Commission, when he says that "it is our task to give them the opportunity they need to create the Europe and the world of tomorrow" (European Commission, 2007). Walther points out that, in many official discourses of the early twenty-first century, youth is treated as a resource for society, and their participation is seen as a form of legitimation for decision-makers. However, when youth deviates from institutionally stipulated life trajectories, they are quickly transformed into a problem or a waste of resources. The author warns that the categories of youth as a problem and youth as a resource are intertwined; that is, when the young person is thought of as human capital (Becker, 1994), it turns into an investment, and when expectations are frustrated, what was once a resource quickly turns into a problem.

Le Bart and Lefebvre (2015) propose the following equivalences: youth = resource = adaptability = legitimacy. This set of equivalences would explain the importance of including young people in the political horizon and directing discourses to youth, as it is they who would provide the necessary legitimacy for the general population to understand a decision as collective. Already in 2007, the European Commission spoke of investing in and empowering youth, introducing a new grammar for youth political participation that incorporated a series of concepts from the economy. Youth would be a resource and, as "human capital", would require investments to develop. Empowered youth would make rational choices and be equipped with the individual capacity for mobilization and political activism.

Souza (2009), in a convergent analysis, researched the discourse of "youth protagonism" as one of the possible statements—present in the discourses of international organizations, governmental bodies, third sector organizations, as well as academics and entrepreneurs—to prescribe a certain model of political participation. It is a discourse that conceives society as an agglomeration of "social actors", which "homogenizes the social to the extent that it conceals class divisions or any other division: a society composed of atoms, among which there are no relations of domination, power, or exploitation, but a relationship of negotiation" (Souza, 2009, p. 14). Within the set of derivations of such discursive production, there would be statements about "resilience", "empowerment", "social capital", and "entrepreneurship" itself.

Goulart (2011), in his thesis "Biopolitical Incursions: Youth Power in the Public Arena", also analysed documents from governments and institutions, such as the United Nations (UN), seeking to identify how "youth power" (Poerner, 1968) became the object of public policies. Goulart considers that this power, "in biopolitical plots, will be both a set of power strategies that target youth as an aim and instrument (Foucault, 2008a), and a production of subjectivity" (Goulart, 2011, p. 12). This power would be a field of forces related to the actions of young people, being both the result of social practices translated into two centuries of discourse production about youth through documents from public, private, and academic institutions and a production of the youth's own actions and organization. For him, the new discourses about youth protagonism also have a regulatory power that defines "forms and modes" of youth participation. However, the author allows reflection on a dialectical movement in which categories and discourses interpellate and produce young subjects but in which these subjects are capable of creating ruptures, which configure resistances.

Thus, it is understood that youth and political youth participation have become categories in the Western world and have become part of scientific, institutional, and public discourses. If youth has become a fundamental resource for legitimizing new movements, it is not surprising that there is an intentional incorporation and summoning of young people into radical right movements. Although activism in such movements is often understood as a "deviant form of participation"—mainly because of its contents—it is understood that there is an influence of discourses about youth protagonism also in the subjective formations of such young people. More broadly, the transformations pointed out by the studies above are interpreted as part of new normativities, constituted within a new political rationality. In the next section, I explore how these normativities are related to the identification processes, understood here as "modes of subjectivation".

2.5 Inaugurating Normativities and Modes of Political Subjectivation

In the face of the 2008 financial crisis in Europe and the United States, many thought they were seeing "the final tolls of neoliberalism", with a "return of the State" in market regulation. The crisis operated in an opposite movement, strengthening reforms and intervention in State regulation, which was translated as "fiscal austerity"[16] and provoked an acceleration in labour market transformations, with intense "uberization" (Pochmann, 2016; Abílio, 2020) and the strengthening of the Gig Economy. Dardot and Laval (2016) anticipated this unfolding, as they pointed out that predictions about the end of neoliberalism revealed a limitation of its understanding as "ideology" or as "economic policy", which was not sustained in the observations of the bases and metamorphoses of such discourses. They also indicated the mistake of focusing only on the destructive aspect of neoliberalism, disregarding the modes of living and feeling that would have been produced over the last 40 years.

The authors present neoliberalism as a new world reason (Dardot & Laval, 2016), having as the main reference the analysis of governmentalities made by Foucault (2008a, 2008b). They analyse neoliberalism from the conception of biopolitics, emphasizing the micropowers and the multiplicity of forces that act simultaneously on individuals, materializing bodies and producing subjectivities. Knowledge in Foucault is not a mirror of reality, as truth and knowledge will transform over the course of history. Through investigations into the different forms of governing the body—prisons, asylums, schools—Foucault seeks to understand how and who is defining the truth, since defining truths is having power. For Foucault (1979, p. 147), "nothing is more material, more physical, and more corporeal than the exercise of power"; even the State is seen as a set of strategies, as the institution does not contain power in itself but creates mechanisms of power that will define conduct and subject bodies.

[16] For Rossi et al. (2019, pp. 2–6), "austerity can be defined as an economic adjustment policy based on the reduction of public spending and the role of the State in its functions as an inducer of economic growth and promoter of social welfare. (…) The theoretical assumption for the success of austerity policies is the increase in the confidence of private agents. Austerity is the instrument and the solution to restore market confidence which, in turn, would be the cause of economic growth. In austere rhetoric, the pursuit of market confidence is very present, both abroad and in Brazil". However, Safatle (2020) explains that the origin of the term is from moral philosophy and that, in practice, there was no economic theory of austerity. Thus, the author understands that by naming such policies as austerity, it also proves how moral values were mobilized "to justify the rationality of social and economic intervention processes" (Safatle, 2020, p. 18).

Foucault proposed a new "analytics of power" from the essays "Security, Territory, Population" (2008a) and "The Birth of Biopolitics" (2008b). The emphasis is that power does not refer to things, possessions, or objects but to strategic situations, to something that continuously transits between individuals. Foucault (1999) proposes the concept of biopolitics as an extension of biopower (power over life, considered in biological terms), differentiating it from disciplinary power, which focuses on individual bodies. In the sphere of biopolitics, the focus is on the bodies of populations as a whole, addressing issues such as health, hygiene, birth rate, mortality, race, and longevity. In this context, "a set of processes such as the proportion of births and deaths, the reproduction rate, the fertility of a population, etc." is analysed (Foucault, 1999, p. 290). Biopolitics encompasses political and governmental interventions aimed at controlling the population's life; in this sense, they are also interventions that define the "making live and letting die".[17] With this backdrop, Foucault will analyse the art of governing and the manuals of government, that is, the discourses tied to government practices and their interpellation in subjects.

Dardot and Laval (2016) describe the encounter between biopolitics and the analysis of neoliberalism in Foucault (2008a), stating that the philosopher had the intuition that he was observing an acute crisis of the dominant forms of power and, by exploring the history of liberal government, was able to notice that what is called economy, since the eighteenth century, has been the foundation of the set of population control devices and conduct orientation, which constitutes biopolitics. Biopolitics will find, in neoliberalism, an unprecedented systematization because, in it, competition and the business model would become a general mode of government, going far beyond the economic sphere, in the usual sense of the expression.

Foucault will, therefore, be a pioneer in treating neoliberalism as a political rationality and will be followed by a series of specific analyses involving Christian Laval, Pierre Dardot, Thomas Osborne, Robert Castel, Wendy Brown, and Melina Cooper. This interpretation has the consequence of admitting that, as a rationality, neoliberalism will dispense with external coercion, whose mastery lies in making the individual conduct themselves in a certain way, interpreting that they are motivated by their own interests. To understand this external coercion, the analyses of neoliberalism (Cooper, 2017; Brown, 2019; Franco et al., 2020) have focused on its precepts, often analysing works originating from three schools: the Austrian School of Economics, whose exponents are Ludwig von Mises and Friedrich Hayek; the German Ordoliberalism, with names like Walter Eucken and Franz Böhm; and the

[17] Athanasiou (2011/2021, p. 167) states that "neoliberal governmentality denotes an authoritarian apparatus of producing expendable and disposable populations and, at the same time, of producing and demarcating normative codes of the human, through the (economic) regulation of vitality, affectivity, potentiality, embodiment, vulnerability, and habitability of subjects. Within this governmentality, the biopolitical imaginary and the management of life and death are reinvented, revitalized, and reconfigured; while resources and vulnerability are differently and unequally distributed among different bodies—bodies differently economized, racialized, and gendered".

Chicago School, influenced by the former but whose most known theorists are Milton Friedman, George Stigler, and Gary Becker (Corbanezi & Rasia, 2020).

The interpretations regarding the incidences of a new rationality are not univocal; however, studying them has as a starting point of the admission that neoliberalism "produces certain types of social relations, certain ways of living, certain subjectivities" (Dardot & Laval, 2016, p. 16). Brown (2018) also emphasizes that neoliberalism is not thought of as an ideology, which would mean:

> Different from ideology—a distortion or mystification of reality—neoliberal rationality is productive, world-making: it economizes every sphere and human endeavor, and it replaces a model of society based on the justice-producing social contract with society conceived and organized as markets and with states oriented by market requirements. As neoliberal rationality becomes our ubiquitous common sense, its principles not only govern through the state but suffuse workplaces, schools, hospitals, gyms, air travel, policing, and all manner of human desire and decisions. (Brown, 2018, pp. 61–2)

Similarly, Safatle et al. (2020) state that neoliberalism constitutes itself as "a way of life in the fields of work, language, and desire", which "recodes identities, values, and ways of life through which subjects truly modify themselves" (2021, p. 10).

We are dealing here, therefore, with the fact that neoliberalism inaugurates normativities that impact modes of subjectivation; that is, new ways are inaugurated for individuals to constitute themselves as subjects for themselves as well as—facing knowledge and powers—constituting themselves as objects for others. In this research, by placing subjects and their discourses at the centre, I seek to understand both the processes of interpellation[18], which operate through "discursive formations" and "systems of representation", as well as processes of political subjectivation, which involve understanding how subjects constitute themselves as such, identifying and positioning themselves in relation to knowledge and powers. For Pineda and Cubides (2012), thinking about political subjectivation as a result of new discursive formations and systems of representation requires thinking historically about the notions of subject and political subject, expanded beyond their modern meanings. Thus, it is necessary to take into account that the subject is socially

[18] The concept of discursive interpellation will be constantly used in this book. Its origin lies in the work of Althusser (1985), when referring to ideological interpellations, and in the work of Foucault (1971), when referring to discursive formations. In a later appropriation, post-structuralist authors will speak of discursive interpellations, which do not define subordination, but the very mode of existence of the subject in language. The subject constitutes itself as social and to whom one can speak, going through processes of discursive interpellation (including naming). Therefore, there is a "summons" to be a social subject through circulating discourses. Part of this summons does not occur at a conscious level; however, a dimension of "forgetfulness" predominates, in which the subject understands themselves to be in full control of their "discursive choices". Interpellation—as a summons also to identification—is a process of signification, through which the subject inserts themselves and uses the "chain and network of signifiers" (Pêcheux, 1975/2009). Discursive formations (matrices of meaning) will, therefore, be signs of the subject's identification with the discourse and originated by the process of discursive interpellation. The fourth chapter of this book delves into this area, seeking to understand what the interpellations are and what subjective positions are offered by the radical right. This also occurs through the identification of the chain of signifiers that gains meaning and articulates with the trajectories of young people.

produced and their self-constitution figures between two fields: the instituted and the instituting. Returning to the etymological definition of the term itself, the subject would be the *subjectus*, that is, the one subjected to, submitted to power devices. Thus, normative technologies would condition and fix the political identities of subjects to institutional recognition, and institutions, therefore, would operate as mechanisms of political normalization.

In this way, identification would consist of a complex act of meaning production through which the subject, by discursively constituting themselves, constitutes a world (Sousa et al., 2022). Political subjectivity is not defined in radical opposition to traditional political practices, as nothing that is instituted can be completely separated from what institutes it. These two fields of force are in progress in the same social field. No one is outside the rules and normativities that configure the dominant social imaginary, and, within the instituted, are the economy, the state, organizations, the family, that is, various hegemonic forces that, through their mechanisms of power and control, produce discourses and offer subjective positions.

The subject is not understood here as the place of full freedom, nor of full subjection. He:

> is immersed in a field of forces, in the relationships and interactions he establishes with the environment, with his own self, with local and global institutional processes, which permanently structure him from a multiplicity of subjective vectors: need, desire, impulses, instincts, interest, language, laws, thought, will, feelings, projects, among others. (Pineda & Cubides, 2012, p. 75)

In this sense, Hall (2000) will speak of modes of subjectivation as processes of identification, which mean a necessary articulation/suturing for the subject, but not a subsumption. Identification, within the discursive approach, is a construction, a process that is never complete. In this sense, it can be sustained or abandoned, but it is of interest to think about which discourses privilege the construction and maintenance of an identity. Hall emphasizes that discourse should not be confused with ideology, as a falsified representation of the world. For this reason, it is not up for analysis to discuss the truth content of discourses but rather the contexts in which they are produced, the "regime of truth" within which the discourse acquires significance, constituting itself as plausible and, consequently, acquiring practical efficacy.

Thinking in terms of identities, it is important to highlight that such a concept has been placed "under erasure" by cultural and post-structuralist studies. That is, although it has been understood and affirmed as fundamental to thinking about human issues, it has been reinterpreted in light of the concept of "difference". One comes to the understanding that identifying always presupposes the marking of difference, which establishes an inside and an outside; what I am and what I deny being. Authors like Hall (2000), Butler (2000), and Brah (1996) also draw inspiration from Foucauldian biopolitics and develop a concept of identity that distances itself from a rigid, uniform, and developmental conception of identity—related to the Enlightenment. They consider identity as a construction that is in continuous movement, and their studies bring the discursive plane to the centre of the analysis. Silva (2000, p. 97) will say that:

> identity is not an essence; it is not a given or a fact—whether of nature or culture. Identity is not fixed, stable, coherent, unified, permanent. Identity is neither homogeneous, definitive, finished, identical, transcendental. On the other hand, we can say that identity is a construction, an effect, a production process, a relationship, a performative act. Identity is unstable, contradictory, fragmented, inconsistent, unfinished. Identity is linked to discursive and narrative structures. Identity is linked to systems of representation. Identity has close connections with power relations.

Costa (2006) explains that language constructs social reality and, in this context, "*différance*" can only be formed within the scope of discourse. The concept of *différance* precisely breaks with the notion of a pre-existing, ontological, and essential difference. *Différance* would arise in the very act of its manifestation, within the fabric of representations, differences, and differentiations. Focusing on *différance* is also recognizing that it is in the relationship with the Other, with what one is not—or even with what is lacking—that identities are constructed. Identities contain within themselves exclusion, hence their effect of forming the "abject". Butler (2000) will also say that the constitution of identities requires the existence of a domain of abject beings, those who will not yet be considered subjects. Thus, a place of feared identification is formed, and this abject exterior will also be within the subject, as its own founding repudiation. Therefore, a threatening spectre is created, and this identification with the abject must be persistently denied through the force of reiterating regulatory norms.

When we stop treating identity as "essence", we also have to observe its strategic dimension, that is, its practical efficacy. Thus, in the course of this book, I do not seek to investigate identity as a collective and true self that remains hidden behind layers or masks, nor do I consider that subjects are merely subsumed by discourses. Identities translate the desire of different groups to secure new opportunities and achieve privileged access to social goods, as well as to spaces of power. Silva (2000) emphasizes that, to understand identities, it is essential to consider the broader power relations, since "identity and difference are never innocent" (Silva, 2000, p. 81).

With these premises, the present investigation focuses on the trajectories and narratives of political activists from the radical right in Brazil and Germany to identify processes of subjectivation/identification, as well as processes of coercion and/or discursive interpellation. Such a distinction is much simpler at a theoretical level, becoming more blurred when encountering the empirical. However, it is essential that this distinction has been made known here so that it is possible to understand the methodological choices of the research that informed this book. The combination of the (re)construction of participation biographies, as well as the (de)construction of narratives into thematic categories, sought to address this task. In the next chapter, I clarify what these methodologies are and how they were applied, in addition to explaining the research path and the ethical and practical challenges faced.

References

Aarão Reis, D. (2020). Notas para a compreensão do bolsonarismo. *Estudos Ibero-Americanos, 46*(1), 1–11.

Abílio, L. C. (2020). Uberização: a era do trabalhador just-in-time? *Estudos Avançados, 34*(98). https://doi.org/10.1590/s0103-4014.2020.3498.008

Abramo, H. W. (1997). Considerações sobre a tematização social da juventude no Brasil. *Revista Brasileira de Educação, 6*, 26–36.

Abramo, H. (2005). Condição juvenil no Brasil contemporâneo. In H. Abramo & P. P. M. Branco (Eds.), *Retratos da juventude brasileira: análises de uma pesquisa nacional*. Fundação Perseu Abramo/Instituto Cidadania.

Abranches, S. (2018). *Presidencialismo de coalizão: raízes e evolução do modelo político brasileiro*. Companhia das Letras.

Adorno, S. (2022). O fracasso do controle legal dos crimes e da violência na sociedade brasileira contemporânea: questões para discussão: como alcançar saídas viáveis e socialmente legítimas sem comprometer a vigência da democracia na sociedade? *Ciência e Cultura, 74*(4), 01–09.

Almeida, E. (2009). Os estudos sobre grupos juvenis: presenças e ausências. In *O Estado da Arte sobre juventude na pós-graduação brasileira: Educação, Ciências Sociais e Serviço Social (1999-2006)* (Vol. 2). Argvmentvm.

Althusser, L. (1985). *Aparelhos ideológicos do Estado*. Graal.

Andrade, C. A. N. (1994). *A organização política dos estudantes da Universidade Federal do Rio Grande do Norte* (1974-1984). [Master's thesis, Universidade Federal do Rio Grande do Norte]. Acervo UFRN. Retrieved from https://app.bczm.ufrn.br/home/#/item/31046

Art, D. (2011). *Inside the radical right: The development of anti-immigrant parties in Western Europe*. Cambridge University Press.

Arzheimer, K. (2019). Conceptual confusion is not always a bad thing—The curious case of European radical right studies. In K. Marker, A. Schmitt, & J. Sirsch (Eds.), *Demokratie und Entscheidung*. Springer VS. https://doi.org/10.1007/978-3-658-24529-0_3

Athanasiou, A. (2021). Estados de emergência, modos de emersão: atuações críticas de "o povo" em tempos de crise. In C. Albino, J. Oliveira, & M. Melo (Eds.), *Neoliberalismo, neoconservadorismo e crise em tempos sombrios*. Editora Seriguela. (Work originally published in 2011).

Becker, G. (1994). *Human capital: A theoretical and empirical analysis with a special reference to education*. University of Chicago Press.

Begeres Bisneto, V. (2019). *Fronts Islamistas no Brasil: prenúncios de uma radicalização incompleta face ao fundamentalismo existencial*. [Doctoral dissertation, Universidade de São Paulo]. Repositório USP. Retrieved from https://www.teses.usp.br/teses/disponiveis/8/8138/tde-12122019-170616/

Bello, E., Capela, G., & Keller, R. J. (2021). Operação Lava Jato: ideologia, narrativa e (re)articulação da hegemonia. *Revista Direito e Práxis, 12*, 1665–1667.

Bertoa, F. C., & Bourne, A. (2017). Prescribing democracy? Party proscription and party system stability in Germany, Spain and Turkey. *European Journal of Political Research, 56*(2), 440–465.

Besen, B., & Walther, A. (2023). Participation on and beyond the borders: Brazilian youth activism in radical right movements. *Youth and Globalization, 5*(1).

Betz, H. G. (1994). *Radical right-wing populism in Western Europe*. Macmillan.

Betz, H.-G. (2018). Populist mobilization across time and space. In K. A. Hawkins, R. E. Carlin, L. Littvay, & C. Rovira Kaltwasser (Eds.), *The ideational approach to populism* (pp. 181–201). Routledge.

Blee, K. M. (2017). How the study of white supremacism is helped and hindered by social movement research. *Mobilization, 22*(1), 1–15.

Blee, K. M., & Creasap, K. A. (2010). Conservative and right-wing movements. *Annual Review of Sociology, 36*(1), 269–286.

Bourne, A. (2011). *The proscription of parties and the problem of "militant democracy"*. Retrieved from http://www.dundee.ac.uk/politics/research/csepp/

Brah, A. (1996). Difference, diversity, differentiation. In A. Brah (Ed.), *Cartographies of diaspora: Contesting identities* (pp. 95–127). Routledge.

Braun, S., Geisler, A., & Gerster, M. (2009). *Strategien der extremen Rechten*. VS Verlag für Sozialwissenschaften.

Bringel, B., & Pleyers, G. (2019). Five years later: Polarization, reconfiguration of activism, and challenges for the Brazilian left. In V. Puzone & L. Miguel (Eds.), *The Brazilian left in the 21st century. Marx, Engels, and Marxisms* (pp. 237–258). Palgrave Macmillan.

Brown, W. (2018). Neoliberalism's Frankenstein: Authoritarian freedom in twenty-first century "democracies". *Critical Times, 1*(1), 60–79.

Brown, W. (2019). *In the ruins of neoliberalism: The rise of antidemocratic politics in the west*. Columbia University Press. https://doi.org/10.7312/brow19384

Buchholz, S., et al. (2009). Life courses in the globalization process: The development of social inequalities in modern societies. *European Sociological Review, 25*(1), 53–71.

Butler, J. (2000). Corpos que pesam: sobre os limites discursivos do "sexo". In G. L. Louro et al. (Eds.), *O corpo educado: pedagogias da sexualidade*. Autêntica.

Caiani, M., Della Porta, D., & Wagemann, C. (2012). *Mobilizing on the extreme right: Germany, Italy, and the United States*. Oxford University Press.

Caldeira Neto, O., & Gonçalves, L. P. (2020). *O fascismo em camisas verdes: do integralismo ao neointegralismo*. FGV Editora, 2020.

Cardoso, R., & Sampaio, H. (1995). *Bibliografia sobre a Juventude*. Editora da Universidade de São Paulo.

Castells, M. (2018). *Ruptura: a crise da democracia liberal*. Zahar.

Cepêda, V. A. (2018). A Nova Direita no Brasil: contexto e matrizes conceituais. *Mediações-Revista de Ciências Sociais, 23*(2), 40–74.

Codato, A., Bolognesi, B., & Roeder, K. M. (2015). A nova direita brasileira: uma análise da dinâmica partidária e eleitoral do campo conservador. In S. Cruz, A. Kaysel, & G. Codas (Eds.), *Direita, volver, o retorno da direita e o ciclo político brasileiro*. Editora Fundação Perseu Abramo.

Cohen, P. (1997a). *Subcultural conflict and working-class community. Rethinking the youth question*. Macmillan Education UK. https://doi.org/10.1007/978-1-349-25390-6_3

Cohen, P. (1997b). *Rethinking the youth question*. Macmillan Education UK. https://doi.org/10.1007/978-1-349-25390-6_8

Cooper, M. (2017). *Family values: Between neoliberalism and the new social conservatism*. MIT Press.

Corbanezi, E., & Rasia, J. M. (2020). Apresentação do Dossiê: racionalidade neoliberal e processos de subjetivação contemporâneos. *Mediações-Revista de Ciências Sociais, 25*, 287–301.

Costa, M. R. (1993). *Os Carecas do subúrbio: caminhos de um nomadismo moderno*. Editora Vozes.

Costa, S. (2006). Desprovincializando a sociologia: a contribuição pós-colonial. *Revista brasileira de ciências sociais, 21*, 117–134.

da Goulart, M. V.S (2011). *Biopolitical incursions: Youth power in the public arena*. [Master's thesis, Universidade Federal do Rio Grande do Sul]. LUME Repositório Digital. Retrieved from https://lume.ufrgs.br/handle/10183/32012

Dantas, B. S. D. A. (2013). Psicologia política das religiões: uma análise dos símbolos e ideologias da Igreja Universal do Reino de Deus. *Revista Psicologia Política, 13*(28), 489–506.

Dardot, P. & Laval, C. (2016). *A nova razão de mundo: ensaio sobre a sociedade neoliberal*. Boitempo.

de Sousa, R. S., de Oliveira Filho, P., Araújo, J. B., & Vieira, D. V. M. (2022). A Identidade da Direita em Narrativas de seus Militantes numa Universidade Brasileira. *Psicologia: Ciência e Profissão, 42*, 1–16.

Decker, O., Kiess, J., & Brähler, E. (2016). *Die enthemmte Mitte. Autoritäre und rechtsextreme Einstellungen in Deutschland*. Psychosozial Verlag.

Díaz, B. (2021). Make (neo-)liberalism cool again'. Rear-view mirrors, creative destruction and right-wing youth political culture in Brazil. *45° Encontro Anual da ANPOCS.*

do O Catão, M., & Pereira, M. C. (2015). Juventude e Criminalidade sob a perspectiva da Escola de Chicago. *Revista da Faculdade de Direito-RFD-UERJ, 28*, 131–156.

Ellison, M., Pollock, G., & Grimm, R. (2020). Young people's orientations towards contemporary politics: Trust, representation and participation. *Zeitschrift für Erziehungswissenschaft, 23*(6), 1201–1226.

Escosteguy, A. C. (1998). Uma introdução aos estudos culturais. *Revista Famecos, 5*(9), 87–97.

European Commission. (2007). *Promoting young people's full participation in education, employment, and society.* Communication from the Commission Youth Council. Retrieved from https://www.cedefop.europa.eu/en/news/promoting-young-peoples-full-participation-education-employment-and-society

Farias, P. J. L. (2009). Respeito às Funções Urbanísticas e a Prevenção da Criminalidade Urbana: Uma Visão Integrada à Luz da Escola de Chicago. *Direito Público, 15*(1), 40–65.

Fernandes, V. J. A., & Machado, D. S. M. (2022). Discurso popular-democrático e o sujeito de negação bolsonarista. *Revista de Ciências Sociais: RCS, 53*(1), 23–56.

Finchelstein, F. (2017). *From fascism to populism in history.* University of California Press.

Foracchi, M. (1972). *A Juventude na Sociedade Moderna.* Pioneira.

Foucault, M. (1971). *A arqueologia do saber.* Vozes.

Foucault, M. (1979). Por uma Genealogia do Poder. In M. Foucault (Ed.), *Microfísica do Poder.* Graal.

Foucault, M. (1999). Em Defesa da Sociedade. In M. Foucault (Ed.), *Curso no Collège de France (1975–1976).* Martins Fontes.

Foucault, M. (2008a). Nascimento da Biopolítica. In M. Foucault (Ed.), *Curso no Collège de France (1978-1979).* Martins Fontes.

Foucault, M. (2008b). Segurança, Território, População. In M. Foucault (Ed.), *Curso no Collège de France (1977–1978).* Martins Fontes.

Franco, F., Castro, J. C. L., Manzi, R., Safatle, V., & Afshar, Y. (2020). O sujeito e a ordem do mercado: gênese teórica do neoliberalismo. In V. Safatle, N. da Silva Junior, & C. Dunker (Eds.), *Neoliberalismo como gestão do sofrimento psíquico* (pp. 47–76). Autêntica.

Freire Filho, J. F. (2005). Das subculturas às pós-subculturas juvenis: música, estilo e ativismo político. *Journal of Communication and Culture, 3*(1), 138–166.

Fuks, M. (2011). Efeitos diretos, indiretos e tardios: trajetórias da transmissão intergeracional da participação política. *Lua Nova: Revista de Cultura e Política, 83*, 145–178.

Gentile, F. (2018). A direita brasileira em perspectiva histórica. *Plural: Revista de Ciências Sociais, 25*(1), 92–110.

Gentile, F. (2020). Uma direita "plural": configurações ideológicas e organizações políticas da direita brasileira contemporânea. In F. G. Faria & M. L. B. Marques (Eds.), *Giros à direita: análises e perspectivas sobre o campo líbero-conservador* (pp. 222–240). Editora SertãoCult.

Giugni, M., & Grasso, M. (Eds.). (2021). *Youth and politics in times of increasing inequalities.* Palgrave Macmillan.

Gonçalves, F. J. (2014). O Combate à Radicalização no Extremismo Islâmico: a Contrarradicalização e a Des-radicalização. *Nação e Defesa, 5*(137), 217–237.

González, R. S., Baquero, M., & Grohmann, L. G. M. (2021). Nova direita ou vinho velho em odres novos? A trajetória conservadora no Brasil do último século. *Revista Debates, 15*(2), 9–44.

Groppo, L. A. (2016). Dialética das juventudes modernas e contemporâneas. *Revista de EDUCAÇÃO do Cogeime, 13*(25), 9–22. https://doi.org/10.15599/0104-4834/COGEIME.V13N25P9-22

Groppo, L. A., & Silveira, I. B. (2020). Juventude, classe social e política: reflexões teóricas inspiradas pelo movimento das ocupações estudantis no Brasil. *Argumentation, 1*, 7–21.

Grossberg, L. (2006). Does cultural studies have futures? Should it? (or what's the matter with New York?): Cultural studies, contexts and conjunctures. *Cultural Studies, 20*(1), 1–32. https://doi.org/10.1080/09502380500492541

Hall, S. (2000). Quem precisa da identidade? In T. T. Silva (Ed.), *Identidade e diferença: a perspectiva dos estudos culturais* (pp. 103–133). Vozes.
Hall, S., & Jefferson, T. (Eds.). (2006). *Resistance through rituals: Youth subcultures in post-war Britain*. Routledge.
Heitmeyer, W. (2003). Right-wing extremist violence. In W. Heitmeyer & J. Hagan (Eds.), *International handbook of violence research* (pp. 399–436). Springer Netherlands.
Heitmeyer, W. (2018). *Autoritäre Versuchungen: Signaturen der Bedrohung (Tentações autoritárias: Assinaturas de Ameaças)*. Suhrkamp Verlag.
Hernández, E., & Kriesi, H. (2016). The electoral consequences of the financial and economic crisis in Europe. *European Journal of Political Research, 55*(2), 203–224.
Hofmann, D. C. (2020). How "alone" are lone-actors? Exploring the ideological, signaling, and support networks of lone-actor terrorists. *Studies in Conflict & Terrorism, 43*(7), 657–678.
Honneth, A. (1995). *The struggle for recognition*. Polity Press.
Huke, N. (2021). *Ohnmacht in der Demokratie: Das gebrochene Versprechen politischer Teilhabe*. Transcript.
Ignazi, P. (1992). The silent counter-revolution: Hypotheses on the emergence of extreme right-wing parties in Europe. *European Journal of Political Research, 22*(1), 3–34.
Kitschelt, H., & McGann, A. J. (1997). *The radical right in Western Europe: A comparative analysis*. University of Michigan Press.
Klandermans, B. (2013). Extreme right activists: Recruitment and experiences. In S. von Mering & T. W. McCarty (Eds.), *Right wing radicalism today. Perspectives from Europe and the US* (pp. 60–84). Routledge.
Klandermans, B. (2020). Life-history interviews with rightwing extremists. In S. D. Ashe, J. Busher, G. Macklin, & A. Winter (Eds.), *Researching the far right* (pp. 225–238). Routledge. https://doi.org/10.4324/9781315304670-14
Klandermans, B., & Mayer, N. (2005). *Extreme right activists in Europe: Through the magnifying glass*. Routledge.
Klüppel, G. S., Cruz, M. M., & Cerri, L. F. (2021). Jovens, uma nova "nova direita" e suas esquerdas: um estudo sobre a posição política de jovens brasileiros. *Revista de História da UEG, 10*(02), e022108–e022108.
Kováts, E. (2018). Questioning consensuses: Right-wing populism, anti-populism, and the threat of "gender ideology". *Sociological Research Online, 23*(2), 528–538. https://doi.org/10.1177/1360780418764735
Krasteva, A. (2016). Occupy Bulgaria or the emergence of post-communist Contestatory citizenship. *Southeastern Europe, 40*(2), 158–187.
Krasteva, A. (2017). Re/De/constructing far-right youth. In G. Lazaridis & G. Campani (Eds.), *Understanding the populist shift: Othering in a Europe in crisis* (pp. 150–178). Routledge.
Laqueur, W. (1997). *Fascism: Past, present, future*. Oxford University Press.
Laruelle, M. (2022). Illiberalism: A conceptual introduction. *East European Politics, 38*(2), 303–327.
Le Bart, C., & Lefebvre, R. (2015). *La proximité en politique: usages, rhétoriques, pratiques*. PU Rennes.
Lewicki, A. (2018). Race, islamophobia and the politics of citizenship in post-unification Germany. *Patterns of Prejudice, 52*(5). https://doi.org/10.1080/0031322X.2018.1502236
Lopes, A. P. H., & Dantas, B. S. A. (2017). Representações sociais da cura divina no contexto neopentecostal. *Psicologia em Revista, 23*(2), 771–789. https://doi.org/10.5752/P.1678-9563.2017v23n2p771-789
Lorenzen, J.-M., Neumann, D., Seehaus, A., & Trappman, V. (2016). Towards political disenchantment and populism? Consequences of precarious working and living conditions in the case of young Germans. In *36th International Labour Process Conference*.
Mannheim, K. (1952). *Diagnose unserer Zeit: Gedanken eines Soziologen*. Frankfurt am Main: Büchergilde Gutenberg.

Mannheim, K. (1982). O problema sociológico das gerações. In M. Foracchi (Ed.), *Karl Mannheim: Sociologia* (pp. 67–95). Ática.

Mayer, N. (2020). Political science approaches to the far right. In S. D. Ashe et al. (Eds.), *Researching the far right: Theory, method and practice*. Routledge.

McCauley, C., & Moskalenko, S. (2011). *Friction: How radicalization happens to them and us*. Oxford University Press.

Meier, J., Bögelein, N., & Neubacher, F. (2022). A biographical perspective on processes of radicalisation. *European Journal on Criminal Policy and Research, 28*(2), 155–176.

Miguel, L. F. (2018). A reemergência da direita brasileira. In E. Solano (Ed.), *O ódio como política*. Boitempo.

Miller-Idriss, C. (2018a). *The extreme gone mainstream: Commercialization and far right youth culture in Germany*. Princeton University Press.

Miller-Idriss, C. (2018b). Youth and the radical right. In J. Rydgren (Ed.), *The Oxford handbook of the radical right*. Oxford University Press.

Minkenberg, M. (1992). The new right in Germany: The transformation of conservatism and the extreme right. *European Journal of Political Research, 22*.

Minkenberg, M. (2017). *The radical right in Eastern Europe: Democracy under siege?* Springer.

Monteiro, E. L. D. S. (2023). *Bolsonarismo e a manipulação do brasileiro autoritário: nazifascismo a serviço do neoliberalismo*. [Master's thesis, Pontifícia Universidade Católica de São Paulo]. Repositório PUC-SP. Retrieved from https://tede.pucsp.br/handle/handle/32246

Mouffe, C. (2018). *For a left populism*. Verso.

Mrozowicki, A., Trappmann, V., Seehaus, A., & Kajta, J. (2019). Who is a right-wing supporter? On the biographical experiences of young right-wing voters in Poland and Germany. *Qualitative Sociology Review, 15*(4). https://doi.org/10.18778/1733-8077.15.4.10

Mudde, C. (1996). The war of words defining the extreme right party family. *West Europeanpolitics, 19*(2), 225–248.

Mudde, C. (Ed.). (2016). *The populist radical right: A reader*. Routledge.

Mudde, C. (2019). *The far right today*. Wiley.

Mudde, C., & Kaltwasser, C. R. (2017). *Populism: A very short introduction*. Oxford University Press.

Nilan, P. (2021). *Young people and the far right*. Springer Nature.

Pasieka, A. (2021). National, European, transnational: Far-right activism in the twentieth and twenty-first centuries. *Societies and Cultures, 35*, 863–875.

Pasieka, A. (2022). "Tomorrow belongs to us": Pathways to activism in Italian far-right youth communities. *Comparative Studies in Society and History, 64*(1), 150–178.

Pêcheux, M. (1975/2009). *Semântica e Discurso: uma crítica à afirmação do óbvio* (4th ed.). Editora da Unicamp.

Perasović, B., Mustapić, M., Ibañez Garzaran, Z. L., Mulari, H., & Hofreiter, R. (2022). Youth in conflict: Space and subculture. *Journal of Youth Studies, 26*, 368–386.

Pereira, M. H. F. (2015). Nova direita? Guerras de memória em tempos de Comissão da Verdade (2012-2014). *Varia Historia, 31*(57), 863–902. https://doi.org/10.1590/0104-87752015000300008

Pettersson, K., & Sakki, I. (2022). "You truly are the worst kind of racist!": Argumentation and polarization in online discussions around gender and radical-right populism. *British Journal of Social Psychology, 6*, 119–135.

Pfaff, N. (2009). Youth culture as a context of political learning: How young people politicize amongst each other. *Young, 17*(2), 167–189.

Pierucci, A. F. (1987). As bases da nova direita. *Novos estudos CEBRAP, 19*(3), 26.

Pilkington, H. (2016). *Loud and proud: Passion and politics in the English defence league*. Manchester University Press.

Pineda, M. C. M., & Cubides, J. (2012). Sujeito e política: vínculos e modos de subjetivação. *Revista colombiana de educación, 63*, 67–88.

Pinheiro-Machado, R., et al. (2019). *Brasil em transe: Bolsonarismo, nova direita e desdemocratização*. Oficina Raquel.

Pleyers, G. (2020). A "guerra dos deuses" no Brasil: da teologia da libertação à eleição de Bolsonaro. *Educação & Sociedade, 41*.

Pochmann, M. (2016). Terceirização, competitividade e uberização do trabalho no Brasil. In M. O. Teixeira, H. Rodrigues, & E. d'Ávila Coelho (Eds.), *Precarização e terceirização: faces da mesma realidade* (pp. 59–68). Sindicato dos Químicos-SP.

Poerner, A. (1968). *O Poder Jovem — história da participação política dos estudantes brasileiros* (2nd ed.). Civilização Brasileira.

Pollard, J. (2007). 'Clerical Fascism': Context, Overview and Conclusion. *Totalitarian Movements and Political Religions, 8*(2), 433–446. https://doi.org/10.1080/14690760701321528

Pollock, G., Brock, T., & Ellison, M. (2015). Populism, ideology and contradiction: Mapping young people's political views. *The Sociological Review, 63*(S2), 141–166. https://doi.org/10.1111/1467-954X.12266

Power, T. (2000). *The political right in post authoritarian Brazil: Elites, institutions, and democratization*. Penn State Press.

Pucci, B. (2020). A Personalidade Autoritária no Brasil em tempos de neoliberalismo e de Coronavírus. *Revista Eletrônica de Educação, 14*, e4538132.

Quintão, G. F. (2017). A nova direita cristã: alianças, estratégias e transfiguração do discurso religioso em torno do projeto de cura gay. *Estudos de Sociologia, 22*(42).

Renström, E. A., Aspernäs, J., & Bäck, H. (2021). The young protester: The impact of belongingness needs on political engagement. *Journal of Youth Studies, 24*(6), 781–798.

Rocha, C. (2018). O boom das novas direitas brasileiras: financiamento ou militância? In E. Solano (Ed.), *O ódio como política*. Boitempo.

Rocha, C. (2019). *"Menos Marx, mais Mises": uma gênese da nova direita brasileira (*2006-2018*)*. [Doctoral dissertation, Universidade de São Paulo]. Biblioteca Digital USP. Retrieved from https://www.teses.usp.br/teses/disponiveis/8/8131/tde-19092019-174426/pt-br.php

Rocha, C., Solano, E., & Medeiros, J. (2021). *The Bolsonaro paradox. The public sphere and right-wing counterpublicity in contemporary Brazil*. Springer.

Rokeach, M. (1960). *The open and closed mind: Investigations into the nature of belief systems and personality systems*. Basic Books.

Rossi, P., Matos De Oliveira, A. L., Arantes, F., & Dweck, E. (2019). Austeridade Fiscal e o Financiamento da Educação no Brasil. *Education and Society, 40*, 2019.

Runciman, D. (2018). *How democracy ends*. Profile Books.

Safatle, V. (2020). A economia é a continuação da psicologia por outros meios: sofrimento psíquico e o neoliberalismo como economia moral. In V. Safatle, N. da Silva Junior, & C. Dunker (Eds.), *Neoliberalismo como gestão do sofrimento psíquico* (Vol. 1). Autêntica.

Safatle, W., da Silva Junior, N., & Dunker, C. (2020). *Neoliberalismo como gestão do sofrimento psíquico*. Autêntica.

Sahd, F. B. (2022). (Neo)fascismo, (pós)fascismo ou (neo)populismo? Um balanço bibliográfico possível de uma calorosa disputa classificatória. *Intellèctus, 21*(2), 94–120.

Salles, L. G. (2017). *Nova direita ou velha direita com wi-fi?: uma interpretação das articulações da "direita" na internet brasileira*. [Master's thesis, Universidade Federal de Santa Catarina]. Repositório Institucional UFSC. Retrieved from https://repositorio.ufsc.br/handle/123456789/183615

Salzborn, S. (2016). Renaissance of the new right in Germany? A discussion of new right elements in German right-wing extremism today. *German Politics and society, 34*(2), 36–63.

Sanfelice, J. L. (2008). *Movimento estudantil: a UNE na resistência ao golpe de 64*. Alínea.

Santos, A. A. (2011). O Estudo sobre Juventude no Brasil. *Revista Segurança Urbana e Juventude, 4*(1).

Savegnado, S. D. O. (2019). Práticas discursivas e sociais relativas aos jovens e à juventude. *Última Década, 51*, 192–224.

Schellenberg, B. (2013). Developments within the radical right in Germany: Discourses, attitudes and actors. In R. Wodak, M. Khosravinik, & B. Mral (Eds.), *Right-wing populism in Europe: Politics and discourse* (pp. 149–162). Bloomsbury.

Scheuch, E., & Klingermann, H. D. (1967). Theorie des Rechtsradikalismus in westlichen Industriegesellschaften. *Hamburger Jahrbuch filr Wirtschafts-und Geselhchaftspolitik, 12*, 11–29.

Schwander, H., & Manow, P. (2017). *It's not the economy, stupid! Explaining the electoral success of the German right-wing populist AfD. CIS Working Paper 94*. University of Zurich.

Schwanenflügel, L., Lütgens, J., McMahon, G., & Liljeholm Hansson, S. (2019). Participation biographies: Routes and relevancies of young people's participation. *Diskurs Kindheits- und Jugendforschung, 14*(4), 431–445.

Sedgwick, M. (2010). The concept of radicalization as a source of confusion. *Terrorism and Political Violence, 22*(4), 479–494.

Severo, G. R., Weller, W., & Araújo, G. C. (2021). Jovens de direita e extrema-direita: posicionamentos políticos no ensino médio. *Linhas Críticas, 27*, 1–24.

Shaw, C. (1966). *The Jack-roller*. University of Chicago Press.

Silva, J. I. A. (1987). *Estudantes e política no Rio Grande do Norte* 1960-1969. [Master's thesis, Universidade federal do Rio Grande do Norte]. Repositório Institucional UFRN. Retrieved from https://repositorio.ufrn.br/handle/123456789/52217

Silva, T. T. (2000). *Identidade e diferença: a perspectiva dos estudos culturais*. Vozes.

Silva, I. H. D. M. (2021). "Liberal na economia e conservador nos costumes". Uma totalidade dialética. *Revista Brasileira de Ciências Sociais, 36*, e3610702.

Singer, A. (2009). Raízes sociais e ideológicas do lulismo. *Novos estudos CEBRAP, 85*, 83–102.

Smith, D. (2022). Pam Nilan: Young people and the far right. *Journal of Applied Youth Studies, 5*, 269–273.

Solano, E. (Ed.). (2018). *Hatred as politics: The reinvention of the right in Brazil*. Boitempo Editorial.

Souza, R. M. D. (2009). Protagonismo juvenil: o discurso da juventude sem voz. *Revista Brasileira Adolescência e Conflitualidade, 1*.

Sposito, M. P. (Ed.). (2009). *O Estado da Arte sobre juventude na pós-graduação brasileira: Educação, Ciências Sociais e Serviço Social (1999–2006)* (Vol. 2). Argvmentvm.

Sposito, M. P., & Tarábola, F. D. S. (2017). Entre luzes e sombras: O passado imediato e o futuro possível da pesquisa em juventude no Brasil. *Revista Brasileira de Educação, 22*(71). https://doi.org/10.1590/S1413-24782017227146

Standing, G. (2014). O precariado e a luta de classes. *Revista Crítica de Ciências Sociais, 103*, 9–24.

Stanley, B. (2008). The thin ideology of populism. *Journal of Political Ideologies, 13*(1), 95–110.

Stanley, J. (2018). *How fascism works: The politics of us and them*. Random House.

Stefanoni, P. (2021). *¿La rebeldía se volvió de derecha?: Cómo el antiprogresismo y la anticorrección política están construyendo un nuevo sentido común (y por qué la izquierda debería tomarlos en serio)*. Siglo XXI Editores.

Stockemer, D., Lentz, T., & Mayer, D. (2018). Individual predictors of the radical right-wing vote in Europe: A meta-analysis of articles in peer-reviewed journals (1995–2016). *Government and Opposition, 53*(3), 569–593.

Taguieff, P. A. (1984). La rhétorique du national-populisme. *Mots. Les langages du politique, 9*(1), 113–139.

Tavares, B. (2012). Sociologia da Juventude: Da juventude desviante ao protagonismo jovem da Unesco. *Sociedade e Cultura, 15*(1), 181–191. https://doi.org/10.5216/sec.v15i1.20683

Taylor B. (2020). Alt-right. In Z. A. Casey (Ed.), *Encyclopedia of critical whiteness studies in education* (pp. 15–22). Brill Sense.

Teixeira, J. M. (2019). *A conduta universal: governo de si e políticas de gênero na Igreja Universal do Reino de Deus*. [Doctoral dissertation, Universidade de São Paulo]. Biblioteca Digital USP. https://doi.org/10.11606/T.8.2019.TDE-30052019-103135

Teixeira, J. M., & Barbosa, O. A. (2022). A mulher e a família: agendas pentecostais na disputa pela gramática dos direitos humanos. *(Syn)Thesis, 15*(1), 89–105.
Thrasher, F. (1927). *The gang: A study of gangs in Chicago*. University of Chicago Press.
Toscano, E. (Ed.). (2019). *Researching far-right movements: Ethics, methodologies, and qualitative inquiries*. Routledge.
Trancoso, A. E. R., & Oliveira, A. A. S. (2016). Aspectos do conceito de juventude nas Ciências Humanas e Sociais: análises de teses, dissertações e artigos produzidos de 2007 a 2011. *Pesquisas e Práticas Psicossociais, 11*(2), 278–294.
Traverso, E. (2019). *The new faces of fascism: Populism and the far right*. Verso.
Wahl, K. (2020). *The radical right: Biopsychosocial roots and international variations*. Palgrave Macmillan.
Wahl, K., Doermer-Tramitz, C., & Blumtritt, J. (2013). *Fremdenfeindlichkeit: auf den Spuren extremer Emotionen*. Springer.
Walther, A. (2012). Participation or non-participation? Getting beyond dichotomies by applying an ideology-critical, a comparative and a biographical perspective. In P. Loncle, M. Cucocnato, V. Muniglia, & A. Walther (Eds.), *Youth participation in Europe: Beyond discourses, practices and realities* (Vol. 1). The Policy Press.
Walther, A., Stauber, B., & Pohl, A. (2009). *UP2YOUTH. Youth -- Actor of social change. Final report*. Institut für Regionale Innovation und Sozialforschung.
Walther, A., Batsleer, J., Loncle, P., & Pohl, A. (Eds.). (2020). *The struggle of participation and young people. Contested practices, power and pedagogies in public spaces*. Routledge.
Weller, W., & Bassalo, L. D. M. B. (2020). A insurgência de uma geração de jovens conservadores: reflexões a partir de Karl Mannheim. *Estudos Avançados, 34*, 391–408.
Whyte, W. F. (2005). *Sociedade de esquina: a estrutura social de uma área urbana pobre e degradada*. Jorge Zahar.
Willis, P. (1977). *Learning to labor: How working class kids get working class jobs*. Columbia University Press.
Zhirkov, K. (2014). Nativist but not alienated: A comparative perspective on the radical right vote in Western Europe. *Party Politics, 20*(2), 286–296.

Chapter 3
Comparing Discourses, Identities, and Meanings of Political Participation

For most of the twentieth century, the economic project[1] was placed at the centre of research seeking to understand politics and its transformations. The introduction of new interpretations is recent and dates back to the linguistic and cultural turn experienced at the end of the century; cultural studies, for example, sought to understand resistance and oppression through the lenses of economy and social classes but began to focus on everyday experiences and symbolic productions. Stuart Hall (2000) proposed a structuralist approach in the field of cultural studies, placing at its centre the significant practices and discursive processes. The articulation of the concepts of culture and discourse with power relations enabled new understandings of the processes of identity/difference production, as well as new perceptions about the political. This articulation brought new questions to the study of politics and identities, enabling the emergence of interdisciplinary studies, like the one presented here.

Cultural studies proposed a pioneering approach to interdisciplinarity that goes beyond the coalition of different areas, where each speaks from within its "specialty". This interdisciplinary approach involves an intellectual risk, in the sense that it must destabilize already established fields and the fragmentation of knowledge, in order to bring forth something new (Grossberg, 2006). This book is based on cultural studies and its encounter with Foucaultian power analytics, as well as Brazilian studies on life narratives conducted by Ciampa (2005). Lima (2007) states

[1] Dardot and Laval (2016), in their Introduction to the English version of *The New Way of the World*, provide an extensive explanation about the historical importance of Marxism and, mainly, its observation on the violent basis of capitalism. However, they state that analysing neoliberalism merely as a transformation of the accumulation regime with the introduction of new ideologies is an approach that still centres on an economic theory, which does not allow for understanding the strong resilience of neoliberalism, as well as its influence on subjects' self-governance forms. For the authors, it is necessary to consider that this normative logic is constituted over initially uncertain battles and often tentative politics. Its elements were gathered, little by little, defining a new set of rules that propose another society, which in turn is a response not to an accumulation crisis but to a crisis of governmentality (Foucault, 1979).

B. Besen, *Youth Activism in the Radical Right of Brazil and Germany*,
https://doi.org/10.1007/978-3-031-87635-6_3

that it was Ciampa who initiated, in Brazil, a critique of essentialist notions of identity, influenced by George Mead, as well as Sarbin and Berger and their studies on social roles. de Souza Filho et al. (2020, p. 295) revisit Ciampa's works and affirm that:

> narratives are not objects, but the methodology itself. As a critical research approach, autobiographical narratives materialize the metamorphoses of an individual's identity, and thus express the singular and particular dimension of experiences, as well as represent the universal dimension of broader events in the social sphere.

This book records research whose methodology centres on the narratives of young activists from radical right movements and constitutes a comparative study, aimed at analysing and comparing the discourses, identities, and meanings of political participation of young people in radical right movements in Brazil and Germany. It seeks to introduce the theme within the tradition of political participation studies, reflecting on the metamorphoses of political identities and the transformations in representation systems and modes of subjectivation.

In this chapter, I discuss the methodological choices in light of the research objectives while seeking to clarify the challenges and changes in course, as well as to discuss, in a more in-depth manner, the instruments and their connection with the theoretical orientations. The chapter is divided to first present the choice and implication of using biographical interviews or life narratives. Then the paths and ethical procedures adopted are presented in more detail, leading, in the end, to a presentation and contextualization of the methods and stages of biographical reconstruction and thematic analysis of narratives.

3.1 The Principle of Openness: Biographical or Life Narratives Interviews

Biographical interviews were introduced by Schütze (1983) in Germany, as early as 1970, to explore the phenomenon of municipal mergers and the process of choosing new names. The research was part of a project analysing decision-making processes and power structures in municipal contexts. The sociologist noted that, in narrating this process, the interviewees intertwined biographical elements to connect such choices to their paths. Initially, Schütze aimed to focus on the specific event of name selection, but, as the experience unfolded, he noticed an advantage in adopting a broader initial question that could give the interviewee freedom to intertwine biographical elements with the specific event being investigated. The methodology began to be adopted in the fields of sociology and education, gaining new contours. Its continued use led the sociologist to identify biographical patterns and highlight the potential of biographies in revealing social structures. One of the elements developed, in collaboration with Rosenthal (2018), was the principle of openness (*Prinzip of openness*), prioritizing the non-hypothesis-driven data collection and providing the greatest possible space for the presentation of experiences and views on the topics addressed, as well as in relation to their own actions.

In the Brazilian case, biographical research or life narratives still occupy a marginal place in the production of empirical research in the fields of sociology and psychology, having greater strength in education studies. An exception occurred in the Center for Studies and Research on Identity-Metamorphosis—NEPIM, led by Antônio Ciampa at the Pontifical Catholic University (PUC) and, more recently, in the research group of Aluisio Lima in the Department of Psychology at the Federal University of Ceará. Symbolic interactionism and ethnomethodology were also strands that adopted the methodology by conceiving that social actors interpret the objects they confront and are endowed with agency. In the case of discourse analysis research, there are controversies and discussions regarding its application to interviews, being more common to find analyses of media and parliamentary discourses, as well as everyday interactions (Iñiguez, 2006).

As evidenced in the previous chapter, there is a huge contingent of research on the far-right that continues to grow, but qualitative methods are still a minority. No previous studies were identified that compare youth activism in radical right-wing movements between countries in Europe and Latin America. Comparative studies have been conducted between European countries but mostly focused on studying participation within political parties (Art, 2011; Klandermans & Mayer, 2005; Caiani et al., 2012; Pasieka, 2020). In the case of studying radical right-wing movements, many studies have been produced analysing the speeches of leaders or legislative representatives (Aguiar & Pereira, 2019; Bernardi & de Morais, 2021; Namise & Rizzotto, 2023), also seeking to understand the normalization or *mainstreaming* of far-right discourses (Ekman, 2022; Mondon, 2022). Research exploring social networks also stands out, including analyses of activities and posts on Instagram and Facebook (Araújo, 2016; Weller & Bassalo, 2020). In the case of interviews, there is also the approach of voters and leaders of parties and movements (Damhuis, 2020; Roy, 2022).

Qualitative studies have still been largely based on secondary data on the subject (Damhuis & de Jonge, 2022). Although they are fundamental for understanding the phenomenon, these data do not contribute to visualizing the complex individual trajectories, nor the "lived worlds of meaning" (Fisher-Smith et al., 2021). One of the challenges of research with interviews or ethnographies with such groups is the possibility of listening to activists on their own terms, maintaining the principle of "openness" to encounter what is distinct and uncomfortable.

To maintain the principle of openness, it is important to adopt a stimulus to narration, avoiding explanatory questions.[2] Biographical interviews are usually composed of three stages. Firstly, a very open question encourages the interviewee to freely describe their biographical trajectory. In the case of the interviews presented in this book, young people were asked to imagine that a biography of their lives was

[2] Clearer examples of explanatory questions are those starting with "why" and "what does it mean". In the narrative case, questions involving "how" or "could you tell me more about" are favoured.

being published and to tell what it would include. In other cases, they were asked about their earliest memory and to recount the trajectory of their lives from there. In the initial phase of the interview, the interviewer's job is to maintain the narrative flow without making substantial interventions. In the second phase, the questioning period, the interviewer asks (immanent) questions about things the interviewee mentioned, seeking to use the elements and language used by the interviewee. In the final stage, the interviewer asks (exmanent) questions about topics the interviewee did not mention but are of interest to the researcher. In this study, the questions in the final stage focused on political perceptions and paths to political engagement, as well as identifying the main activities and reference points of the interviewees.

The choice of this method is justified by considering that biographies are capable of reflecting on processes in social spheres, as well as reflecting the agency and practices of individuals. In Ciampa's view (2003), in biographies, we seek the revelation of material and cultural conditions, as well as ideologies; in a post-structuralist view, we seek to reveal the discourses and systems of representation, which conceal mechanisms of power, as well as constitute "realities". Silva (2000, p. 6) explains that, for post-structuralists, representation is a system of signification and "like any system of signification, a form of meaning attribution. As such (…) it is a linguistic and cultural system: arbitrary, indeterminate, and closely linked to power relations". Despite the particularities, both perspectives allow reflection on life narratives as powerful lenses for observing broader processes concerning the relationships between individual and society and/or between subject and knowledge.

3.2 Path and Strategies: Reflections on Positionality and Ethics in Research

3.2.1 Recruitment Strategies and Ethical Procedures

One of the first methodological challenges of the present study was to list which were the actors, movements, and groups that would be understood as part of the radical right. In the first chapter, I discussed the conceptual choice to approach these movements as radical right. Such a choice, evidently, also defined the methodology and the selection of groups. It is understood that the radical right consists of actors, parties, movements, and groups that are positioned at the far end of the political spectrum to the right, pointing to inequalities (which may be racial, cultural, or economic) as natural and/or positive—or even understanding that the state should not function as a regulator of them (Bobbio, 1996).

Furthermore, these groups or movements are critical of some characteristics of liberal democracy, especially in terms of the rule of law, more specifically, when it comes to the constitutional protection of minorities. It is perceived that the concept is broad, but it also serves to differentiate these groups from those understood as extreme-right, which remain marginal to democratic political processes, expressing rejection of the constitutive elements of liberal democracy. Despite this differentiation, the influences between the radical right and the extreme-right are not ignored, including in terms of joint expansion, as evidenced in the Brazilian case by the tireless studies of anthropologist Adriana Dias[3] on the increase of neo-Nazi cells and groups in Brazil.

The chosen strategy for approaching and accessing potential interviewees was the creation of a professional Instagram in 2020.[4] On it, I added and followed actors, movements, and groups that were presented in the media as leaders of the new right. From these, I dissected posts and tags, seeking to identify and add other groups and movements, as well as young people who identified as activists. For several months, I observed the posted content, confirming that there were direct attacks on minorities or their constitutional rights, as well as on the state in its policies of regulating inequalities. With this strategy, I began to follow about 250 profiles.

Initially, young people who identified as activists on their social media profiles or who were tagged in posts by radical right movements were invited to participate in the interviews. Subsequently, the "snowball" method (Vinuto, 2014) was employed, which led me to interviews with young people belonging to the same groups and movements. After these strategies, I also decided to connect directly with movements and parties, to which I sent messages via Instagram, as well as through institutional emails. In my messages, I introduced the research and extended the invitation for young participants to be interviewed. The recruitment strategy through social networks—more specifically Instagram—was the most effective, resulting in a set of 12 interviews with young people aged between 18 and 33.[5] Through the snowball method, I obtained four more interviews, which were not incorporated into the research due to the criteria that will be presented below. Initially, the interviews were planned to be in person. However, due to the Covid-19 pandemic, regional distances, and security issues, I chose to carry out online interviews via video calls. This entailed limitations, such as the impossibility of using non-verbal information analysis and ethical concerns of confidentiality (Germani

---

[3] Adriana Dias passed away in January 2023, and her research represents an immeasurable contribution to studies on the far-right in Brazil. The anthropologist's thesis, *Observing Hate: Between an Ethnography of Neo-Nazism and the Biography of David Lane*, published in 2018, highlights that, in these groups, hate figures as the centre of the social life of activism. The researcher managed to map the networks and connections between American and Brazilian groups, warning of an expansion of the groups during the government of former president Jair Bolsonaro.

[4] There is a broad literature being produced about cyberethnography (Keeley-Browne, 2011; Araújo, 2016), which is defined as a research methodology that expands the notion of "field", as cyberspaces are observed to understand human processes, including the composition of collective identities, previously investigated at a face-to-face level. Despite the time and intensity of network observation, and the inspiration from these studies, I do not consider that a cyberethnography was constructed. However, I emphasize that, regarding the construction of thematic categories, which will be better defined in the next section, elements of this observation were used to enrich and strengthen the analyses.

[5] Accepting this interval reflects the view that youth today is a social condition and a type of representation, which is reflected more in terms of phase than in terms of age group (Dayrell, 2003).

et al., 2022). The research project was submitted and approved by the Brazilian Research Ethics Council, and a consent form was formulated in Portuguese and German. In the German case, the consent form was inspired by that used by the PARTISPACE research group, which compared styles and practices of participation in Europe.

The consent forms were sent by email before the interviews and signed by all participants. The form included clarification of the general objective of the research, the methods, and the guarantee of data protection and anonymization. The form established the objective of understanding and comparing the perspectives and trajectories of political activism of young people in Brazil and Germany. The interviews were conducted to meet the ethical requirements of preserving the confidentiality of the identity of the young people involved, through the anonymization of the transcribed text, including the alteration of names of places and people that could be directly associated with the interviewees. The interviews—conducted between January 2022 and January 2023 via Skype and Zoom platforms—were not saved in the cloud. The interviewee's right not to answer questions was reinforced and pointed out in the consent form, in addition to declaring the voluntary nature and the right to withdraw participation at any time.

In the Brazilian case, it was possible to conduct 11 interviews with activists who identified as men and women. In the German case, there was greater difficulty in finding potential interviewees, resulting in a total of five interviews, involving only interviewees who identified as men. It is not possible to establish a single reason, but a relevant hypothesis is the fact that I, as a foreigner, was identified as having an immigrant background. In this topic, it is interesting to mention that researcher Nicole Roy (2022) researched the activism of women within the AfD and FPÖ and generously shared her thesis with me before its availability in the online archive. The researcher, of German origin, managed to interview 21 German women, but only from medium and high classes, questioning whether this might be related to a distrust of the lower classes in relation to the researchers. This situation was not reproduced in the present research, highlighting that, often, it is not possible to identify a sufficiently strong hypothesis for something that appears in the research, requiring work with the available material and that the limitations be included and considered in the analyses themselves.

Faced with the set of 16 interviews, I chose to make a selection, favouring a variety of contexts. This criterion was based on the observation that, when transcribing the general set of interviews, some narrative similarities became evident due to active participation in the same space, whether physical or virtual. This finding represented a barrier to critical thematic analysis, as identifying discursive patterns within such a restricted group of interviews could result only from interactions stemming from these common spaces of participation. Thus by diversifying contexts and movements, a more comprehensive reflection on the systems of representation of radical right-wing groups in Brazil and Germany was sought.

As it is a qualitative research, there was no need to constitute a sample. However, it is relevant to highlight that, among the Brazilian interviewees, there are young people residing in the northeast and southeast regions, with the majority coming from the latter. In the German case, young people from the regions of former East and West Germany were interviewed. Regarding gender, there was a predominance of interviewees who identify as men; however, efforts were made to ensure the inclusion of interviews with women, dedicating a specific category for the discussion of related issues. For the analysis of this category, the findings of Roy's research (2022) were considered, especially his interviews with young women.

Regarding race and ethnicity, only one young person declared themselves black, and another claimed to belong to a family of Arab origin. Considering these particularities and the relevance of social markers of difference (Crenshaw, 2017), attention was given to the specific narratives that emerged in the interviews with these young people. That is, both in the analysis of reconstructions and narratives, the incidences of gender, race, ethnicity, and place of origin markers were taken into account.

3.2.2 *Reflexivity and* Ethics of Care

Segers et al. (2023) state that research with the far-right brings inherent challenges related to power, justice, and ethics. The researchers understand that, to navigate such issues, it is essential to adopt an *ethics of care*. This ethics involves both attention and care for the emotions and effects of the research on the researched group and on the researcher. Thus, they emphasize the importance of reflexivity throughout the research process, ensuring that the thesis or report allows for visualization of how navigation through this universe was conducted, as well as observing the motivations related to decision-making during the process.

Therefore, beyond the issues related to recruitment strategies and ethical procedures, it is also essential to address the issue of reflexivity and *ethics of care*—that is, the effects of my positionality (Massey, 1994) on the research and the interviewees, as well as issues related to safety. In the case of interview and ethnography work with the extreme-right, it is understood that there is a greater risk to the safety of researchers, as most activists conduct their activities anonymously and the practice of actions of direct violence is part of their recurring strategies. Even with the clarity that my focus was on radical right-wing groups, I decided, before contacting interviewees in the German context, to get in touch with other researchers. One of the first contacts was with a German researcher with extensive experience with interviews with former female activists of the far-right. Despite expressing enthusiasm for the research, she warned me that approaching the interviewees would be very dangerous due to my foreign origin, which could be identified as immigrant. However, meeting other researchers, such as David Meiering (Meiering et al., 2020), and the publication by Damhuis and de Longe (2022) about interviews with the radical right encouraged me to proceed, accepting the limitations and potentials that the condition of "immigrant researcher" could bring.

Damhuis and de Longe (2022) recently published an article on the experience of interviewing leaders, voters, and activists of radical right-wing groups. According to them, one of the main issues would be the difficulty of establishing openness due to the lack of proximity, defined as a reciprocal distance between the researcher and the activists. They argue that many researchers are generally voters and supporters of left-spectrum parties (including green parties), frequenting different spaces and, consequently, presenting different interests, lifestyles, and social identities. I understand that this also applies to this research; however, I would list some fundamental mitigators. Firstly, during my years of work in the Heliópolis favela, in the city of São Paulo, Brazil, some young people with whom I interacted daily in the projects began to identify with radical right-wing groups. This did not alter the coexistence but generated moments of greater tension. It was also through some of them and their posts, still in 2017, that I began to reflect on the interpellative force of radical right-wing discourses, prompting me to approach, rather than distance myself, from these young people.

Furthermore, I consider it important to mention that I developed work of gathering evidence on hate speech and conducted a historical survey—in open and academic sources—for a report on active far-right and radical-right groups (the entirety of the *far-right*) in Brazil. This work required a 3-month deep dive and included, for example, neo-Nazi groups and cells, neo-fascists, dissidents from the Brazilian Society for Tradition, Family, and Property, and various religious fundamentalists. This immersion was crucial to visualize the networks formed by such groups, perceive the mutual influence between the radical right and the extreme-right in Brazil, as well as to visualize transnational patterns and international influences on the organization of Brazilian groups. Finally—and as is customary for research of this nature—many of my readings and audiovisual content were selected due to their relation to the theme.

I consider, in light of the facts presented above, that the research presented in this book was built over years of immersion in the theme and the universe of radical rights. One of the consequences I can identify, which might be interpreted as something negative, was a level of "naturalization"—in the sense of losing the capacity for shock. However, this is a double-edged sword as it was also what ensured the openness that had been built in previous years through almost daily contact within the realm of social networks.

I must also highlight that, influenced by my social position, origin, and trajectory, I made choices from the conception of the research to the conduct of interviews and subsequent analysis. Identifying and often being identified as white and middle class in Brazil, I occupy a privileged position, which often generates the necessary sense of security to take on the challenge of collecting primary qualitative data, as well as dealing with exclusionary and hateful discourses, such as those that emerged in the interviews. In Germany, I faced different challenges and, although privileged, I experienced barriers and a sense of displacement due to language, immigrant origin, and my non-traditional academic trajectory in terms of disciplines. However, I also relied on my institutional protection, often using the university as an entry point into spaces. In both contexts, however, I identify and am identified as a woman, having been affected by the discourses and facing fears regarding the factual and potential outcomes of the research—which included unknown and evidently extremist male profiles adding me and knowing my identity on Instagram.

Finally, I consider it relevant to highlight that I am part of a non-Orthodox Jewish family. Tradition, more than religiosity, has always been part of family life. In the Brazilian context, such identification was presented naturally in everyday encounters, not generating fear or apprehension. In some countries I had the opportunity to visit, people approached me spontaneously as Jewish or assumed an Israeli origin. Such naturalness changed when I was in Germany and during visits to Eastern Europe. There, I witnessed reactions ranging from astonishment at choosing Germany as a destination and research subject to excessive curiosity about my family's trajectories from Poland to South America. Aware of the anti-Semitism that characterizes European far-rights and considering the intersections in radical rights, I began to avoid addressing and even concealing this identification in certain environments. In the context of the interviews, however, I could not notice any type of reaction or evident hesitation related to this.

This point leads me to discuss the issue of the interviewees' reflexivity, regarding which I need to adhere to hypotheses. One of them is the connection between the university and the academic field with a tendency towards left-wing positioning on the political spectrum. Some interviewees stated they were excited about the possibility of speaking and being heard in an academic setting. Such a statement was often articulated with the idea of "persecution" and "false judgement" by society and, more centrally, by the left (and the green parties, in the German case), in relation to them and their movements. There were also some young people who started the interviews cautiously, in the sense of experimenting with more moderate speeches regarding their positions, combined with attention to my reactions. With my continuous listening and intentional encouragement to speak, which included even smiles and small sounds, the young people continued and tended to become more emphatic. However, it was clear that many of the narratives also constituted justifications.

In this sense, the experience presented by Klandermans (2020) regarding his investigation with far-right activists is considered interesting. The author points out that the use of life history interviews adds an intriguing dimension precisely because the interviewees do their best to understand why they engage in the movements. For him, the element of justification can be so important precisely because participation in a far-right organization can be something strongly condemnable in the eyes of the broader social environment, in which the interviewer may be included. Thus, the use of justifications would not have a negative connotation as it would reveal the discourses and processes of legitimizing political participation in these movements. Furthermore, I understand here that the process of justifying oneself is also a result of self-reflection about one's positions in the world, which can also be interpreted as a "reflexive positioning" (Constanza, 2015).

Regarding the choice not to confront, I admit that I had no difficulties during the interviews—which I also attribute to 10 years of psychoanalytic clinical practice. However, in the process of transcribing the interviews, I experienced difficult moments, in which I realized that I seemed to consent to statements that violated my convictions, in addition to noticing that the contents as a whole—which totalled about 250 pages—also contained hate and exclusionary discourses. I understand that, ethically, I followed the principle of openness that aligned with the proposed methodology; on the other hand, I imagine that such action could cross the individual boundaries of many researchers. Thus, I can only conclude that by seeking the consent of the interviewees through the terms and allowing them to express themselves freely, while taking all precautions with the anonymization of the material, I was able to respect ethical issues and ensure transparency. However, when we think about issues related to a possible normalization of discourses, we enter a grey area.

The conviction I hold is that my analysis does not operate in this sense and that my praxis is committed to critique and social transformation. However, during the research, I remained firm in the proposal I had when constituting and choosing the methodology of biographical interviews—that is, to listen and explore what was brought by individuals in its entirety—seeking to build analyses based on what had been collected, in light of the articulation with the available literature. Certainly, many of my limits have been "expanded"[6] over the years, but I remain guided by a view of inequalities as non-natural and results of power relations, which leads me to understand that the promotion of social justice must be an ethical commitment of the State, but also a horizon of struggle.

3.3 Biographical Reconstructions and Thematic Analysis of Narratives

The reconstruction process is part of the tradition of German interpretative social research. Through the reconstruction of trajectories, the aim is to organize, in a sequential order, biographical elements that were brought throughout the interview, seeking to do justice to the system of relevance presented by the interviewee (Rosenthal, 2004). In this research, it was considered fundamental to present elements related to growth—focusing on childhood and adolescence—centring more on the description of trajectories of involvement with politics and activism. For the reconstructions, I conducted a repetitive process of writing and returning to the transcribed material, seeking to incorporate the elements and avoid emphasizing

[6] In the field of ethnography with the far-right, Deodhar's (2022) article extensively discusses issues of positionality and the influence of ethnic identities, emphasizing her experience as a non-white researcher investigating a white ethnic nationalist party. She references Lichterman (2017), highlighting how "interpretative reflexivity" can be a practice of incorporating the effects of positionality not just as a methodological issue but as an integral part of data analysis. Although there are substantial differences between conducting interviews and ethnography, in both cases, Teitelbaum (2019) observes that the process can involve a solidarity that sometimes approaches immorality. This means understanding that certain findings may not be accessible if the researcher's stance is exclusively confrontational, instead of collaborative and open, even in the face of antagonistic worldviews.

elements that were brought tangentially. The reconstructions aim to capture the "accumulation of biographical experience" (Alheit & Dausien, 2000), distinguishing and then relating the "told" lives to reflect on the constellations of engagement biographies.

Such methodology allows for an in-depth analysis and illustration of the points identified as fundamental in engagement, as well as the particularities in the trajectories (Walther et al., 2021). In the reconstruction, we can also investigate what individuals experienced and what meaning they attributed to their actions. The choice to present 12 interviews, with a larger number of Brazilians, was due to the potential to visualize more trajectories of activists who identified as women. The issue of gender has a significant influence on trajectories and political agendas, which will be discussed through analyses and categories.

After the reconstruction process, a (de)construction of the interview narratives was carried out, using the methodology of thematic analysis of narratives (Braun & Clarke, 2006). This qualitative research method is frequently used in psychology to analyse and interpret the meaning and patterns within a given discourse or text. In the context of the research, the data underwent an analysis using the NVivo software. There, the coding process and the development of thematic categories, based on the articulation with the literature, were developed.

When we deal with a thematic analysis of narratives, the focus is on identifying and examining recurring themes. Braun and Clarke (2006) propose a definition and systematization of thematic analysis as an important research method, widely used but often not recognized as a distinct method. The authors argue that thematic analysis can be considered a method in its own right, and not just a step within other qualitative approaches, such as grounded theory, discourse analysis, and narrative analysis.

Clarke and Braun emphasize the importance of making explicit the epistemological assumptions when applying the method and argue against the idea that themes "emerge" from the data objectively, highlighting the active role of researchers in identifying and selecting themes. Thematic analysis involves the identification, analysis, and reporting of patterns (themes) in the data. The prevalence of a theme is not necessarily determined by quantitative recurrence but rather by its relevance to the research question and the theoretical framework adopted. It can be used to describe and organize selected data, as well as to interpret different aspects of the research topic. Such analysis can be combined with different theoretical frameworks and approaches, allowing for a flexible and detailed analysis of the data.

The process of thematic analysis began during data collection, with the identification of recurring patterns, and involved constant interaction between the data, coding, and analysis report. In the context of this research, a critical perspective was adopted in the construction of categories. Cannella and Lincoln (2015) described critical perspectives as those that recognize power and seek, in their analyses, to scrutinize the archaeology of perspectives taken as truth to understand how unjust and oppressive social conditions came to be reified as "historical data" (Cannella & Lincoln, 2015, p. 244). Critical methodologies advance the ability to deconstruct the "archaeology of knowledge" and identify how human discourse is linked to systems of representation. Discourse is, therefore, constitutive of the social, relating to hidden and public strategies of domination, as well as to practices of resistance (Jaramillo, 2012). When one looks at a set of discourses, an intertextual chain is formed. Foucault (1979) described intertextual chains by arguing that all knowledge is formed from a "network of references" that must be unveiled and broken (Lawless & Chen, 2019).

Thematic analysis, therefore, works well for integrating a critical perspective, revealing that there are modes of interpreting social reality that can be understood through the revelation of social representation systems. Thus, the intersections of discourses (and networks of references) were considered to constitute a set of categories that can parameterize the exploratory and comparative dimension of the research. The coding involved two phases, presented below.

1. **Open coding**: The first step is open coding, which involved staying as close as possible to the interviewees' discourse. Guided by repetition, recurrence, and forcefulness, special attention was given to what the discourses revealed, indicated, or identified in terms of salient and significant discursive patterns for the interviewees, whether individually or collectively. In this layer, what was actually said was referenced through the interviewees' words.
2. **Closed coding**: Once the first coding process was done, the process of connecting the interview discourses with broader social discourses and devices was initiated. In this phase, I began questioning the functions and workings of the emerging themes, as well as their articulation with the literature.

This process was carried out using NVivo software. Regarding the software, this book underwent an initial translation process into English through software, followed by a native reviewer.

In the case of the transcriptions, the coding process was done, in the first phase, with the original languages, to preserve and analyse the idiomatic particularities. The transcription initially used free software generating about 250 pages. However, the free versions were quite precarious, relying on audio playback for word adjustments and the addition of emphases marked in capital letters, as well as notes on laughter (marked as "laughs") and pauses (indicated by "…").[7] Finally, given the development of artificial intelligence and the expansion of free software, I noticed an exponential increase in the quality of translations, which led to the decision to translate all interviews into Portuguese for a final phase of analysis. In this phase, I used NVivo software to perform a word recurrence analysis. This analysis was used for the construction of categories and presented in Chap. 5. Despite considering the limitations of a quantitative dimension, I understand that it was used as another

[7] For the interview excerpts reproduced in the book, subtle changes were made, including the elimination of repetitions, syntactic breaks, and other marks of orality that may get in the way of understanding their transcription, in addition to a few specific cuts that preserved the fluency and the meaning in the original languages. The words or phrases in brackets were not explicitly stated by the interviewees but refer to previous excerpts or are implicit in the contexts of the interviews, being added to ensure greater clarity.

"look" at the material, still prevailing the qualitative character of the research, which favours the combination with the analysis of the context and the limits of the findings.

Souza et al. (2011) state that qualitative analysis software has the function of providing the integration of collected material and its visualization to expedite the work of categorization and familiarization that was already common to qualitative researchers. By generating various forms of visualization, including through pattern searches that might go unnoticed, such software stimulates the creation of questions and new paths of analysis. Thus, it is understood here that the function of the software should not be underestimated but dimensioned. They have an auxiliary function, always leaving it to the researcher to formulate and question what is found. Thus, the word recurrence analysis was the last step, which generated the possibility of new questions and perspectives on the material that were considered enriching given the exploratory potential of the research.

However, regarding the limits, it is important to consider that the survey of word recurrence in a universe of three languages and a small number of interviewees can generate errors or incorrect "dimensioning". Firstly, because translations have limits in terms of capturing idiomatic particularities. Terms can have ambiguous meanings, and the final selection, even if based on the context of the sentence, does not guarantee precision. Moreover, it is necessary to make a selection in front of the universe of words, which defines a specific bias. In the case of the research presented in this book, it was decided to select nouns or terms that could have this function. This meant the exclusion of verbs, adverbs, and adjectives. Finally, it is possible that an interviewee presents some "language habit", which stresses the use of a term and influences the result. Given such consideration, I reiterate here that the maintenance of such analysis in the research is based on its exploratory potential and the fact that the identified dimensions are complemented by the previous process of coding, contextual analysis, and articulation with the literature.

For this reason, I understand that the study's objective—to analyse and compare the discourses, identities, and meanings of young people's political participation in radical right movements in Brazil and Germany—is realized through the use of a set of methodologies and analyses. The adoption of life narrative interviews aimed to ensure access to trajectories and narratives to provide a view of the engagement processes, as well as the main identities and practices presented by the youth. Furthermore, and in a complementary manner, the biographical reconstructions, as well as the (de)construction of narratives into thematic categories, illustrate what the young people presented as knowledge and their ambiguities, allowing for the exploration of the discourses' interpellations and representation systems. Considering that representation systems are shaped according to historical time and local particularities, the adopted methodologies also prioritized understanding how and if similar discourses, identities, and practices emerged in the context of activism in both countries. In the next two chapters, I present and explore the research results.

References

Aguiar, B. S., & Pereira, M. R. (2019). O antifeminismo como backlash nos discursos do governo Bolsonaro. *Agenda Política, 7*(3), 8–35.

Alheit, P., & Dausien, B. (2000). Biographicity as basic resource of lifelong learning. In P. Alheit et al. (Eds.), *Lifelong learning inside and outside schools. Conference proceedings*. RUC.

Araújo, C. J. N. (2016). *Jornadas de Junho: a rede em rede.* [Master's thesis, Universidade Federal do Rio Grande do Norte]. Repositório Institucional UFRN. Retrieved from https://repositorio.ufrn.br/jspui/handle/123456789/23106

Art, D. (2011). *Inside the radical right: The development of anti-immigrant parties in Western Europe*. Cambridge University Press.

Bernardi, A. J. B., & de Morais, J. A. (2021). Fascismo à brasileira? Análise de conteúdo dos discursos de Bolsonaro após o segundo turno das eleições presidenciais de 2018. *Política & Sociedade, 20*(48), 300–327.

Bobbio, N. (1996). *Left and right: The significance of a political distinction.* University of Chicago Press.

Braun, V., & Clarke, V. (2006). Using thematic analysis in psychology. *Qualitative Research in Psychology, 3*(2), 77–101. https://doi.org/10.1191/1478088706qp063oa

Caiani, M., della Porta, D., & Wagemann, C. (2012). *Mobilizing on the extreme right: Germany, Italy, and the United States*. Oxford University Press.

Cannella, G. S., & Lincoln, Y. S. (2015). Deploying qualitative methods for critical social purposes. In G. S. Cannella, M. S. Pérez, & P. A. Pasque (Eds.), *Critical qualitative inquiry: Foundations and futures*. Left Coast Press.

Ciampa, A. C. (2003). A Identidade social como metamorfose humana em busca de emancipação: articulando pensamento histórico e pensamento utópico. In *Anais do XXIX Encontro da Sociedade Interamericana de Psicologia – SIP*.

Ciampa, A. C. (2005). *A estória do Severino e a História da Severina*. Brasiliense (Work originally published in 1987).

Constanza, W. A. (2015). Adjusting our gaze: An alternative approach to understanding youth radicalisation. *Journal of Strategic Security, 8*(1–2), 1–15.

Crenshaw, K. (2017). *On intersectionality: Essential writings*. The New Press.

Damhuis, K. (2020). *Roads to the radical right. Understanding different forms of electoral support for radical right-wing parties in France and the Netherlands*. Oxford University Press.

Damhuis, K., & de Jonge, L. (2022). Going nativist. How to interview the radical right? *International Journal of Qualitative Methods, 21*, 1–11.

Dardot, P. & Laval, C. (2016). *A nova razão de mundo: ensaio sobre a sociedade neoliberal*. Boitempo.

Dayrell, J. (2003). O jovem como sujeito social. *Revista Brasileira de Educação, 24*, 40–52. https://doi.org/10.1590/s1413-24782003000300004

de Souza Filho, J. A., Gonçalves Neto, J. U., & de Lima, A. F. (2020). Metamorfoses no projeto de Antonio da Costa Ciampa: da proposta analítica a uma teoria de identidade. *Psicologia Revista, 29*(2), 285–309. https://doi.org/10.23925/2594-3871.2020v29i2p285-309

Deodhar, B. (2022). Inside, outside, upside down: Power, positionality, and limits of ethnic identity in the ethnographies of the far-right. *Journal of Contemporary Ethnography, 51*(4), 538–565. https://doi.org/10.1177/08912416211060666

Dias, A. A. M. (2018). *Observando o ódio: entre uma etnografia do neonazismo e a biografia de David Lane.* [Doctoral dissertation, Universidade Estadual de Campinas]. Biblioteca de Teses e Dissertações. Retrieved from https://bdtd.ibict.br/vufind/Record/UNICAMP-30_a1547fc82f28a37df1cb70dfb8b94adb

Ekman, M. (2022). The great replacement: Strategic mainstreaming of far-right conspiracy claims. *Convergence, 28*(4), 1127–1143.

Fisher-Smith, A., Sullivan, C., Macready, J. D., & Manzi, G. (2021). Methodology matters. In S. D. Ashe, J. Busher, G. Macklin, & A. Winter (Eds.), *Researching the far right. Theory, method and practice*. Routledge.

Foucault, M. (1979). Por uma Genealogia do Poder. In M. Foucault (Ed.), *Microfísica do Poder*. Graal.

Germani, A. C. C., Conceição, M. I. G., Cabral, I. E., Oliva, I. L., Bastos, D. F., & de Souza, A. R. N. D. (2022). Narrativas: o que aprendemos sobre métodos online durante a pandemia? *New Trends in Qualitative Research, 10*, 526–526.

Grossberg, L. (2006). Does cultural studies have futures? Should it? (or what's the matter with New York?): Cultural studies, contexts and conjunctures. *Cultural Studies, 20*(1), 1–32. https://doi.org/10.1080/09502380500492541

Hall, S. (2000). Quem precisa da identidade? In T. T. Silva (Ed.), *Identidade e diferença: a perspectiva dos estudos culturais* (pp. 103–133). Vozes.

Iñiguez, L. (2006). *Analisis del Discurso. Manual para las Ciencias Sociales*. El Ciervo.

Jaramillo Marín, J. (2012). Representações sociais, práticas sociais e ordens do discurso. Uma abordagem conceitual a partir da análise crítica do discurso. *Entramado, 8*(2), 124–136.

Keeley-Browne, E. (2011). Cyber-ethnography: The emerging research approach for 21st century research investigation. In G. Kurubacak & V. Yuzer (Eds.), *Handbook of research on transformative online education and liberation: Models for social equality* (pp. 330–238). IGI Global.

Klandermans, B. (2020). Life-history interviews with rightwing extremists. In S. D. Ashe, J. Busher, G. Macklin, & A. Winter (Eds.), *Researching the far right* (pp. 225–238). Routledge. https://doi.org/10.4324/9781315304670-14

Klandermans, B., & Mayer, N. (2005). *Extreme right activists in Europe: Through the magnifying glass*. Routledge.

Lawless, B., & Chen, Y. (2019). Developing a method of critical thematic analysis for qualitative communication inquiry. *Howard Journal of Communications, 30*(1). https://doi.org/10.1080/10646175.2018.1439423

Lichterman, P. (2017). Interpretive reflexivity in ethnography. *Ethnography, 18*(1), 35–45.

Lima, A. F. (2007). Para uma reconstrução dos conceitos de massa e identidade. *Revista Psicologia Política, 7*(14).

Massey, D. (1994). *Space, place and gender*. University of Minnesota Press.

Meiering, D., Dziri, A., & Foroutan, N. (2020). Connecting structures: Resistance, heroic masculinity and anti-feminism as bridging narratives within group radicalization. *International Journal of Conflict and Violence (IJCV), 14*(2), 1–19. https://doi.org/10.4119/IJCV-3805

Mondon, A. (2022). Populism, public opinion, and the mainstreaming of the far right: The "immigration issue" and the construction of a reactionary "people". *Politics*. https://doi.org/10.1177/02633957221110472

Namise, D. K., & Rizzotto, C. C. (2023). Trollando em tempos de crise: uma análise dos discursos de Bolsonaro durante a pandemia. *Revista Eco-Pós, 26*(01), 168–189.

Pasieka, A. (2020). In search of a cure? Far-right youth activism and the making of a new Europe. In F. Duina & F. Merand (Eds.), *Europe's malaise (Research in political sociology)* (pp. 85–102). Emerald. https://doi.org/10.1108/S0895-993520200000027009

Rosenthal, G. (2004). Biographical research. In C. Seale et al. (Eds.), *Qualitative research practice* (pp. 48–64). Sage.

Rosenthal, G. (2018). The narrative interviews. In I. G. Rosenthal (Ed.), *Interpretative social research: An introduction* (pp. 133–147). Götting University Press.

Roy, N. (2022). *"We are just normal women": Narratives of far-right women members of the AfD and FPÖ*. [Doctoral dissertation, University of York]. White Rose eTheses. Retrieved from https://etheses.whiterose.ac.uk/33153/1/Roy_FinalThesis_CentreforWomensStudies.pdf

Schütze, F. (1983). Biographieforschung und narratives interview. *Neue Praxis, 13*(3), 283–293.

Segers, I. B., Gelashvili, T., & Gagnon, A. (2023). Intersectionality and care ethics in researching the far right. *Feminist Media Studies*, 1–6.

Silva, T. T. (2000). A produção social da identidade e da diferença. In T. T. Silva (Ed.), *Identidade e Diferença* (pp. 73–102). Vozes.
Souza, F. N., Costa, A. P., & Moreira, A. (2011). Questionamento no Processo de Análise de Dados Qualitativos com apoio do software WebQDA. *EduSer-Revista de educação, 3*(1), 19–30.
Teitelbaum, B. R. (2019). Collaborating with the radical right: Scholar-informant solidarity and the case for an immoral anthropology. *Current Anthropology, 60*(3), 414–435. https://doi.org/10.1086/703199
Vinuto, J. (2014). A amostragem em bola de neve na pesquisa qualitativa: um debate em aberto. *Temáticas, 22*(44), 203–220.
Walther, A., Lüküslü, D. G., Loncle, P., & Pais, A. (2021). Regimes of youth participation? Comparative analysis of youth policies and participation across European cities. *Young, 29*(2). https://doi.org/10.1177/1103308820937550
Weller, W., & Bassalo, L. D. M. B. (2020). A insurgência de uma geração de jovens conservadores: reflexões a partir de Karl Mannheim. *Estudos Avançados, 34*, 391–408.

Chapter 4
(Re)Constructing the Trajectories of Political Participation from the Biographies of Young Activists

This chapter presents 12 reconstructions of trajectories of young activists in the radical right of Brazil and Germany, revealing political engagement as a site of tension between institutional normativities of democratic participation and liminal practices. By examining in Sect. 4.2, how meanings attributed to political action—from social mobility to religious missions—interweave in individual experiences, it demonstrates how education systems and welfare regimes shape perceptions of activism. While in Brazil academic dedication and grassroots mobilisation emerge as political capital, in Germany the pursuit of private careers is intertwined with everyday practices in party-affiliated spaces. These dynamics illuminate a contemporary paradox: the need for 'youth protagonism' to legitimize political projects, even when such projects are not acknowledged as aligned with the principles of liberal democracy. The notion of 'liminal participation' is presented in Sect. 4.3, not merely as an analytical category but as a tool to understand how contemporary subjects construct effective 'identity collages,' negotiating power spaces in a landscape marked by intersections between normative discourses and practices of subjectivation.

4.1 Reconstructions of Trajectories

In this section, 12 trajectories of political participation are reconstructed from the narratives obtained in biographical interviews.

B. Besen, *Youth Activism in the Radical Right of Brazil and Germany*,
https://doi.org/10.1007/978-3-031-87635-6_4

4.1.1 Alexander: "A Line of Tradition that Follows into the Future"

Alexander is 18 years old and presents himself as part of the state leadership of the youth organization of a radical right-wing German party. His parents are "Russian Germans", but the young man was born in Germany. His early years were spent in a house shared by his parents and grandmother, who had a significant influence on his interest in painting and the arts, which faded over time. His father never adapted to the country and was in a cycle of coming and going, having left for the first time when Alexander was 3 years old. It was his grandfather who "took on the role of father", being the person who most "shaped him as a man". The death of his grandfather in 2016 was a moment of sadness for the young man, who describes himself as introverted.

Alexander visited the country and city of his parents' origin, where he experienced an emotional moment upon finding the new house built by the part of the family that had remained in the rural area. His education was "rigorous", and through the influence of his parents, who "express themselves quite conservatively", he acquired his "common sense" and "good reasoning". He attended the *Gymnasium* and, for a long time, his favourite subject was geography; he enjoyed identifying countries and their borders. However, from the ninth grade, things changed with the introduction of topics like climate change. Alexander does not believe that humans are the cause of such changes. History is also a subject he likes, but he feels uncomfortable with the "ideological approach" to certain topics, especially National Socialism.

His political positions began when a refugee camp was set up in the area where he lived, causing reactions in the family. After having contact with his organization, the young man was able to look back and notice that the arrival of refugees was not only related to terrorist episodes but also to smaller changes, such as loud music in the neighbourhood and increased litter on the streets. Despite aligning with conservatism, Alexander prefers to be identified as a nationalist. Unlike other conservatives, he does not miss the past; he just believes that "somehow, there is a line of tradition that you follow into the future".

Currently, Alexander has no friends at school as they are all more leftist and socialist. There, the young man expresses his thoughts without fear, including those related to opposition to the European Union and discomfort with the restrictive measures related to Covid-19. This leads some classmates to call him a Nazi or extremist, but this does not inhibit him from speaking his mind. The young man only regrets the loss of a friend, who was an important companion during the first year of the pandemic but stopped calling him and communicating with him due to Alexander's positions on restrictive measures.

It is in the party's youth where he finds people with whom he can talk about political topics, as well as other aspects of life. His routine includes biweekly meetings, in which they discuss transmitting the interests of young people to the party, as well as the entrance of new members to the party. There is also public relations work, which is related to postings and organizing events to engage other young people. As an advisor on the Executive Committee, he organizes meetings such as summer festivals and larger gatherings with the national committee. In the future, Alexander wishes to continue his studies and find a good job. Regarding the party, he would like to take a position on the board and continue contributing and being able to live a daily life he considers "exciting".

4.1.2 Aline: "I Owe Nothing to Feminism!"

Aline is 20 years old and lives in a city in the interior of the southeast region of Brazil. She presents herself as a pro-life activist. In the past, she was bullied and persecuted at school; her mother—a "single mother"—is her main partner in life and politics. The young woman lives in the same house where she grew up, which over time gained "wires and electricity" to ensure the safety of the two women. Therapy has been a part of her life since childhood, first to help her cope with the absence of her father and sister, later to help her deal with the bullying she suffered at school. Both her mother and father have other children, but the young woman does not have a close relationship with any of her siblings or extended family. In the case of her maternal family, there were always many conflicts—mainly due to "financial interests"—which led her mother to choose a more distant life. As for her paternal family, they even demanded a DNA test to prove paternity, which at least guaranteed the right to alimony, providing the money that now allows the young woman to pay for pharmacy school.

Aline has gone through various religious experiences, involving important moments in the evangelical church. It was a friend who took her to a youth "cell", a space that helped her face negative experiences at school. During adolescence, however, she recognized herself as an atheist, living a "more rebellious phase". More recently, a boyfriend introduced her to the book *Infinite Light*. This is how Aline began to take an interest in and research Judaism, finding along this path the Bnei Noach[1] denomination group, which follows the Noahide laws.[2] Aline understands

---

[1] Jovegelevicius (2018) conducts a detailed research on the approach of evangelicals to Judaism and, in this context, also situates the Bnei Noach, about whom he explains: "the Bnei Noach, 'sons of Noah', are a group of non-Jews who have been advised by figures of Jewish orthodoxy in fulfilling the seven laws of Noah. Like much of the practices of Brazilian Jewish orthodoxy, the movement was imported from the United States and offers religious assistance to those who seek to approach Judaism, without converting them" (Jovegelevicius, 2018, p. 31). Supported by other references (Costa, 2017), the researcher points out that such an approach is based on an attempt to distance and differentiate from Catholicism, in addition to an approach to orthodox practices that define more rules and foundations for daily life. Additionally, the identification with the right seems to relate to a specific promotion of the State of Israel, which is increasingly gaining authoritarian contours, being protected and defended by the orthodox community spread throughout Brazil.

[2] Aline explains that all humans are descendants of Noah and emphasizes that she follows the seven laws, which are summarized as (1) do not kill, (2) do not steal, (3) do not worship false gods, (4) do not commit adultery, (5) do not eat any part of a living animal, (6) do not blaspheme, and (7) administer justice through courts.

that conversion is very difficult, so she has been involved with the group and identifies as a "Judaizer".

The start of her activism coincided with the 2018 presidential election campaign, when she and her mother began to observe and follow the candidates' speeches "in full". Displeased with the "gender ideology" represented by the Workers' Party candidate, the two embarked on a journey of support for candidate Jair Bolsonaro, participating in rallies and demonstrations. These demonstrations formed another essential bond between mother and daughter, who became fans of various influencers and public figures of the new right. Several trips to São Paulo and Brasília were exhausting adventures, involving various setbacks and efforts for the two. However, meeting such personalities, as well as other activists, made it worthwhile.

Over the last 3 years, Aline has started producing content focused on the anti-feminist agenda. The central statement of her first post that gained traction was: "I owe nothing to feminism!" Stemming from a process of studying YouTube videos, the young woman says she discovered reading, admiring mainly the books of Ana Campagnolo, such as Feminism: Perversion and Subversion. In the last 2 years, Aline has joined different political movements, often invited because of her activism on social media. Through these contacts, she has already travelled to the country's capital, participating in two conservative movement congresses, including CPAC[3] (Conservative Political Action Conference). Today, Aline can already work in the field, having completed pro-life courses in international organizations. Due to her activism, Aline reports receiving constant threats on her social networks. One message contained the image of a girl that had been hung with the suggestion that she do the same.

At the time of the interview, she was sure that Bolsonaro would have the majority of votes in the 2022 elections. If he lost, she pointed to the possibility of a civil war. Aline reports a strong identification with the Brazilian Independence Anthem, which says "either the Fatherland will be free, or we will die for Brazil". Until she marries and has children, which she highlights as her main life goal, she wants to fight for Brazil.

[3] The CPAC began in the United States and arrived in Brazil in 2019. Today, it is conducted by the Instituto Conservador Liberal (Conservative Liberal Institute), representing a fundamental platform for leaders, *influencers*, and politicians of the radical right. Sanders and Jenkins (2023) analysed the importance of the CPAC Coalition for the transnational diffusion of authoritarian anti-feminist policies. The authors analysed the context of the North American conferences, seeking to highlight the internationalization of a discourse that seeks to promote the control of education and the production of knowledge, as well as the defence of the constitution of authoritarian leaders. At the core of these discourses, anti-feminism was also identified, which, in the Brazilian case, has gained repercussion through an extensive editorial production, whose most well-known name is Ana Campagnolo.

4.1.3 Thomas: "A Point of View from East Germany"

Thomas is 22 years old and is from a city in former East Germany. Since 2020, he has been attending the regional university, where he studies political science. The young man describes himself as someone engaged in politics and a participant in the civic association of a German party. As a child, he had a great passion for building Lego, playing with miniature model cars, and hiking. Some of these hobbies have been lost, but hiking remains a daily activity that he shares with his family. The family also influences another of his favourite activities—reading. His appreciation for reading is long-standing and involves, especially, political works, history, and subjects related to antiquity and the Middle Ages. Additionally, he is a fan of printed newspapers, which he receives weekly.

His parents are separated, and Thomas currently lives with his mother and stepfather. After a turbulent time due to the separation, he rebuilt a close relationship with his father. The young man associates the differences between his father, stepfather, and mother with the marks of the former division of Germany. While his father served in the West German army, his stepfather served in the East German army. He, his mother, and stepfather are "typical East Germans", while his father is a classic "Bavarian Seppel".

Regarding his father, the main divergences are due to their positions on refugees. Today, Thomas has questions, while his father adopts a position more aligned with the UN. As for his stepfather, the main conflict concerns the idealization of the United States. His moral values do not allow him to believe that the United States are heroes, while his stepfather—who lived 18 years in the country—does not believe that Americans should be held accountable for war crimes in Vietnam. While his father has opted for the Greens, his stepfather is a regular CDU voter—and a fan of Angela Merkel—and his mother has always opted for the SPD (Social Democratic Party of Germany). Coming from a "social-democratic" family, he always felt that he "would become more conservative".

At the age of 13, the young man was already concerned with politics, being critical of proposals coming from the Alternative for Germany (AfD). In daily life, he began participating in discussions of his city's municipal council, but gradually, the desire to get actively involved grew. It was in this way that, in 2019, he joined the youth of a left-wing party. He stayed there for a short time, realizing there were contradictions and a lack of real proposals. It was mainly at university that he noticed that the left and the Greens are extremely intolerant, demanding that right-wing symbols be censored while those of the left remain. Moreover, they advocate for the existence of more than 20 genders but ignore that biologically there are only two sexes.

Thomas does not consider himself very conservative but rather someone who bases himself on facts. In terms of facts, he observes that Germany is not managing to solve its own problems, becoming a society that is no longer purely capitalist, but "a mix of capitalism and socialism", in which the federal government does nothing for the market. He currently participates in municipal "round tables" (*Runde Tische*) and is part of the party's association. His party created an exclusive organization for young people, which has been seeking to expand its influence in the region. His group is still stigmatized but always manages to enter the German Federal Parliament (the *Bundestag*). In 20 years, Thomas believes they will be a fundamental part of the *Bundestag*. His current focus is on his studies and progress, but an idea he has been considering is joining the armed forces. Politically, he intends to remain active in his region, prioritizing his hometown and policies that can benefit it.

4.1.4 Carlos: "I Could Have Been a Criminal"

Carlos is 19 years old and lives on the outskirts of a capital city in Southeast Brazil. He presents himself as a law student and conservative activist. Throughout his childhood, he moved from house to house, being considered a problematic child by his family. As the older brother, he soon became responsible for taking care of his sister as his mother worked and spent a lot of time away from home. In elementary and high school, he attended schools close to his home. In class, he would stay together with a minority of black classmates like him. There and in the neighbourhood, he did not experience prejudice, but in *shopping centres*, he noticed that those who "misbehaved" received strange looks.

From an early age, he also attended a neighbourhood football club. Despite his passion for the sport, situations of internal corruption at the club[4] prevented him from achieving his desired career. At the same time, his mother got involved in urban homeless movements in her search for access to homeownership. Although she participated in many of the movement's activities, she was not granted an apartment. These experiences allowed Carlos to perceive the problem of corruption in the country. Additionally, they were also impulses to start seeking possibilities to become an entrepreneur and be his own boss.

The year 2021 was marked by losses, especially that of his grandfather, who was a great role model for the young man. Both his former football school coach and his grandfather taught him that discipline is the foundation of life. His activism began with an interest in entrepreneurship and liberal theories. Videos on the subject led him to discover the "philosopher" Olavo de Carvalho. Through his videos, he began a process of rethinking Brazilian history, especially the communist threat in the country. Carlos joined a liberal right-wing movement at a Brazilian public university for the first time, but he found weak participants who were only interested in money. Since 2018, he has been part of a movement that does "grassroots activism work" for the Brazilian right. The first meeting with his current friends from the

[4]The young man mentions realizing that, to achieve positions in professional teams, more than talent, it was necessary to have resources to participate in informal financial agreements. This would have been one of the first situations where he felt disappointment, which translated as a realization that corruption existed in Brazilian institutions.

movement took place at a pro-gun demonstration, organized and convened via Facebook.

The young man is proud to be a committed and studious young person who refused a predestined future as a criminal in the periphery. Recently, he was honoured at the high school he attended. However, he was persecuted for his conservative position and prevented from expressing his convictions in educational spaces. As these spaces are marked by leftist political indoctrination, he dreams of being a university professor and being able to transform this from within.

Today, he actively participates in study groups and demonstrations organized by his movement, maintaining particular contact with the leadership. For him, former Brazilian President Jair Bolsonaro betrayed his conservative convictions and "sold himself as something that he is not". Being a centrist politician, Bolsonaro was not a strong enough leader. Carlos sees the future of conservatism beyond the former president and closely related to the grassroots and study work that his movement carries out in Brazil.

4.1.5 Nissin: "A Process of Personal Development"

Nissin is 23 years old and presents himself as an engineering student who spends most of his time at university and is quite politically active. Having been born in a predominantly Muslim country, he arrived in Germany at the age of one and a half. His father had immigrated to the country before marrying his mother, as a political refugee. In her country of origin, his mother studied her native language, but after immigrating, she developed small cleaning jobs, dedicating herself mainly to the care of her children and the home. She was the one who taught Nissin to read even before entering primary school, contributing to his good performance.

During most of his adolescence, the young man stayed with friends in his village, practicing karate and playing the guitar. A few years ago, he visited his native country, which seemed "very poor" to him, reflecting the image of "a third-world country". He still has relatives there, but the contact is not constant. Although his parents introduced aspects of their culture, Nissin was confronted[5] more intensely by German culture. During secondary school, his performance declined, and he did not achieve a good grade in the *Abitur*.[6] The young man was admitted to the engineering

[5] In some of the reconstructions, the words originally used are maintained, as these will be important for subsequent analysis. Additionally, there are some terms that have multiple meanings and translations in English. Sometimes, it is understood that such translations do not alter the final discourse, while at other times, the choice between the two words will produce a very distinct meaning. This is the case of "confronted", which can mean just the encounter, but also denotes "confrontation" and "shock", especially considering that he uses the term culture.

[6] The *Abitur* is a secondary school leaving examination in Germany. It is taken by young people aged only12 or 13 years old, varying according to state regulations. The exam defines entry into most German universities, also being accepted in other universities in Europe and the United States. The exam is usually exclusive to those who will enter the *Gymnasium* for high school. The

course, an event explained by the "shortage of engineers in the country", which led the university to "accept anyone". Despite having entered with low grades, the young man has discovered himself to be very good, currently working as a tutor.

About 3 years ago, Nissin experienced a crisis in which he felt he had no purpose and knowledge about life. During this period, he met a colleague who had a lifestyle that inspired him. Led by her to the church, he decided to get baptized. His parents still do not know about his baptism, but he stopped attending church due to reactions at home. His parents are also conservative, but in profoundly different ways: While they are "conservative Muslims", he is "conservative in a German Christian way". In Islam, people follow many rules to be saved, while evangelical people follow the religion because they are saved. Nissin feels that in Christianity, there is a recognition that people commit sins and that no path will be perfect.

After his baptism, the young man underwent many transformations, cut his long hair, and changed his "nerd" *appearance*. This was a process of personal development (*self-improvement*),[7] also related to the new perceptions he acquired about women and relationships. Dating was a frustrating subject in the past, but through studies, he learned that women are evaluated by appearance and men by success. Since such a transformation, he has been much more noticed and respected.

During the pandemic, he joined a movement within the university to fight against the government's restrictions in response to the coronavirus pandemic. A close friend recommended it, but the group was difficult to find. Still, he managed to participate in several demonstrations. More recently, another friend introduced him to a more significant movement related to a German party. He is participating in some events and has identified with politicians who emphasize that the German government spends too much on foreign countries instead of its citizens, who are "its own people". In 2023, he will work to experience life as a politician. If he becomes one, he would like to discuss topics such as family and marriage. However, his main focus is to invest in his engineering career, as through this path, he will achieve more success and consequently be ready for a serious relationship.

German educational system has an orientation towards vocational positions defined quite early (Walther, 2022), as explained in footnote 8.

[7] It is interesting to highlight that the discourse about a process of personal development (*self-improvement*) is identified as central in some spaces of the "manosphere" (Ironwood, 2013), centrally among the "*red pill*" communities. Fields explains that the term "*red pill*" "is derived from the movie *The Matrix*, posits that men become enlightened to perceived misandry (i.e., contempt or prejudice toward men) and feminist 'brainwashing.' The online community in the 'manosphere' is described as seeking to make both men and women 'great again' by rebuilding traditional gender roles and a focus on men's 'self-improvement'" (Fields, 2024, p. 1). Although Nissin does not directly mention these communities, his description of the learnings regarding gender roles and the focus on this process as personal development indicates a connection with such groups, which are expanding in the two countries studied.

4.1.6 Simon: "We Just Want to Take Care of Our Country"

Simon is 22 years old and is a board member of the youth organization of a German party. He presents himself as someone who did not have a "political education" and who gradually became interested in the subject. Having grown up in the same house since childhood, he began living only with his mother after the age of 3—when his parents got divorced. The mother then needed to work outside, leaving him in the care of his grandparents, who live close to his home. Despite political differences, the relationship with them is extremely loving.

Simon attended a *Realschule* but always lived next to a *Hauptschule*[8] and a *Gymnasium* and, in this sense, was able to observe how the two types of education function in Germany. The *Gymnasium* creates a two-class society, where Germans are the majority and those with migratory backgrounds face prejudice. In the *Hauptschule*, the reality is more diverse, which seems better to him, as everyone should be treated equally, especially if they were born in the country and speak German. Today, he is pursuing an *Ausbildung* (vocational training course) that prepares him to be a wholesale and foreign trade manager.

His friendships are the most important part of his life, as friends are those who have always been by his side, in good and difficult times. Some of these friends have very different political positions from his, but it is important to "judge the person by the person themselves, not by their political attitude". Simon is gay and loves being able to talk with other gays about his support for the party. However, he assumes this is a taboo, which leads to rejection and breaking ties with some people. At school, he is admired for arguing with all the teachers. Despite the good experiences with discussions, he is unfairly demonized when he expresses his convictions, which range from issues about the type of energy production in Germany to the need to restrict immigration.

His interest began around the same time as the founding of the AfD party, around 2013. At that time, one of the central arguments presented in YouTube videos and talk shows by the representatives was the fight against the euro and against Germany's support for the Greek crisis. In 2017, he joined the youth organization.

[8] The German educational system generally consists of three tracks: "(1) *Hauptschule* (traditional duration of 5 years after 4 years of primary school), generally attended by students with average or below-average grades, offering basic education and preparation for vocational training that requires practical skills; (2) *Realschule* (traditional duration of 6 years after 4 years of primary school), generally attended by students with average grades, offering extended basic education and preparation for almost all types of vocational training; (3) *Gymnasium* (traditional duration of 8 or 9 years after 4 years of primary school), generally attended by students with above-average grades, offering academic education and preparation for university" (Salden & Hertlein, 2020, p. 117). Such a description allows understanding of the system; however, several works (King & Koller, 2009) have discussed this as a process that promotes early exclusion. Simon's description reflects the issue that students with immigrant backgrounds or immigrants from lower classes rarely access the *Gymnasium*. Beach et al. (2019), through ethnography, also confirm the higher incidence of immigrant youth in the *Hauptschule* but point out that experiences of segregation are also related to residential areas.

However, he was disappointed to understand that the movement was independent of the party. Thus, he left and returned in 2019, during the pandemic. Being forced to stay at home, he rebelled against the restrictive measures and decided to mobilize. Currently, his group is trying to reach the minimum number of participants to launch a district association. Additionally, Simon gained a position on the national youth executive committee.

Being a "contrarian" party, the participants of his group are commonly labelled as Nazis. One of the roles of his organization is precisely to show young people that they are needed in the party and that the demonization of the group is not fair. What they really want is to "take care of their country", especially concerning "culturally strange" people (kulturfremdem Menschen). These workers have come with the justification of solving the shortage of skilled labour, but they cannot even write or speak their own language.

Today, Simon organizes party events, in addition to maintaining activity on social networks like Instagram and X (formerly Twitter). A fan of Trump since 2016, he has a flag in his room and follows all his speeches. The politician fulfilled his campaign promises by building a wall to contain immigration. In the future, the young man would like to be part of the National Parliament, where he could make speeches and propose bills, being an active voice in the country. In 2 years, he intends to already be a candidate in local elections.

4.1.7 Vinícius: "Conservatism Is Not an Ideology, It's a Lifestyle"

Vinícius is 25 years old and was born in a peripheral region of a coastal city in the southeast of Brazil. He presents himself, from the beginning, as a studious young man who has been involved in politics since childhood. Both his mother and grandmother worked for a "royal family" in his city, which called him to be a young campaigner at the age of 8. He handed out leaflets and accompanied the parliamentarian throughout the city. The experience was "the spearhead" for his involvement in politics, "a theoretical childhood game" that he ended up liking. When he was little, he lived with his mother, grandmother, and siblings; nowadays, he lives only with his mother, as two of his brothers and his grandmother have passed away, and his older sister lives with her husband.

In high school, he joined several student councils, the student union, and the Catholic Church. One of the highlights was Luzia, his Portuguese teacher, who, besides being a teacher, also gave life advice—a kind of "coach". Around 2013, in the face of a "certain anti-PT trend", he approached the Free Fare Movement and participated in the June 2013 Journeys. He joined the demonstrations because he felt anger and anguish seeing Brazil being robbed. There, he got involved in violent actions by the black blocs and ended up having problems with the police, realizing the radical and disorganized nature of the left. During this same period, he discovered the YouTube videos of Olavo de Carvalho—the "teacher"—who is a reference for "everything he knows to this day". Olavo was the one who revealed the existence of the São Paulo Forum, something that did not appear in the traditional media; Olavo was also the bridge to meet Jair Bolsonaro, of whom he is also a "devotee".

At the centre of his activism is the defence of freedom and Judeo-Christian morality. Vinícius lived in a community and saw many "people get lost" with drug trafficking and banditry. His brother, imprisoned seven times and now deceased, ended up choosing "the wrong life". As a child, he visited his brother in jail along with his mother. Seeing the suffering of his mother and that of the mothers of other detainees, he decided he did not want that life, realizing that his studies and attachment to morality and ethics would protect him from repeating such a fate. Conservatism "marvelled him" and became a "lifestyle", reflecting positions he already had on issues like abortion, drugs, public safety, and family.

Last year, he participated in an organized movement, where he met important figures, but was dismissed due to internal disagreements related to his resistance to campaign for a candidate from another city. Today, he has expanded his participation in grassroots work and humanitarian actions, conducting more independent activism. He uses social networks to support the electoral campaigns of legislative candidates in his city. His dream is to follow a long career in politics, moving from the position of parliamentary advisor to deputy. The family for which his mother and grandmother worked admires his career and supports him. Recently, he moved from the periphery to a more central area, but he is still saving to, in the future, move to an even better neighbourhood.

4.1.8 Igor: "Defending a Noble Ideal"

Igor is 23 years old and presents himself as a law student and political activist who fights for the restoration of the monarchical system in Brazil. Coming from a family of federal jurists, he attended private schools throughout his life. Today, he lives with his parents in a "middle-class neighbourhood" of a northeastern Brazilian capital; however, he was born in a smaller nearby city. During his teenage years, he didn't go out much, feeling uncomfortable in environments with loud music, people drinking, and "partying". Being a "shy guy", he preferred staying home reading comics and watching Japanese animations.

His interest in politics began at 17, after the election for class representative at his school. An authoritarian young woman was chosen, leading him to question forms of government and confront his classmates. His first involvement was through Twitter (now X), a space where those who are shy or have difficulty taking a stand express their opinions. Identifying as a skeptical conservative, he began actively questioning politicians. This position was mirrored in his father, for whom he has enormous admiration. Regarding his mother, many conflicts arose because she supported the left and imposed her ideas through "moral authority". However, the pandemic represented a time of change in which he learned to listen and relate better to others.

Two years ago, Igor experienced a crisis and dropped out of university, feeling that his path had been too influenced by his parents. Since then, he has undergone significant changes but decided to return to studying law and complete his education. Since 2015, the young man has admired the fight against corruption led by Operation Car Wash. It was his support for Judge Sergio Moro who led him to get involved and support the electoral campaign of former President Jair Bolsonaro. For the young man, the 2018 elections were a "critical moment" in the country, where political views that were not prominent began to appear in the public arena. This is how he accessed liberal and conservative economic theories. During the campaign, he was also introduced by a friend to the monarchist cause. Today, he studies the topic and organizes pro-monarchist demonstrations in the streets, facing the challenges imposed by the internal divisions of the movement. His identification with the cause extends even to his hobbies, which involve reading monarchist content and drinking tea.

A fundamental memory from his past refers to the day he went to mass in the fourth grade, being the only one to kneel and show respect. There, he distinguished himself from his classmates, feeling like a stranger among them. Such a past is a sign of his attachment to conservatism. The young man finds it difficult for Brazil to adopt a parliamentary monarchy, but his activism is based on the "defence of a noble ideal". His discontent with the left involves neglect regarding family and respect. Additionally, he feels particularly bothered by feminist movements, as he lives and experiences life as a man, needing to defend his gender. In the future, he wants to secure a public position in the field of law and continue activism in pro-monarchy movements.

4.1.9 Nuria: "Society Is Getting Crazier"

Nuria is 19 years old and presents herself as a law student living in a city in the interior of southeastern Brazil. Since she was born, she has had an interest in "discovering the history of the world". Her family, which is "her foundation and base", has always encouraged reading. Through family encouragement, she developed the ability to interpret texts and grasp stories. This ability also helped her during high school when she attended a technical school in foreign trade. Among her favourite books are also works of fiction, which allow her to access the world of fantasy and "travel to other worlds and times".

Raised by her mother and grandparents, Nuria had her father as an inspiration to choose a career in law. He passed away when she was 1 year old. During childhood and adolescence, she faced hearing and speech problems, which were not well handled by her teachers. Movements between schools were due to this inability, combined with financial issues. Her political engagement began in 2018, during Jair Bolsonaro's campaign, which was a time when "many people mobilized with politics", including young people. From that time, she highlights an interview that Jair Bolsonaro gave to the Jornal Nacional, in which he exposed the existence of very wrong sexual education in schools, which encouraged children to become promiscuous through a "gay kit". In recent years, she has attended demonstrations in her city and capitals, as well as organized and participated in conservative seminars.

During the pandemic and in her last year of high school, she was locked at home and began sharing her indignations and studies on social media. During this time, she studied political topics and, at the same time, college entrance exam topics. Through TikTok, she managed to reach many followers. It was there that she found her true friends, who fight for the same causes. In high school, she experienced many problems at school, with the entry of very mean people who spoke badly of her behind her back and "exposed her in a very ridiculous way on Twitter". Such an experience made her stronger, showing that she should not care about what people say, only about what Christ thinks of her. Christ is also responsible for her wisdom and political struggle.

The young woman has difficulty identifying people who want good, "because society is getting crazier". Recently, she joined a party and seeks to collaborate on the campaigns and mandates of councillors. The main changes she would like to see are in the field of culture and education, mainly with the end of ideological indoctrination. In this sense, she is inspired by Olavo de Carvalho—the one who most changed her life and serves as a "base for everything". In the last year, she was encouraged by a group of adults from the street movement she is part of to spread her information and knowledge with other young people. Thus, she founded a new conservative movement with friends. The plan is to help millions of people, spreading the truth, collecting food for people in need, and helping women in vulnerable situations.

4.1.10 Moritz: "Young People Are Getting Dumber and More Degenerate"

Moritz is 23 years old and was born in a small town in the western part of Germany. He lived with his parents until he was 21, when he moved to a larger city, sharing an apartment with two university friends. His school journey "was not spectacular", as he never achieved very high grades nor stood out. His parents always had high expectations regarding his performance. During his childhood, they worked a lot, leaving him with his grandparents, with whom he no longer has a strong connection.

He moved out from his parents' house due to a worsening relationship with his father. The relationship had always been bad, but it reached a chaotic point where he felt something bad could happen. With his mother, however, Moritz always had an excellent relationship, considering her one of the most important people in his life. As a child, he dreamed of becoming a doctor but soon understood that only candidates with the best grades could access the course. Thus, he ended up opting for pharmacy, a course he quite likes.

At the beginning of college, he faced many difficulties related to the speed of the subjects and exams, even repeating some courses. This made it difficult to establish close friendships in his class. The pandemic was another challenge, but it was what led him to get involved in a university movement, where he found friends with ideas similar to his. The movement sought to oppose the measures imposed by the German government regarding Covid-19, mainly the 3G rule.[9] The movement did not attract many students, as most saw them as conspiracy theorists.

Moritz found the group on WhatsApp and began meeting with other students and organizing some strategies so they could be heard. The abolition of the 3G rule happened some time later, not due to the influence of his movement but because the government finally accessed the research and understood what Moritz already knew. Through the knowledge acquired in his pharmacy studies, the young man identified that it was not possible to define the effects of the vaccine, besides there being no need for healthy young people like him to be vaccinated. This knowledge also supported his decision to remain unvaccinated.

In the past, the young man saw himself as more conservative; however, the changes he experienced did not lead him to abandon his convictions. Such convictions are related to the "importance of traditional values and family for civilization and society". Another topic that mobilizes him is the issue of the free market as there is excessive state influence in the economy. His conservatism today is related to the fact that he does not go to parties nor enjoy spending money on things he does not need.

The future is something difficult to predict because today we live in "times when things can change very quickly". One of the factors is a downfall in general society, in a time when "young people are getting dumber and more degenerate". They no longer choose important careers that can contribute to society. For Moritz, German society, after World War II, created wealth that is being lost by the new generations. Despite being active in the movement, he intends to focus on his studies and pursue a master's degree in his field.

4.1.11 Letícia: "An Unarmed Population Is a Population that Cannot Have Its Rights"

Letícia is 32 years old and lives on the coast of southeastern Brazil. Currently, she is pursuing her second degree in medicine at a private university. Her parents are married and the family—which includes a brother—is very close. The young woman always attended private schools, never giving her parents much trouble due to her focus and determination. When she was still 4 or 5 years old, she wrote in a

[9] The 3G rule (*3G Regel*) was defined by the German government in 2021 and adopted by universities, stipulating that access to all facilities and classes was conditioned on the presentation of proof of vaccination, recovery, or a negative test conducted within the last 24 hours.

school assignment that her mother "did nothing" because she was a housewife. Although this thought seems ridiculous to her today, it was this phrase that served as a "turning point" in her mother's life. Shocked by what she read, her mother decided to go to college, becoming the most educated person in the family. Childhood was a happy period, spent with family and friends from the building she lived in. Friendships were always cultivated and many still remain.

When she was 18, Letícia started working in the service industry but ended up suffering an episode of exhaustion due to the demanding shifts that involved swapping days for nights. Upon resigning, she began to take her first degree and faced difficulties re-entering the job market. In 2012, the family went through a deep financial crisis that affected their purchasing power. Before, each member had a car and international trips were common. The crisis required sacrifices from everyone to ensure that she and her brother could finish college. During this period, her father had an episode of depression due to financial losses. To support herself, Letícia combined an extra job with her pre-university course.

Her interest in politics began back in 2005, during the referendum on guns. This was a topic that engaged her, as gun ownership would guarantee her and her family's safety. Given her interest, she joined groups, still on Orkut. Later, she also began participating in a shooting club, concluding that "an unarmed population is a population that cannot have its rights". In 2018, she was already in the habit of posting her opinions on social media, gaining attention by discussing topics such as the free market. A close couple of friends invited her to lead the directory of women from the then party of former president Jair Bolsonaro—with whom she already shared convictions.

This experience was fruitful but ended marked by disagreements. In the directory, what united people was the desire for change, which was personified by Bolsonaro and, mainly, by the Minister of Economy Paulo Guedes. Letícia identifies as a libertarian and, although she is right-wing, she does not consider herself part of the conservative spectrum. Some people label her this way because, in Brazil, "people's political views generally lack depth and research". Today, in medical school, she stands out in leadership activities, being recognized for her skills in dialoguing with diverse groups and seeking to understand perspectives different from her own.

Currently, she is part of a group that organizes almost daily live broadcasts to discuss news, focusing mainly on topics related to Latin America. Her greatest interest is the economy and the defence of the free market, including reading authors like Ludwig von Mises, Friedrich Hayek, and Adam Smith. Letícia believes that libertarian ideas will gain ground in Brazil in the coming years, and she plans to continue contributing to this movement.

4.1.12 Catarina: "My Values Do Not Come from the Right, They Come from the Bible"

Catarina is 20 years old and is studying psychology at a university located on the southeastern coast of Brazil. She presents herself as a homebody, whose most important moments in life were lived in the church and with her family. The young woman has always lived in the same house and grew up with her two older sisters and her parents, in a childhood full of "fun and disasters". At school, she was never very popular and ended up distancing herself from the only close friend she had, still during high school. Catarina still holds many memories of the "turmoil" she experienced during this period, but currently, she no longer has to go through that.

Her earliest memories are from her childhood at the church that she and her parents still attend. Catarina is an evangelical Christian, and it was the people from the church who contributed to her personal development. It was there that she learned to play the guitar and sing, activities that are still her passions and began at the age of 14. Her interest in politics was sparked by an activity promoted by her philosophy teacher in high school. The activity involved strings that defined who asked and who answered the questions. The young woman could not answer the question if "a good criminal is a dead criminal", realizing that it was a political question. At the time, she felt her answer leaned towards yes, but she decided to study, seeking to better understand the meaning of political systems. Currently, her opinion has changed as her anti-abortion and pro-life stance led her to consider that all life must be preserved. Today, she identifies as someone on the right, but "her values do not come from the right, but from the Bible", which also defines the importance of speaking and preaching to others about politics and religion.

In the 2018 elections, she got involved in campaigns, supporting Jair Bolsonaro. However, after that, she returned to dedicating herself to the church, going through conversion, a moment when she "handed her life project to God", putting everything under His control. Before that, her lifestyle was not that of a Christian—conversion meant "removing a blindfold from her eyes and living according to God's standards". The choice to study psychology was also part of this "calling", involving the possibility of working and understanding people's minds. Additionally, in college, Catarina has been able to study human development "from the embryo", helping in preparation to be a good mother, as well as gaining knowledge and arguments to defend the pro-life cause.

In November 2020, after the end of a relationship, she felt lighter and ready to start discussing and expressing her opinions on social media. The young woman was already part of an anti-feminist group and brought political and religious discussions to her profile. After 2020, she also began acquiring books on the topic of anti-feminism. Her first book was *Pocket Guide Against Feminist Lies* by Ana Campagnolo. Today, she has the habit of acquiring and reading books and PDFs, commenting on them on her networks. Her priority for the future is to get married and have children, but as a psychologist, she would like to work with pregnant women, mothers, and babies.

4.2 Main Dimensions of Reconstructions and Trajectories of Activism

The biographies presented above reveal a diversity of forms and meanings concerning participation in radical right-wing movements, reinforcing the idea of heterogeneity among activists and their engagement trajectories. However, some similarities stand out, mainly in the form of self-representation and identification with radical right-wing movements and their agendas. The following section presents selected results according to the analysis of the reconstructions, complemented by some narratives.

4.2.1 Trajectories and Self-Representation

The analysis of the trajectories of the young interviewees reveals that the social and family history of participation does not determine participation in radical right-wing movements in a unidirectional way, as is generally assumed in relation to formal participation (Giugni & Grasso, 2021; Fuks, 2011). Some trajectories, like that of Alexander (18 years old, Germany) and Catarina (20 years old, Brazil), demonstrate that the family can have a direct influence on the identification with a political spectrum or even in finding a space for participation. However, there are experiences, like Aline's (20 years old, Brazil), which demonstrate that engagement can arise from a joint experience or, as in the cases of Nissin (23 years old, Germany), Thomas (22 years old, Germany), and Moritz (23 years old, Germany), involve the rejection or denial of family expressions. In all trajectories, the family is identified as a fundamental core in which values are transmitted, which can be followed or denied; however, class issues did not emerge as defining in the form of political participation of these young people, but translated into diverse expectations regarding political participation, as we will see below.

Indeed, the 12 interviewees vary in relation to social class. Here, the existence of a variety of interpretations regarding social class is considered, but a classification related to the types of work performed by parents and/or caregivers is adhered to. Thus, it is understood that, despite speaking of a totality of families and young people who depend on their salaries, there is a varied distribution among the lower, middle, and upper classes, with a prevalence of the middle class. This distribution corresponds to what has been found in the literature, which confirms that support for radical right-wing movements in Brazil and Germany is spread across different social classes (Solano, 2018; Schwander & Manow, 2017). It is understood that the class issue may diverge in the contexts of the two countries, due to average incomes and levels of inequality. In Brazil, it is noted that some types of public competitive jobs can provide access to an upper class—due to the average income in the country—even though we are still dealing with salaried employees (Ribeiro, 2014). In Germany, teachers, public employees, and technicians usually conform to what is interpreted as a middle class. Despite this difference, I emphasize that all young people mention the need to enter the salaried labour market, even if some have plans to undertake or take public exams.

It is notable, however, that even among interviewees from the middle and upper classes, there is the expression of experiences of instability, precariousness, and injustice in their lives, whether they are constant processes of change, family changes, or an absent father (which is a widespread condition in many Brazilian families; cf. Costa & Marra, 2020; Fernandes, 2021), as well as experiences of bullying in school, university, and other contexts. Some of the young people referred to themselves as shy or introverted and presented the experience of being part of a movement as a way to deal with these experiences and find peers and belonging. Although individual experiences are diverse, the corruption scandals and the pro-impeachment movements against President Dilma Rousseff in 2015 and 2016, as well as the 2018 elections in Brazil, were pointed out as decisive turning points in collective experiences of injustice. In the case of Germany, the Covid-19 pandemic and the "refugee crisis" of 2015 were listed as central triggers for engagement in movements. By relating their lives to collective experiences of injustice, young people legitimize the framing of their individual experiences as "unjust".

It is perceived that the existence of "conflicts" or "crises" is quite present, with greater evidence in the life stories of Nissin (23 years old, Germany), Letícia (32 years old, Brazil), and Igor (23 years old, Brazil); however, these are situations that are present, indirectly, in the experience of other young people, including those who describe themselves as extroverted and included. There is no intention here to particularize the crisis experience to the lives of young radical right-wing activists but to raise the hypothesis that moments like these—in which emotions such as fear and insecurity are associated with experiences of displacement—can function as pivotal points for the beginning of the interpellation of radical right-wing discourses. In these moments, some "theories", including conspiratorial ones, would account for the frustrations and would later align with specific "political agendas". I put it this way because the reconstructions of the trajectories highlight the processes of radicalization, in which many begin engagement through specific contact with an agenda or theory that is in tune with their frustrations and/or expectations. The expansion of this to the identification with a set of values and with the movements seems to be gradual or may not even happen. I emphasize here that radicalization is not equated with a process of imminent threat or an approach to security.

Gaspar et al. (2020) indicate that the approach that equates the concept of radical to the practice of violence has caused more harm and stimulated non-democratic measures to deal with the issue. The authors emphasize that radicalism is not a "political evil" and that radicalization will not always lead to "political violence" (Gaspar et al., 2020, p. 14). The young people mentioned here did not describe any direct physical act of violence; however, they all shared exclusionary discourses, which defined that groups of individuals should have reduced rights, be persecuted, and even eliminated. The emphasis on the idea of processes and trajectories and the perception that young people build diverse paths—often tortuous and almost always contradictory—highlight the fact that elements of their lives are re-signified in light of contact with the agendas and discourses of radical right-wing movements. In this sense, Meiering et al. (2020) emphasize the existence of framing processes within groups, which assume the fundamental role of directing subjective experiences of injustice. According to the authors, these framings intensify feelings of belonging, concretize conceptions of the enemy, and shape the discursive formulation about external political events. Moreover, they depend on the presentation of narratives, which the researchers call "linking narratives"—emphasizing their ability to provide a bridge between groups, reinforcing collective identities.

Referring to the articulation between individual experiences and collective experiences, it is possible to identify different meanings for politics: Politics can be a source of upward social mobility (Vinicius), a form of social integration (Nissin), a strong family bond (Aline and Alexander), the denial of a predetermined future (Carlos), a proof of "nobility" (Igor), an act of rebellion (Simon), an attempt to order the world (Nuria), a validation of one's knowledge (Moritz), a (re)elaboration of the marks of the German division in the family (Thomas), a search for security (Letícia), and a religious mission (Catarina).

Regarding Vinicius (25 years old, Brazil), it is noteworthy that his participation is linked to upward social mobility, that is, a concurrent process in which involvement in politics symbolically and objectively guarantees him differentiation from his place of origin. In front of those who were the "bosses", he gains admiration and support for his new conservative lifestyle. It is conservatism that ensures he does not repeat his brother's trajectory. As for Thomas (22 years old, Germany), it is possible to observe an association between family political positions and the former division of the country. As a "typical East German", he resents the economic failure of his region, especially for what "his city could be, but never became". Faced with family references that also reflect the division of the past, he seeks to position himself differently, denying what he understands went wrong in the past, without abandoning his East German identity.

In the case of Nissin (23 years old, Germany), the desire for social integration stands out, as the process of engagement is concurrent with what is presented as a process of personal development, in which baptism and transformations in terms of appearance guarantee him a new perspective and respect towards the culture he describes having confronted. Both in Aline's (20 years old, Brazil) and Alexander's (18 years old, Germany) trajectories, politics seems to have a connection with family ties. Regarding the young woman, she and her mother adopt politics as a joint journey, where "adventures and misadventures" further propel engagement. Alexander reinforces that his positions reflect a family tradition, with the discovery of a potential space for participation through a cousin. For him, choosing this path is related to "common sense", but which we can extend to a "common sense", in the sense of what is shared and common among those who "shape him as a man".

Regarding Carlos (19 years old, Brazil), the idea stands out that, for him, there was a defined trajectory from the beginning, due to his class origin and place of residence. Unlike Vinicius (25 years old, Brazil), Carlos returns and continues living in the peripheral region after involvement with politics. His desire does not seem to be focused solely on ascension but on the possibility of proving his resilience and denying a predestined fate, differentiating himself from within. In the case of Igor (23 years old, Brazil), the encounter with the monarchy seems to reflect the desire to show himself more "noble" than his peers, understanding nobility here, not only as wealth but especially as habits and practices that conform to an "imaginary" about being special. Drinking tea, being homey, and not liking those who indulge in "partying" place him in a more "noble" position than his colleagues.

For Simon (22 years old, Germany), the meaning of political participation that stands out is rebellion, the need to oppose what might be expected of a young gay man. Positioning himself as someone always ready to displease, he recounts the reaction to a Twitter post, stating that "when the left hates you and when the far-right hates you, then it's perfect". For Núria, the intensity and "flood" of speeches and arguments also seem to provide a way to process the experiences she had with so many "bad people". By saying that society is getting crazier, the young woman also seems to indicate that politics can provide an "ordering" for all this that is difficult to understand and grasp. Arguments provided by her as data and facts form a new chaos but now apprehensible among the peers of the radical right. In the case of Moritz (23 years old, Germany), the meaning seems more diffuse and difficult to identify. On one hand, there is the validation of the "knowledge" he sought to establish, at some cost, in the face of the difficulties he faced and his identification as a "non-exceptional" student. With a certain pessimism about his own youthful condition, the young man is the only one who prefers not to define the future, as things seem too unpredictable.

When it comes to Letícia, it is impossible not to highlight the impact of the financial crisis moment, which takes away all the "security" the family imagined having. It is from there that she emphasizes the need to act to cope and "ensure" what the State does not provide. By changing careers and engaging in new movements, Letícia also seems to try to reorganize and return to a state of "security". Finally, in the case of Catarina (20 years old, Brazil)—one of the few with this characteristic, although often identified as a general image of the radical right—political participation seems to emerge as a religious mission, also related to family history, but reflecting a "calling", in which the definition of feminism as "diabolical" calls her to live and act as a Christian, propagating and spreading her faith.

Beyond the particular elements, in all trajectories, political participation also seems to translate the desire to encounter spaces of belonging and recognition (Honneth, 2011). In this sense, Nilan (2021) points out that studies on social movements always highlight the sociability and solidarity experienced within the movements as determining factors for engagement. Klandermans and Mayer (2005) also indicate that the activists interviewed in their research describe that, in their movements, they gained a respect that was denied to them in the outside world, describing feeling demarginalized or finally recognized.

Besides the majority of respondents identifying with conservatism, the young people also position themselves as "libertarians", "nationalists", "paleolibertarians", "liberals" focused on the free market and individual freedom, or even "monarchists". In the German case, one of the young people also pointed out a difference between what he called "Flügel" and the "bürgerlich-konservative". While the

Flügel wing may be more inclined towards nationalist, anti-immigration, and identity positions, the bürgerlich-konservative would tend to be more moderate and focused on "liberal-conservative" economic policies.

Brazilian young women report being "anti-feminists" and point to feminism and LGBTQI+ movements as major threats to the traditional family and Brazilian society. Like Aline (20 years old, Brazil) and Catarina (20 years old, Brazil), other young women interviewed for the study refer to anti-feminist or pro-life agendas as the main drivers that led them to activism. Although all respondents mentioned being Christian, with a majority of Catholics, religion was only a main theme in the trajectories of young Brazilian women identified as evangelicals. This aligns with research indicating that, in the Brazilian context, there is a neo-Pentecostal influence on agendas and adherence to radical right-wing movements, centrally influencing women's trajectories (Teixeira & Barbosa, 2022).

Regarding the trajectories, some particularities stand out. In the case of Nissin (23 years old, Germany) and Moritz (23 years old, Germany), it is notable that their entry into movements was related to the fight against Covid-19 pandemic restrictions and vaccination. It is striking that these two young people did not describe having a particular interest in politics or participation experiences. For Nissin, this movement was a gateway to involvement with a party organization. In the case of Alexander (18 years old, Germany) and Simon (22 years old, Germany), both joined youth party organizations directly but note that the pandemic was the period of engagement. The topic has not yet been widely explored in the literature—especially concerning young people—but there is a perception of "stricter" restriction measures in Germany. Faced with broader aid policies, there was a requirement for isolation of a much larger group than in Brazil. In light of such measures, most young people interviewed in the German context stated they felt attracted to groups that interpreted such policies as state "abuse" or "tyranny". Simon (22 years old, Germany) describes

> And in 2020, I joined [my group] for the first time because of all these Covid lockdowns, which I found more useless than anything else, and then regulations like 2G, 3G, which were bad for all people my age, because you couldn't go anywhere, couldn't do anything. Even if you were vaccinated, you had to take a test in the end. And then I thought to myself, you absolutely have to start contributing in some way to fight this, because otherwise nothing would ever change.[10]

Many young people also pointed out that the pandemic revealed the limited power of organization and influence of young people in institutional decisions, including

[10] As mentioned in Chap. 3, for the reproduction of interview excerpts in the book, small modifications were made that included the elimination of repetitions and language habits, as well as specific cuts that favoured the fluidity and maintenance of the meaning captured in the original languages. The words or phrases in brackets were not explicitly said by the interviewees but refer to previous excerpts or are implicit in the contexts of the interviews, being added to ensure greater clarity of the text.

the universities they attended.[11] However, Moritz (23 years old, Germany) expresses doubts about the movement's impact, saying that:

> Moreover, there are other groups at the university that labelled other people who disagreed with these rules as conspirators, conspiracy theorists, and so on. But we had to live with that and accept the fact that other people don't like what we say. But, yes, as I said, we didn't have such a big impact on the opinion of the university administrations. I don't even know if they noticed we existed.

In this sense, Lewandowsky et al. (2023) state that, at the beginning of the pandemic, the AfD was present in all state parliaments (Landtage), as well as in the federal (Bundestag), quickly positioning itself as the voice of the people and those suffering from the government's restrictive measures. Strategically, the party would have redefined the crisis, shifting the issue from public health to a dictatorial abuse of power—also summarized as an attack on democracy. This discourse was not absent in the narrative of Brazilian young people; however, the pandemic was not presented as a "turning point". Most respondents pointed to the 2018 elections as this turning point.

Another particularity is identified in the trajectories of Vinicius (25 years old, Brazil) and Thomas (22 years old, Germany), with them mentioning previous involvement with movements located on the "left" of the political spectrum. In this case, we can more directly relate the literature on the biographies of formal participation of young people, which involve experimentation with different spaces and styles of participation (Lüküslü & Walther, 2021). In the case of Vinicius (25 years old, Brazil), there is also an entry into another radical right-wing movement, in which he describes encountering obstacles and experiencing misunderstandings. The existence of conflicts—which may relate to projects but also to group relations—seems to generate the search for other places of participation. After leaving, it is noted that such groups are reinterpreted and positioned as not being coherent with current ideas and/or political struggles.

4.2.2 Significant Others: Virtual and In-Person Spaces and the Virtue of Studying

The process of engagement is generally stimulated and supported by other people, who may be family members, friends, or famous right-wing leaders, such as Olavo de Carvalho, known as "the teacher" or "the philosopher" of the New Right and also mentioned as a model for dealing with the criticism and judgement experienced

---

[11] In the German case, a student movement was formed that directly opposed the measures adopted by the government during the Covid-19 pandemic. The movement was decentralized—several Instagram pages were found in different cities across the country—and they shared the initiative to promote debates where they presented their central position, which was opposed to mandatory vaccines. The idea of returning to "normality" was part of their slogan, emphasizing that imposed rules like the 2G and 3G should be banned. The demonstrations were directed at universities but occupied the streets, sometimes mingling with the acts called by the AfD.

when becoming a conservative. Some of the interviewees also reported what Roy (2022) termed as "taking the red pill". She used this term to refer to the narratives in which female activists and leaders of the AfD and FPÖ describe that reality was revealed from the encounter with the party. In the same way, we can see Vinicius (25 years old, Brazil), Alexander (18 years old, Germany), Nissin (23 years old, Germany), and Igor (23 years old, Brazil) describing moments of "revelation", where the encounter with some experience—which, in this case, was not only focused on the encounter with the party and the movement—gave rise to a reinterpretation of reality. It can be understood that these young people also operate the reinterpretation of previous experiences from new encounters, but it is understood that the process of greater institutionalization within a party can lead to a more pronounced division between a "before" and an "after". It is noticed that the before and after only appears as a fundamental division in Nissin's discourse when he talks about his baptism and the process of personal development. For the rest of the young people, the process has more nuances, and only Olavo de Carvalho and, more indirectly, Ana Campagnolo were portrayed as figures capable of "unveiling" reality.

Although other significant people have been pointed out as models regarding the development not only of a political perspective but also of conservative values, most interviewees point to social networks (Facebook, Twitter (X), Instagram, and TikTok) as spaces where they found the first groups and invitations to demonstrations. YouTube is referred to as a source of information and a fundamental space for building the first elements of a conservative identification. In their comments on digital activism, some interviewees referred to numbers of followers and viewers, as most combine in-person activities with intensive production of digital content. The young people, in the face of using multiple platforms, still seem to seek an "expressive coherence" (Polivanov, 2019), producing a "narrative of self" whose performative dimension is connected to the ideal of authenticity—which will be discussed later.

This relationship between digital space and politics has been extensively explored in academic literature, as evidenced by previous studies (Dias et al., 2017; Bordignon & Bonamigo, 2017; Machado & Miskolci, 2019). These studies address the influence of social networks on the trajectories of political engagement of young people, as well as on the formation of their identities and discourses.[12] However, with the specific objective of this research in mind, I choose to focus the analysis on what young people say they find and present in digital spaces. Thus, I highlight that the digital content reported alludes to a literature "distributed by publishers that" direct "their offerings to an audience interested in authors intellectually linked to the right-

---

[12] Polivanov (2019) argues that contemporary identities are characterized by dimensions of performance, self-reflexivity, fluidity, and dynamism, directly linked to the dynamics operated on social networks. However, she points out that the operation through algorithms, responsible for selecting and directing content, has delineated and shaped the "profiles" of activists. I highlight here that this research sought to transcend the "digital profiles", evidencing that the homogenizing character is not reproduced in the trajectories and self-representations of the young interviewees. This finding does not contradict the emphasis given to social networks in the expansion of radical right-wing movements but shifts the focus to their discursive interpellations, linked to the construction of representation systems that will be addressed in the next chapter.

wing political field" (Silva, 2018, p. 83). This element calls our attention, especially in the Brazilian context, in which all interviewees seek to reference a conservative and libertarian literature, as well as the habit of reading as a legitimizer of their political positions.

Curcino and Pereira call this a "political phenomenon of editorial nature, or even an editorial phenomenon of political nature" (Curcino & Pereira, 2022, p. 197). The researchers report an expansion and consolidation of a book segment oriented towards an audience of readers identified or with potential identification to the political gradient that ranges from the right to the far-right. Such a segment also has distribution through national and local events, organized by movements and institutes. Aline (20 years old, Brazil) mentions:

> CPAC[13] is the largest conservative event in the world, it didn't start in Brazil, it started in the USA, right? It's been going on for years, but in Brazil, the first edition was in São Paulo, in 2019. Then the pandemic came, it couldn't [happen in 2020], and in 2021, it was in Brasília. In Brasília, there were two days of events, with several speakers, it's 12 hours of lectures. It's exhausting as hell. It happened again this year in Campinas, and I went too. This time, with my mother, in Campinas. But in Brasília, I also went alone, some friends picked me up at the airport.

In the German case, there was no such clear reference to a "referential" body of literature, and only Thomas (22 years old, Germany) focused on the specific study of literature from the political field. The others presented themselves as dedicated students and professionals, giving more strength and value to participation in councils and municipal or state representative bodies of their parties. In this sense, it is observed that the German radical right-wing militancy is more directly linked to political parties, while the Brazilian has found resonance is greater in movements and groups. This can be associated with differences in political regimes, but it also seems to influence what is understood as "fundamental activities" of an activist.

In the Brazilian case, most young people chose to study law. Carlos (19 years old, Brazil), Nuria (19 years old, Brazil), and Catarina (20 years old, Brazil) relate their career choices directly to their political activity. In the German case, professional careers and political activity seem to occur in parallel. One hypothesis is the

[13] Sanders and Jenkins (2023) highlight that the Conservative Political Action Conference (CPAC) events are fundamental platforms for the dissemination of transnational anti-feminism. In this sense, it is not surprising that Aline, as an activist focused on this agenda, has attended the conferences. They are platforms for both national and international politicians and *influencers*, bringing together activists who select their lectures. Today, the conference in Brazil is already the second largest in the world. Hoeveler (2020) points out that the event's organization was carried out by Eduardo Bolsonaro, who now leads the Conservative Liberal Institute. She explains that: "its main organizer is the American conservative lobbyist Matt Schlapp, president of the American Conservative Union (ACU). Connected to the Koch brothers, he is a professional political activist, having worked on several presidential campaigns such as George Bush Jr.'s, for which he was awarded a position in the White House. His wife is the chief communications advisor to President Donald Trump, who himself attended a CPAC event in the United States back in 2019. Having apparently grown in size and influence, CPAC is adopting the strategy of internationalising its nationalist and obscurantist discourse: besides Brazil, in 2019 CPAC also takes place in Australia, South Korea, Japan, and Ireland" (Sanders & Jenkins, 2023, p. 83).

very structure of German education, where different types of careers are defined and selected early on and have less relation to "individual trajectories", especially in the middle and lower classes. The three educational paths produce segregation and "immobility"[14] that could explain the impossibility of decisions based on individual trajectories. In the Brazilian case, it is important to consider that the massive expansion of access to higher education also occurred through the multiplication of private educational institutions.[15]

It is noteworthy that, in the sample of Brazilian interviewees, all accessed higher education through private colleges. Notably, none of the interviewees mentioned having been covered by or having accessed public policies for access to higher education, such as the University for All Program (ProUni).

All Brazilian interviewees referred to the process of "studying" as a fundamental part of their activism, highlighting their roles as active students who base their opinions and political analyses mainly on studies and readings. Participation in anti-feminist groups, for example, led Aline (20 years old, Brazil) to start reading books.

> I and my mother were never used to reading, you know? I always hated reading; it always made me sleepy. I still don't like to read, but I force myself, you know?" I came to say: "no, I have to force myself." Because I know that books have content that videos don't have. Since then, I force myself to read books and other things, right? Another world other than videos (…). And since then, I got interested, I also took the course Brazil For Life, I learned a lot, I bought it. "I had already bought the book; however it was more with the book We Need to Talk About Abortion, it was more with this book that I became very interested. I bought five books to read, and this was one of them, and I started reading and loved it. And this book has several arguments, several things, that I use, that I study and everything else. To use against the pro-choice agenda, or abortion agenda." And nowadays I debate, nowadays I create content.

[14] Fernandez-Kelly (2012, p. 93) states that the German educational system, despite being public, remains profoundly "unequal", "hierarchical", and "exclusive". Salden and Hertlein (2020, p. 117) say that "to understand the German educational system (which actually consists of several systems due to different regulations among the 16 federal states), it is necessary to return to its origins and historical development, as well as the sociopolitical contexts that explain its current characteristics. This includes, for example, early segregation after the fourth year into different schools in the three-tier school system, which has its roots in the nineteenth-century three-class society. (…) International comparative studies on school performance (e.g., PISA) have indicated that students from poor families and/or families with migration experiences were considerably disadvantaged by the educational system".

[15] Sguissardi (2015) questions whether the process of expanding private higher education can be understood as equivalent to a democratization process. He points out that this process intensified during the government of Luiz Inácio Lula da Silva, at the beginning of the twenty-first century, but maintains segregation due to the services and quality of education offered by spaces oriented by a market logic. Despite this, it is important to reflect that, during these years, beyond ProUni, the University Reform also involved the expansion of federal universities, as well as the creation of quotas and the National High School Exam (Enem). Thus, despite the questions about massification and a supposed "exclusion of the included", there is a change in the structure of access to Higher Education in Brazil that expands to other social classes.

She mentions this almost as an obligation but emphasizes that it is in these books that she finds the arguments she uses in debates and on social media. This same argument is brought by Vinicius (25 years old, Brazil).

> Through information, through reading, through a lot, a lot of study." But, generally, it is more information. I follow, I follow some groups in the city, like specific groups on WhatsApp. As I also publish on my Facebook profile, you know? I publish something, some information, some text, some analysis of mine. And that's how I do it, you know? That's how I do this work of mine, you understand?

Most Brazilian interviewees pointed out the process of study and research as a fundamental "task". Nuria (19 years old, Brazil) points to reading as a process of developing her capacity to interpret the world.

> My main base, to tell the truth, my base, right? Because my foundation is Jesus Christ, but my main base is them, my family, and they always encouraged me to read. Always, when I read a book, they said the following, "oh, you can write a story based on what you read." I said, "no, I will do it!" And more and more, this improved my reading comprehension," mainly in the sense of capturing stories, of understanding more about that world of fiction, right? (...) But later, as Mortimer Adler says, who is the guy who taught how to read books, if you are in an initial phase, like a phase where you only know how to read those certain books, you should not continue in that. You should climb higher and higher to increase your reading level.

Thomas (22 years old, Germany) is the only activist from the German radical right who highlights his particular interest in reading, pointing this out as a characteristic that has accompanied him since childhood. He is the only one who refers to reading printed newspapers.

> However, I, at that time, was already involved with politics. And, yes, you are obliged to deal with it, read newspapers. I know that nowadays people do everything at once, but I am a big fan of printed newspapers. I still receive weekly about two, three, four editions of newspapers, including the Neue Zürcher Zeitung and others. I also read a regional newspaper, the Mitteldeutsche Zeitung, abbreviated as MZ, which brings local news.

While, in the German context, young people relate the paths of activism to participation in local committees, in addition to increasing their "representativeness" within their organizations and parties, the Brazilian activists point to education and grassroots activism as means to expand their political groups and their own capacity for action. Some Brazilian interviewees stated that grassroots activism was associated with leftist movements and that one of the main transformations of the new right-wing movements was identifying the need to organize and reach out to the outskirts, educating and mobilizing people. Grassroots activities are also linked to humanitarian actions, such as donations and volunteer work.

Most Brazilian interviewees referred to activism as an unpaid activity and as a step towards a future career as a representative or parliamentary assistant, teacher, or counsellor. In contrast, young people in the German context spoke of politics and professional careers as parallel activities; some already had specific aspirations within their political groups, such as achieving a position on regional or state councils. Simon (22 years old, Germany) was the only one who spoke of the direct desire to run as a candidate. Generally, when mentioning the professional path, the interviewees from Germany do not seem to be referring to a political career, emphasizing their technical or university courses in various fields. An exception was Nissin (23 years old, Germany), who mentioned the invitation to "experience" life within politics next year. It is unclear if this was a job offer, but the young man says his current pursuit is to establish himself as a successful professional in the engineering career.

I highlight that, at the beginning of the interviews, some young people presented their trajectory in an organized and "prepared" manner, emphasizing their distinctions. Through this effort, several of them showed the desire to differentiate themselves from "normal young people". However, for those from peripheral areas in Brazil, such differentiation was also connected to their motivation and resilience, which ensured the possibility of breaking away from a tragic fate—related to drug use and involvement in crime. Carlos (19 years old, Brazil) says:

> If you look at my trajectory, I could have been a criminal, right? For everything I went through there... while other people, who went through the same thing, took other paths. I can say that I am the most successful of all, you know? So much so that the school even made a picture of me, right? The school where I studied said "the guy went to college. He is following his path." (...) So, it was a very big problem, and we managed to finish high school. It's a struggle!! To be honest, what I say here is with pride because it is indeed a struggle. Finishing high school without using any kind of drug, because at my age, if I used that kind of drug, as I noticed with several of my friends, I would really go downhill, right? Go downhill to a very bad path and would be nothing, would have no worldview, right?

This "struggle" manifests as a distinguishing mark when we talk about young people who present themselves as residents of the outskirts. Their experiences with politics intertwine with the expectations of breaking away from a predestined future, also involving the desire for social ascent. Both Carlos (19 years old, Brazil) and Vinicius (25 years old, Brazil) mention that their political choices and convictions guaranteed them a distinguished place compared to other young people, or, in the case of the latter, compared to their own siblings. For such young people, presenting themselves as responsible and engaged in studies does not seem to be important only to be recognized as "politicized" but also as a form of distinction in their original living spaces. Additionally, these are the two young people who defined that members of their family would be conservative, not due to a political position but because of the "teachings" that were transmitted. Vinicius (25 years old, Brazil) comments about his mother:

> Oh, yes, there's no way. My mother! My mother always advised me to lead an honest life, you know? A decent life, a structured life, always encouraged me to study, always encouraged me not to harm others, to respect others, to respect the elders, to love God above all things. Anyway, it is in this part that I see my mother as a conservative person. For informing me about these drug issues, you know? That drugs can ruin my life. So, that's how I started identifying as conservative. And I see my mother as one of the most conservative people I've ever known.

Carlos (19 years old, Brazil) mentions that his grandfather

> (...) was conservative by nature," like, he had a conservative life, yes. "There are many such cases in Brazil, the person is conservative but doesn't know it." They don't know yet, don't

> identify as a conservative. But you see the person's lifestyle, what they think about the State, about freedom, and you see that it's conservatism, do you understand? My grandfather, he was like that, but he just didn't care about politics, you understand?

Such narratives are consistent with the statements made by the two young people regarding what conservatism would be. Carlos defines it as a "philosophy of life", and Vinicius as a "lifestyle".[16] It seems interesting, however, to reflect that such a narrative has been fostered by radical right-wing groups when they express that the way of living of "ordinary" people has been under attack in recent years. There is a discourse about the possibility of "discovering oneself" as conservative, observing not political projects but aspects of daily life and "moral values". This interpellation seems to provide an important subjective position for such young people—who indeed had to be resilient to ensure a future in the face of a daily experience of violence and death in the outskirts of Brazil.[17] However, it also seems to resonate with

[16] Regarding youth participation, the idea of a "lifestyle" is connected to the existence of "cultural movements". Although young people associate such "paths" and "behaviours" with conservatism, I highlight that *rap*, as a cultural movement from the peripheries that emerged in the 1990s, has a very close relationship with what is identified as a "survival recipe in the peripheries" and with the "construction of mechanisms to face adversities". Silva and Soares (2004) discussed that, in the lyrics of the songs, which also shaped the rules of coexistence in *rap* spaces, problems were denounced, as well as paths to overcome them being provided. The researchers point out that there was a responsibility placed on the individual, who, through personal effort, should not get involved with drug trafficking and consumption, considered dangerous and destructive. Furthermore, "the strengthening of family and friendship ties", as well as "education", are also seen as "solutions" (Silva & Soares, 2004, p. 975). Considering that such values have gained a fundamental place in the significant network of peripheral life, we can assume that the interpellation of conservatism as a "lifestyle" that connects to these "teachings" that come "from family" has even greater discursive efficacy.

[17] In the same 11-year period (from 2009 to 2019) in which the infant mortality rate was significantly reduced—dropping from 22.14 to 12.4 deaths per 1000 live births (Fundação Abrinq, 2021)—333,330 young people between 15 and 29 years old were murdered (Cerqueira et al., 2021). The data highlight an essential contradiction: The same State that seeks to ensure sanitary and welfare conditions to prevent the death of children faces significant difficulties in keeping its young people alive. The *Atlas of Violence* from 2019 reveals that young men, single, of black race, with up to 7 years of education, and who are on the streets during the hottest months of the year, between 6 PM and 10 PM, are the most likely to suffer an intentional violent death in Brazil (Cerqueira et al., 2019). Carvalho (2006) and Rodrigues (2012) point out that the introduction of the ideology of war against drug trafficking and crime in Latin America functioned as a justification for a permanent state of exception, that is, for the consolidation of the continuous exercise of illegal violence, mainly by the military police. The literature that addresses the political and psychosocial trauma generated by dictatorial regimes has emphasized that systematic human rights violations continue to be practiced in democratic contexts (Lira, 1993; Pinheiro, 1997). Created during the period of the military dictatorship in Brazil, the military police, as the State's ostensive force, has been both a cause and a victim of the effects of this permanent violence. In Brazil, there is an alarming number of murders of young people and police officers (Cerqueira et al., 2021), which occur predominantly within the spaces of the favelas. Dialectically, it is possible to point out that police violence has its origin in its institutional structure (Cerqueira, 1996), but it contributes to the wear and tear and rupture of the social fabric, of which the police themselves are a part of.

other young people who associate conservatism with a way of positioning themselves as young in the world. Igor (23 years old, Brazil) will say:

> I think that, because I am generally a more conservative guy, I maintain this thing of not being very party-going, not liking drugs, uh… I even had a habit of drinking alcohol in the past, but I've already quit. Yeah. Occasionally I would go, I would go to the bar on Fridays, have some drinks and read. But today, I'm even tired of that. I don't like tattoos, I don't like promiscuity. I've never used illicit drugs. I think that's it.

Other young people also described conservatism through habits and practices, often indicating opposition to what "would be expected" from the youthful condition. Observing this element in the trajectories raises the question of the interpellation of conservatism as a subjective position for young people who "feel outside" the existing normativity regarding youth as transgression. In this sense, I refer back to Nilan (2021), who states that movements, beyond conservatism, have as their main offer to young people a horizon of radical action. In this sense, the transgression that is not practiced in terms of habits considered "inferior" occurs in the position of a countermovement.

4.2.3 Being in a Countermovement: The Demand for Authenticity and Self-Responsibility

All the young people interviewed were concerned with presenting their desire to be agents of change, pointing to activism as a responsibility. On one hand, activists present themselves as responsible, courageous, and/or engaged individuals, often embodying the image of a "*self-made man/woman*".[18] This can be understood as a reflection of adherence to an order of recognition that establishes conditions of preparation and education for formal participation, which transforms in the twenty-first century. In the face of the influence of neoliberal normativity in forms of organization and political participation, there is an interpellation for young people to be responsible and self-entrepreneurs. Bueno (2021) analyses the changes in the social order, which involve an increasingly strong demand for self-responsibility and authentic self-realization of individuals. Thus, there would be a growing:

> demand to "be yourself" or, as suggested by a popular self-help book, your *Best Self: Be You, Just Better*—in a context of declining social support and increasing inequality, competition, and precariousness. (…) Instead of being guided (and limited) by universal and broadly fixed standards of rationality, this new subject would be driven by the possibility (and demand) to continuously sustain a singular and authentic life: a life that is discovered and created by the individual themselves, emotionally communicative and flexibly adapted to the constantly changing market conditions. (Bueno, 2021, p. 48)

---

[18] The figure of the "*self-made man/woman*" was developed as an "ideal participation profile" characterized by "career orientation, pursuit of self-efficacy or attribution of responsibility for oneself and others in their identities" (Lüküslü & Walther, 2021) in the context of the PARTISPACE research that compared styles and practices of participation in Europe.

Added to the notion of responsibility, which is represented by the diligent, studious, and engaged positioning, there is also the idea of authenticity in involvement with radical right-wing movements. The idea of involvement in a "countermovement" is a common element identified in the interviews. Most of the young people interviewed present themselves as those who go "against the current", which is reflected in their dissatisfaction with the State and opposition to what they refer to as a "hegemonic left-wing culture" (in the German case, this also includes "the Greens"[19]). Even during the presidency of Jair Bolsonaro, the Brazilian interviewees attacked the State, criticizing the deficits in providing people with the minimum conditions of dignity. In various narratives, the State is presented as an enemy that abuses its power and limits individual freedom, and other times, it is classified as a "communist or socialist" state.

Stefanoni (2021) is bold in his work *Has Rebellion Become Right-Wing?*, discussing that, by advancing and deepening a discourse about political correctness, the left opened doors for the "anti-systemic" temperament to be adopted by emerging conservative movements. In the midst of radical right-wing movements, it was accepted to renounce the assumptions of traditional right-wing to embrace a traditionalism that positioned itself as a "countermovement".

In terms of the trajectories of young people, it is perceived that, on one hand, identifying as part of a countermovement or reinforcing the idea of going against the flow meets a demand for being original and authentic. But, beyond that, establishing what is outside—the difference—also makes it more accessible to share common feelings of injustice and the formation of collective identity. In this sense, there is a constant differentiation with other political groups that are, in most cases, treated as enemies that hold a hegemony. Carlos (19 years old, Brazil) states:

> Even being a private college, it doesn't help, the left dominates everything, so sometimes you will see a lot of people who kind of don't understand what they're talking about, but are reproducing what they learned in college. They never reasoned about what they say, about what they were told, and everything else, but they follow the herd, right? Yeah... I find quite a lot of students, but they are afraid to express their opinion, because you have to be a person with a lot of personality to stand against the current, because the left-wing people, in college, they are very loud, and they are very dirty, right? You have to be a real man! You have to be a real woman to go against the consensus, right?

Here, we see the encounter between the idea of authenticity, when the young person claims to have "a lot of personality to speak against what is the current view [or consensus]", and the establishment of negative and depreciative characteristics for the groups that are understood as "opponents". The idea of being unfairly labelled is present in all the interviews, with the young people stating that adjectives like "extremist", "radical", "Nazi", or "fascist" do not translate their own identification and position. For them, the attacks are elements that reinforce their position as counter-hegemonic. Simon (22 years old, Germany) will say that:

[19] Klandermans and Mayer (2005) also found anti-communism as an essential part of the collective identity of far-right groups, understanding that, in the case of some countries, such as Germany, the "Greens" came to serve as a substitute or complementary enemy.

> And we always act like our government and our media, as if we were doing well, which is simply not true. And we have to do something about it, and it's not always just us who swing the baton. But we are called Nazis every time we say something different from the public opinion. Everything always works very well here until you are against it. Are you against filling the whole country with wind turbines? Are you a Nazi? Are you against welcoming an uncontrolled number of people and us? I can't think of the word I would use without being "checked" and verified. Are you a Nazi? Are you in favor of deporting people who are not allowed to stay here according to German law? Then, you are a Nazi. This is the STANDARD way of insulting and belittling people who have a different opinion.

It is noticeable that what Simon lists as a source of conflict and insult is the divergent opinion, and not what is presented. To distance themselves from these identifications, many point out the existence of much more "radical" positions within the movements, also highlighting the differentiation of their group with what we address here as an extreme-right. Finally, it is also common to emphasize the left (understood as a cohesive and unique group) as the true "radicals", who "police" the discourse and impose their agenda, which does not reflect the will of "common" or "normal" men.

4.3 Translating the Dynamics as Forms of "Liminal Participation"

The analysis reveals a dynamic combination of applying recognized practices and positions of democratic political participation, such as the organization of demonstrations, grassroots activities, studies, and involvement with official councils and committees, while the contents and claims transgress the limits of what is widely understood as democratic, that is, they promote exclusion by questioning equality of opportunities, human rights, and the Rule of Law. These practices move between subject positions and differ according to the paths and levels of engagement. The attacks on political correctness—referred to as a boredom of the left and a lack of freedom of expression—contradict the growing power of the radical right in countries but allow young people to occupy new spaces and fight to expand the limits of what can be shared in the public sphere.

These constellations have been explored in terms of "mainstreaming" or "normalization" of far-right discourses (Vieten & Poynting, 2022). Although Nilan (2021) and de Sousa et al. (2022) interpret the position of the right as victim and marginalized minority fighting for freedom and pluralism as a strategy, and not as a condition, the analyses of biographies and narratives also reveal constellations of liminal participation. In the data, we find evidence that young people involved in radical right movements are aware that their claims may be seen as non-democratic and negotiate these limits through recognized and democratic forms of participation.

In the Brazilian case, the tension becomes more obvious in the conflict between the relevance attributed to study as a form of activism and participation and the propensity to transgress the limits of what is widely considered a consensus of democratic dialogue, that is, accepting hate speech and exclusion as part of political participation. The *liminality* of these positions can be seen in the apparent contradiction, where, on one hand, activists follow the norms of formal participation and, on the other hand, also neglect these rules and their underlying principles. However, it is understood that this is not the only contradiction and that the paths and trajectories are also marked by tensions and conflicts. de Sousa et al. (2022, p. 13) state that "another way to give unity to this militancy is to look at its antagonistic exterior, at the instance that antagonizes and paradoxically constitutes it". In this sense, it is observed that the constitution of an antagonistic exterior has a fundamental importance in affirming collective identities and in sharing the idea of "going against the flow". The individual experiences of injustice and the collective discourses of antagonism—from which activists and the collective movement acquire an identity—seem to be key pieces to understand this constellation (Mouffe, 2013).

Collective identities can only be maintained through the constant reference to shared feelings of injustice that activists use to legitimize their crossing of boundaries (Pitti et al., 2021). *Liminality* refers to the relationship between opportunities and limitations of public and institutional recognition. At the same time, it also seems to be related to a project of expansion in which change and the occupation of "intermediate" positions allow activists to formulate goals that provide collective identity, coherence, and agency. The interpretation of young people's participation in radical right-wing movements as liminal emphasizes, therefore, the dynamics of the *movement*, as opposed to stability and a fixed position. The conflicting and non-harmonious potential of participation is highlighted (cf. Schwanenflügel & Walther, 2022).

In this perspective, as in other cases of liminal participation, participation is less a *status* associated with compliance with existing norms and more a practice that integrates different constellations of interest and identity. Pitti et al. (2021) apply the concept of *liminality* to spaces between recognized positions of political subject: As a heuristic category, liminal participation refers, consequently, to practices in public spheres through which individuals express claims of belonging and participation, even if they are not recognized as such by others. Butler (2015) has suggested that the notion of the public sphere be extended beyond institutionalized public spaces to encompass any "spaces of appearance".

Indeed, analysing the public sphere in terms of spaces of appearance helps to bring to light claims of belonging and participation that do not meet the criteria of the dominant order of recognition. The concept of *liminality*, developed by van Gennep (1909/1960) in his systematization of life course transitions, denotes a phase that separates an old *status* from a new one, characterized by an "intermediate" situation that lacks a recognized social *status* (cf. Turner, 1969). However, *liminality* is not simply temporal—as a phase mode suggests—but includes the spaces where movements between subject positions occur. Formally institutionalized transitions, in particular, involve specialized transitional spaces that seek to prepare individuals for a new position, such as schools, pre-professional schemes, counselling centres, retirement homes, or formal youth participation environments, like youth councils.

Andersson (2015) proposes that political socialization be conceptualized as a situated process that arises when individuals move through public spaces and attempt to transform these spaces into meaningful places, where the political assumes different meanings, not only for each individual but also in contradiction to what is institutionally recognized (cf. Skelton, 2015; Kallio, 2018). Therefore, practices that evolve in liminal spaces should be considered as a structural constellation of being "between" (Pitti et al., 2021) and should not be confused with individual movements of "not participating" to participate in the "right" way.

Applied to youth political participation, *liminality* refers to a condition of "intermediation" that differs from "marginality", which "describes the relationship between a given centre and the periphery", while "*liminality* shifts attention to the movements between two (or more) clearly defined reference points" (Pitti et al., 2021, p. 7). This implies viewing participation as a concept that not only describes constellations of negotiation and harmonious political dialogue but also those of social conflict. In this way, conflict is interpreted as an integrative element of youth political participation rather than as an exception to democratic participation. As a heuristic concept, liminal participation emphasizes how participation practices can oscillate between recognized and unrecognized subject positions, through which the boundaries between participation and non-participation become blurred.

Based on reconstructions, youth activism in radical right-wing movements is interpreted as a form of "liminal participation" rather than non-democratic or deviant. An argument in this regard is the way young activists present themselves as victims of injustice, which they use to legitimize the transgression of the boundaries of the democratic order. This can also be seen in their attempt to balance compliance with the norms and rules of formal participation in their positioning while simultaneously transgressing and violating constitutional protections. The reconstruction of trajectories suggests complex processes of relationship between diverse individual experiences of conflict with collective discourses offered as possibilities of recognition through activism, as well as the transformation of everyday practices. Although the data show a legitimization of hate speech and exclusion in the expansion of radical right-wing discourses in the public sphere, the biographical perspective reveals a diversity of constellations of conflict and identification with an antagonistic position in a countermovement.

Interpreting these constellations as cases of liminal participation, firstly, gives visibility to emerging practices in which young people are active in public spheres, although their practices are not always recognized as "participation". This reflects a normativity that not only denies the legitimacy of all their claims but also questions whether there can be experiences of injustice. Secondly, the application of this concept to youth participation in radical right-wing movements emphasizes that engagement is a dynamic process and that participation practices are in constant transformation, involving conflicting interests and meanings for different actors. On a biographical level, it is recognized that participation trajectories in radical right also describe learning processes, in which the subject relates to knowledge, skills, and spaces in a process of experimentation and negotiation. Finally, interpreting such activism in this way also has consequences for the ways of constructing democratic exits to radicalization. By referring to constant movements and varied constellations, we reinforce the "difference" that exists between these actors as something that "remains" and can be explored as a source of transformation and dialogue.

Considering the complexity of this contemporary phenomenon that is in full swing, the present analysis does not seek to establish generalizations but centrally offers the possibility of analysing this activism as an experience of politicization and an expression of participation. This does not mean neglecting the fact that both the claims and practices aim to exclude other groups from power and recognition or deny the responsibility of young people regarding their choices. Although these liminal forms of participation represent a tensioning of liberal scripts, they can also be interpreted as a product of new forms of subjectivation and the interpellation of discourses centred on antagonism. In the next chapter, I will seek to explore the discourses that interpellate young people, redirecting the focus to the incidences of institutions, as well as to the systems of representation.

References

Andersson, E. (2015). Situational political socialization: A normative approach to young people's adoption and acquisition of political preferences and skills. *Journal of Youth Studies, 18*(8), 967–983.

Beach, D., Fritzsche, B., & Kakos, M. (2019). Stigmatisation, identity, and educational exclusion in postindustrial societies: A qualitative synthesis of research from UK, Germany, and the Nordic countries. *Diaspora, Indigenous, and Minority Education, 13*(1), 54–67.

Bordignon, C., & Bonamigo, I. S. (2017). Os jovens e as redes sociais virtuais. *Revista Pesquisas e Práticas Psicossociais, 12*(2), 310–326.

Bueno, A. (2021). What comes after depression? The crisis of neoliberal subjectivity and the new authoritarian wave in Brazil. *Krisis, 41*(1), 45–64.

Butler, J. (2015). *Notes toward a performative theory of assembly*. Harvard University Press.

Carvalho, S. (2006). Política de guerra às drogas na América Latina entre o direito penal do inimigo e o estado de exceção permanente. *Crítica Jurídica Nueva Época, 25*, 261–275.

Cerqueira, C. M. N. (1996). Remilitarização da Segurança Pública: Operação Rio. *Discursos Sediciosos – Crime, Direito e Sociedade, 1*(1), 141–168.

Cerqueira, D., et al. (2019). *Atlas da violência 2019*. IPEA, FBSP.

Cerqueira, D., et al. (2021). *Atlas da violência 2019*. IPEA, FBSP.

Costa, R. V. E. (2017). *O novo templo de Salomão: o projeto de expansão da Igreja Universal do Reino de Deus para o Brasil e o mundo*. [Master's thesis, Universidade Católica de Pernambuco]. Repositório TEDE UNICAP. Retrieved from http://tede2.unicap.br:8080/handle/tede/1548

Costa, F., & Marra, M. (2020). Famílias brasileiras chefiadas por mulheres pobres e monoparentalidade feminina: risco e proteção. *Revista Brasileira de Psicodrama, 21*(1), 141–156.

Curcino, L., & Pereira, T. A. C. (2022). Livros, política e populismo: a "nova direita" brasileira e seus best sellers. In M. A. Marques et al. (Eds.), *Populismo(s) e suas linguagens Textos selecionados*. Edição Húmus.

da Silva, L. N. (2018). O mercado editorial e a Nova Direita brasileira. *Teoria e Cultura, 13*(2), 73–84.

de Sousa, R. S., de Oliveira Filho, P., Araújo, J. B., & Vieira, D. V. M. (2022). A Identidade da Direita em Narrativas de seus Militantes numa Universidade Brasileira. *Psicologia: Ciência e Profissão, 42*, 1–16.

Dias, D. L., Doula, S. M., & Cardoso, P. O. (2017). Participação política nas redes sociais: um estudo com jovens universitários. *Revista Sociais & Humanas, Santa Maria, 30*(1), 124–143.

Fernandes, P. (2021). *Família monoparental feminina:* desafios de ser mãe solo [Doctoral dissertation, Universidade de São Paulo]. Repositório Digital UNESP. Retrieved from https://repositorio.unesp.br/items/39c832cb-5f12-464a-832f-61802e044962

Fernandez-Kelly, P. (2012). The unequal structure of the German education system: Structural reasons for educational failures of Turkish youth in Germany. *Spaces & Flows: An International Journal of Urban and Extraurban Studies, 2*(2), 93–112.

Fields, M. L. (2024). *Taking the red pill: A content analysis of ambivalent sexism and precarious manhood in alpha male podcasts* [Master' Dissertation, Eberly College of Arts and Sciences, West Virginia]. Retrieved from https://researchrepository.wvu.edu/etd/12548

Fuks, M. (2011). Efeitos diretos, indiretos e tardios: trajetórias da transmissão intergeracional da participação política. *Lua Nova: Revista de Cultura e Política, 83*, 145–178.

Fundação Abrinq. (2021). *Cenário da Infância e Adolescência no Brasil*. Abrinq. Retrieved from https://www.fadc.org.br/sites/default/files/2021-04/cenario-da-infancia-e-da-adolescencia-2021.pdf

Gaspar, H. A., Daase, C., Deitelhoff, N., Junk, J., & Sold, M. (2020). Radicalization and political violence–challenges of conceptualizing and researching origins, processes and politics of illiberal beliefs. *International Journal of Conflict and Violence (IJCV), 14*, 1–18.

Giugni, M., & Grasso, M. (Eds.). (2021). *Youth and politics in times of increasing inequalities*. Palgrave Macmillan.

Hoeveler, R. C. (2020). A reorganização da extrema direita latino-americana no ascenso bolsonarista: fóruns e redes organizativas. In F. G. Faria & M. L. B. Marques (Eds.), *Giros à direita: análises e perspectivas sobre o campo líbero-conservador*. Editora SertãoCult.

Honneth, A. (2011). *Verwilderungen des sozialen Konflikts: Anerkennungskämpfe zu Beginn des 21. Jahrhunderts. MPIfG Working Paper, No. 11/4*. Max-Planck-Institut für Gesellschaftsforschung.

Ironwood, I. (2013). *The manosphere: A new hope for masculinity*. Red Pill Press.

Jovegelevicius, J. C. (2018). *Entre a cruz e a estrela: um estudo sobre algumas aproximações de setores evangélicos com o judaísmo*. [Undergraduate thesis, Universidade Federal do Rio Grande do Sul]. LUME Repositório Digital. Retrieved from https://lume.ufrgs.br/handle/10183/182701

Kallio, K. P. (2018). Not in the same world: Topological youths, topographical policies. *Geographical Review, 108*(4), 566–591.

King, V., & Koller, H. C. (2009). Adoleszenz als Möglichkeitsraum für Bildungsprozesse unter Migrationsbedingungen. Eine Einführung. In V. King & H. C. Koller (Eds.), *Adoleszenz — Migration — Bildung*. VS Verlag für Sozialwissenschaften. https://doi.org/10.1007/978-3-531-91459-6_1

Klandermans, B., & Mayer, N. (2005). *Extreme right activists in Europe: Through the magnifying glass*. Routledge.

Lewandowsky, M., Leonhardt, C., & Blätte, A. (2023). Germany: The alternative for Germany in the COVID-19 pandemic. In I. N. Ringe & L. Rennó (Eds.), *Populists and the pandemic. How populists around the world responded to COVID-19*. Routledge.

Lira, E. M. (1993). Trauma político y memoria social. *Psicología Política, 6*, 95–116. Retrieved from https://dialnet.unirioja.es/servlet/articulo?codigo=2826352

Lüküslü, D., & Walther, A. (2021). "I wanted to take on a lot of responsibility". Reconstructing biographies of young people engaged in formal participation. *Journal of Youth Studies, 24*(8), 1068–1084.

Machado, J., & Miskolci, R. (2019). Das jornadas de junho à cruzada moral: o papel das redes sociais na polarização política brasileira. *Sociologia & Antropologia, 9*, 945–970.

Meiering, D., Dziri, A., & Foroutan, N. (2020). Connecting structures: Resistance, heroic masculinity and anti-feminism as bridging narratives within group radicalization. *International Journal of Conflict and Violence (IJCV), 14*(2), 1–19. https://doi.org/10.4119/IJCV-3805

Mouffe, C. (2013). *Agonistics. Thinking the world politically*. Verso.
Nilan, P. (2021). *Young people and the far right*. Springer Nature.
Pinheiro, P. S. (1997). Violência, crime e sistemas policiais em países de novas democracias. *Tempo Social, 9*(1), 43–52. https://doi.org/10.1590/S0103-20701997000100003
Pitti, I., Mengilli, Y., & Walther, A. (2021). Liminal participation: Young people's practices in the public sphere between exclusion, claims of belonging, and democratic innovation. *Youth & Society, 0*(0), 1–20.
Polivanov, B. B. (2019). Identidades na contemporaneidade: uma reflexão sobre performances em sites de redes sociais. *Revista do Centro de Pesquisa e Formação, 8*, 103–119.
Ribeiro, C. A. C. (2014). Mobilidade e estrutura de classes no Brasil contemporâneo. *Sociologias, 16*, 178–217.
Rodrigues, T. (2012). Narcotráfico e militarização nas Américas: vício de guerra. *Contexto Internacional, 34*(1), 9–41. https://doi.org/10.1590/S0102-85292012000100001
Roy, N. (2022). *"We are just normal women": Narratives of far-right women members of the AfD and FPÖ*. Tese de Doutorado, Women Studies, Universidade de York.
Salden, S., & Hertlein, J. (2020). Is it fair? The German education system and its stumbling blocks for adolescents. In M. Watzlawik & A. Burkholder (Eds.), *Educating adolescents around the globe. Cultural psychology of education* (Vol. 11). Springer. https://doi.org/10.1007/978-3-030-37900-1_7
Sanders, R., & Jenkins, L. D. (2023). Patriarchal populism: The conservative political action coalition (CPAC) and the transnational politics of authoritarian anti-feminism. *The International Spectator: A Quarterly Journal of the Istituto Affari Internazionali, 2023*, 1–19. https://doi.org/10.1080/03932729.2023.2225660
Schwander, H., & Manow, P. (2017). *It's not the economy, stupid! Explaining the electoral success of the German right-wing populist AfD. CIS Working Paper 94*. University of Zurich.
Schwanenflügel, L., & Walther, A. (2022). Learning to participate in and through conflict. In Z. Becevic & B. Andersson (Eds.), *Youth participation and learning critical perspectives on citizenship practices in Europe* (pp. 37–55). Springer.
Sguissardi, V. (2015). Educação superior no Brasil. Democratização ou massificação mercantil? *Educação & Sociedade, 36*, 867–889.
Silva, V. G. B. D., & Soares, C. B. (2004). As mensagens sobre drogas no rap: como sobreviver na periferia. *Ciência & Saúde Coletiva, 9*, 975–985.
Skelton, T. (2015). Young people, children, politics and space: Youthful political geography scholarship 2003-2013. In K. P. Kallio & J. Häkli (Eds.), *The beginning of politics: Youthful political agency in everyday life* (pp. 123–136). Routledge.
Solano, E. (Ed.). (2018). *O ódio como política: a reinvenção das direitas no Brasil*. Boitempo Editorial.
Stefanoni, P. (2021). *¿La rebeldía se volvió de derecha?: Cómo el antiprogresismo y la anticorrección política están construyendo un nuevo sentido común (y por qué la izquierda debería tomarlos en serio)*. Siglo XXI Editores.
Teixeira, J. M., & Barbosa, O. A. (2022). A mulher e a família: agendas pentecostais na disputa pela gramática dos direitos humanos. *(Syn)Thesis, 15*(1), 89–105.
Turner, V. (1969). *The ritual process: Structure and anti-structure*. Aldine de Gruyter.
Van Gennep, A. (1909/1960). *Rites of passage*. Routledge.
Vieten, U. M., & Poynting, S. (2022). *Normalization of the global far right: Pandemic disruption?* Emerald Group.
Walther, A. (2022). Welfare states as transition regimes: Reconstruction from international comparisons of young people's transitions to work. In B. Stauber, A. Walther, & R. A. Settersten (Eds.), *Doing transitions in the life courses—Practices and processes* (pp. 37–55). Springer.

Chapter 5
(De)Constructing the Narratives into Thematic Categories

In this chapter, the focus is shifted from the *trajectories* to the *themes* identified in the narratives, in order to outline the identifications and discursive formations as effects of interpellations and normativities. Through the process of open and closed coding, as well as the survey of the recurrence of terms in the transcripts, thematic categories were created, illustrated both by the narratives and by the dialogue with the literature. I seek to propose, within the thematic categories, articulations and reflections, revisiting some and inaugurating other paths of analysis and comparison of the phenomenon of youth engagement and activism, as well as the expansion of the radical right in Brazil and Germany.

5.1 The Process of Analysis and Construction of Categories

The thematic analysis of the narratives involved an initial process of open coding in which broad categories were identified. The first phase began during the interviews, through attention to recurring themes, but was complemented by the use of the *software* NVivo, which allowed for the merging of all transcripts for a systematic analysis and coding. The coding process was initially done using the transcripts in the original languages (seven in Portuguese, two in English, and three in German). In a second phase, I translated all the texts into Portuguese. Thus, in the final phase of analysis, it was possible to develop a recurrence analysis of terms within the *software* NVivo.

Given the theoretical tradition adopted in this research, it is understood that the terms can be interpreted as "signifiers". In post-structuralism, the meaning and signifier are in mutual relation, making it essential to investigate how the subject appropriates the signifier and assigns it meaning. We will notice that, throughout the categories, many of the signifiers illustrated in the "word cloud" gain articulation, forming chains that can be interpreted as "networks of representation". A set of "chains of signifiers" may, in the end, give indications about the grammar of the political projects of the radical right, which, through the force of enunciation and repetition, have been configured as "regulatory norms" (Butler, 2000). Also in the

B. Besen, *Youth Activism in the Radical Right of Brazil and Germany*,
https://doi.org/10.1007/978-3-031-87635-6_5

narratives, I sought to perceive what remains and escapes from such normativities. Thus, there was a double movement: to highlight how coercion operates but also to illustrate what are the fissures and paths of resistance.

The list of initial codes, as well as the word cloud, are presented in Table 5.1 and in Fig. 5.1, and will be mentioned throughout the chapter, and can be revisited. I remind you that, in the case of the word cloud, only nouns or words that could function as subjects were retained, excluding the names of the interviewees. As discussed in the methodology, the present research uses the *software* as an "assistant", whose main function is to provide a "compilation" and faster handling of a huge amount of information, generating forms of visualization. Such forms of visualization prompted questions and did not provide answers. Thus, as I will develop below, the categories constitute themselves as questions, that is, they reflect the search for understanding about the conditions of formation of discourses and identifications that were frequent and/or striking in the narratives. The formation of categories happened through the joint observation of interviews from both countries; thus, even the particularities that are outlined throughout the chapter could lead to the proposition of unified categories, which seek to explore possible common systems of representation, generating diverse agendas and issues.

Table 5.1 List of generated codes

Generated codes in open coding
Accusations of persecution
Anti-feminism or gender
Presentations
Gun is power!
Parental absence
References to the collective past (historical memory)
Conspiracy
Countermovement
Taking care of the country
Statements about leadership
Defence of the group against criticism
Definitions of freedom
Definitions of politics
Definitions and references to masculinity
Detachment from Bolsonaro
Disbelief in social change
Disbelief in racism
Description of the place of residence
Description of life overcomings
Description of engagement
Descriptions of the left

(continued)

Table 5.1 (continued)

Discourse about war
Hate speech
Distinction and criticism of other political groups
Entrepreneurship
Effort and dedication
State as enemy
Dedicated students
Experience in school
Experiences classified as unjust
Experiences of frustration and/or disappointment
Family experiences with politics
Negative experiences in school
Positive experiences in school
Religious experiences (religion)
Expression of fundamental values
Formation (experiences)
Formation (people)
Collective future
Hegemony of the left
Hegemony of the greens and the left
Ideology
Importance of social networks
Impressions about the pandemic
Justification of political agendas
Mentioning political violence
Mentioning about madness
Mentioning about security
Alternative media
Naturalization of violence
Pro-gun agenda
Power
Reference politicians
Gateway
Position regarding immigration
Positions of resistance
Projecting individual future
Reference to Bolsonaro (negative)
References to anti-Semitism
References to Olavo de Carvalho
Relations between the individual and political dimensions
Relations with friends
Routine of movements
Feelings of injustice
Pessimistic views of the future
YouTube and social networks

Source: Prepared by the author, 2023

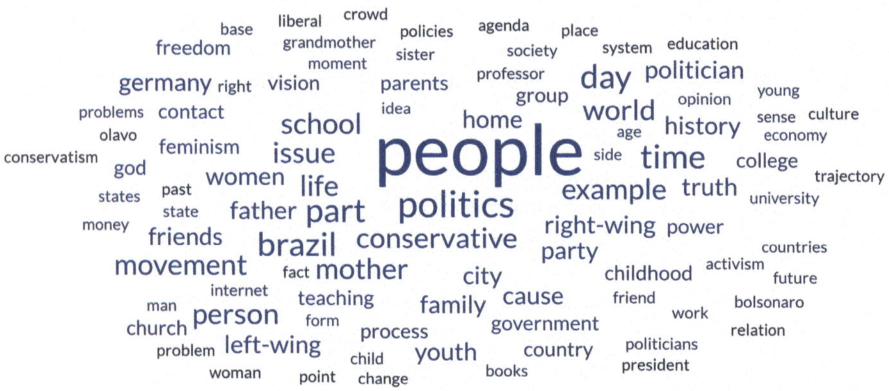

Fig. 5.1 Word cloud of terms with seven characters or more characters generated using *NVivo* software (adapted to English). Source: Prepared by the author, 2023

5.1.1 Familism and the Moralization of Crises: Neoconservatism and the Völkisch *Discourse*

Familism was defined and discussed, as early as 1962, by Rogers and Sebald, as a subordination of the individual's interests to those of the nuclear family group. Sabogal et al. (1987)[1] will define familism as a strong identification and attachment of individuals to their families, developing feelings of loyalty, reciprocity, and solidarity among members. In the field of sociology, initially, familism was defined as a facet of social altruism. However, the exploration of power structures and gender hierarchies in the nuclear family—mainly stemming from feminist theories—led to questioning this relationship. Browning (2003) speaks of the emergence of a critical familism, which has sought to highlight the normative contents of theories and discourses about family and marriage. The unfolding of such a critical reading has allowed for the possibility of reflecting on the conditions of emergence of norms about the family, understanding familism as a discursive construction.

Within this perspective, it was identified that in interviews with young activists, both in Germany and Brazil, familism was present. In a manifest way, narratives were identified that addressed the need for maintenance/recovery of the centrality of the—traditional and nuclear—family in Western society. I emphasize here that the

[1] A review of the use of the concept indicates that, in the past, it was especially used in the context of analysing Hispanic immigrants in the United States, emphasizing that the place of family and family obligations would be distinct and defined by cultural issues. In the context of the mentioned research, the investigation of immigrants from different Hispanic countries would reveal that familism is a central characteristic of Hispanic culture, remaining even in the face of processes called "acculturation". Another line of studies emerges by exploring familism in the context of the *Welfare State*, that is, familism understood as a hypervaluation of family functions to which state responsibilities would be transferred (Moraes et al., 2020).

appreciation of family emotional ties is not questioned within the present research. It is understood that young people may express attachment to family relations, as well as affirm the centrality of the family in their lives. The normative content of familism is questioned, highlighting that, in the case of the interviewees, diverse family configurations were identified, with a recurrence in the biographies of the absence and neglect of the father.[2] In view of this diversity of configurations, it is questioned, therefore, what are the possible discursive interpellations that configure the defence of the traditional and nuclear family, as well as its positioning as an "institution under attack".

To begin such reflection and analysis, I present here some of the narratives. Nuria (19 years old, Brazil) defends the family as something natural to humanity.

> What I value is this. That our culture, which is so mixed, may perpetuate, the positive things. And what about the issue of family? Yes, the natural family is what I preach about. But of course, regarding gays, lesbians, if they want to form a family, great. That's no problem at all because it's their choice. I will respect people, what people are. That is, as I said before, their character. If they want, for example, to create a family, a family unit. Personally, I don't see a problem, I just don't think it's right, for example, that some people from the LGBT movements want to destroy this feeling of family, which is something of humanity, it's our characteristic to have a natural family unit.

Aline (20 years old, Brazil) considers the family the foundation of conservatism and society.

> [Being] conservative is defending morality, the family, because the family is the foundation of society. It has been shown, in history, that the family has always been the foundation in society; there has always been a family structure that served as a foundation for all kinds of people, influence, country, right? The kingdoms themselves are made of families. So the family is defended by conservatism. Conservatism is not in favour of not changing bad things; on the contrary, we want to preserve what is good and reform what is bad. We don't want to revolutionize, right? We think it's no use breaking the house from the ground up. We have to break the house from the roof, and if the problem is in the roof, we have to redo the roof; we don't have to demolish the whole house. So we think we have to preserve the good things, like the family.

Nissin (23 years old, Germany) associates his involvement with politics with his studies on family and marriage.

> I read a lot of literature about dating, about social dynamics, about how men and women are different when it comes to life. One thing I remember is this literature. The literature says this: Women are measured by appearance, and men are measured by success. And that was one of the main moments when I realized: "Yeah, I never thought about that". And it really changed my view of life and how the dynamics between men and women are. (...) Actually, I would say that this is the family and, yes, everything related to family, to marriage. And I know a lot about this topic since I started to study and improve myself. I started self-improvement and read a lot of literature about, as I mentioned, dating and marriage. And I know many statistics about it. I think this also changed my political view.

---

[2] In the past, it was common for a research tradition to seek to relate such family configurations as markers of propensity for deviant behaviors (Markowitz & Ryan, 2016). In the case of the present research, such a view is repudiated, which may stem from the same normative roots.

Moritz (23 years old, Germany) advocates for the presence of both parents and the non-interference of the State in the family.

> It means having traditional values. It does. So, for me, personally, it means that the family is important for civilization, for society. That children need to have both parents, because, for example, single mothers can sometimes be a problem, as there are statistics that say that people, when, for example, it comes to criminals and there are statistics, statistics that, for example, I don't... I don't know if it's a correct number, but, for example, 70% of all criminals were raised in homes with single mothers. And, for example, this is important. It's important that children receive both parents. And I also think that the government should not interfere in how parents raise their children.

As seen, the articulation of the theme within the narratives gains diverse outlines. In general, there is an attempt to stabilize gender roles and the reference to a "human nature" that is organized through the format of the traditional family and marriage, that is, the ideal that there would be a natural and ordered state to which humanity could return. At times, this "something natural" seems to be revealed through the encounter with conservatism (in this sense, the idea of taking the "magic pill" mentioned in the previous chapter is revisited).

However, the inflection that seems to gather the contents and mobilize the majority of young people is the idea that there is an "attack on the centrality and ordering of the family", that is, the discourse about the left and movements based on differences as destabilizers and destroyers of what is "natural" and "morally valid". This would happen both because these groups admit that the State should act as a regulator of social relations and inequality, and because of the developments—experienced both in Brazil and in Germany—of affirmative policies that protect the rights of the LGBTQIA+ population and women, destabilizing gender roles.

To analyse this phenomenon, we seek to reflect on how discourses from various political fields found resonance in the common denominator of the family, as a nucleus that must be restored and/or preserved. Revisiting what was presented about the need to know the "systems of representation", I reflect—based on the work of Dardot and Laval (2016), sociologist Melinda Cooper (2017), and philosopher Wendy Brown (2019)[3]—that this system is based on the intertwining of neoliberal and social conservative[4] discourses, understood by Almeida (2009) as a neoconservative hegemonic turn.

---

[3] It is interesting to highlight that Wendy Brown's work undergoes a shift since her 2015 book, *Undoing the Demos: Neoliberalism's Stealth Revolution*, in which she centralized that neoliberalism had the primacy of transferring the economy to all social relations. For this reason, she saw an incompatibility between conservative social and neoliberal normativities. In the new 2019 book, *In the ruins of neoliberalism: The rise of antidemocratic politics in the West*, she legitimizes this intertwining as a "moral" project aimed at protecting traditional hierarchies by nullifying the concept of society and politics as based on the "common good". However, she understands that the result we observe today has a "Frankensteinian" dimension, in the sense of reassembling the original discourses—with special attention to Hayek—but promoting alliances and a functioning that would not be aligned with the original neoliberal project.

[4] When Cooper (2017) addresses neoliberalism, he refers centrally to the North American schools of new economic liberalism that emerged in different universities in the United States, such as

Cooper (2017) is the one who states that, for a long time, the cultural history (genealogy) of neoliberalism was told without considering the role of the family, which was isolated from a critical perspective and often interpreted—even within the left—as a "sign" of strong and lasting social ties. Cooper's book offers a reading of the period from 1960 to 1980 in the United States, highlighting that Gary Becker, an exponent of the Chicago School, when constructing his *Treatise on the Family*, even in 1981, already stated that "the family in the Western world has been radically altered, some claim it has almost been destroyed, by the events of the last three decades" (Becker, 1981, p. 1). Cooper interprets that there is a collapse of the Fordist family—already in the 1960s—which functioned as a fundamental mechanism in the normalization of gender and sexual relations, as well as a centre of work, race, and class organization in the mid-century (Cooper, 2017).

Through the works of Cooper (2017) and Brown (2019), it is possible to understand how feminism and the liberation movements of the 1960s—in their quest for greater gender equality and the redefinition of traditional roles in the family—were factors that contributed to the flexibilization of labour relations and the deconstruction of a standard family structure. Cooper's book proposes a fundamental inversion, in which these changes are no longer seen as a product, but rather as causes of neoliberal transformations. In this way, it is emphasized that neoliberal normativities expand as an adaptive and accommodating response to such destabilization.

Already in the 1970s and 1980s, with an economic scenario of high inflation and an environment of uncertainty and insecurity for many American families, neoliberal economists, such as Milton Friedman and Friedman (1980) and Gary Becker (1981), began to argue that inflation was eroding family values and the traditional family structure; centrally, such figures said that inflation was undermining the family's ability to fulfil its central role in society as an institution of stability and economic security. Such discourse already established the private family as the first line of defence against economic uncertainty, stating that financial security should be sought within the family sphere rather than relying exclusively on the Welfare State.

In this context, social conservatives would have found common ground with neoliberals, as they interpreted the crisis as a decline in public and private morality reflected centrally within the family. The convergence between the two political groups strengthened the constitution of a "family moral agenda", placing it as a central theme of various political campaigns that spread across the West. In this way, Cooper allows us to understand that, despite not being based on transcendental

Chicago, Virginia, and Los Angeles, mainly in the 1960s and 1970s. These schools and authors are brought to Brazil still in the 1980s, as discussed in Rocha's thesis (2019). However, considering that Cooper is based on Foucauldian studies, I understand that the comprehension of neoliberal political rationality involves all the schools that develop from the Walter Lippmann Colloquium in 1938. In this way, ordoliberalism (Austrian School) is also addressed, as a European exit, which brings common normative roots, but particular developments regarding the positioning of the State, as will be discussed later. The new social conservatism refers to the conservative movements that emerged at the end of the 1960s, including the neoconservative movement, Lawrence Mead's new paternalism, the new religious right formed by Catholics and evangelicals, as well as the communitarian movement.

virtues, the neoliberal logic admits "an immanent ethic of virtue, as well as a natural order of family values, conceived as emerging automatically from the mechanisms of the free market" (Cooper, 2017, p. 57). Therefore, within the "regime of truth" of neoconservatism, the idea is constituted that, if the family is responsible for the economic security of its members, then the State must guarantee moral values that sustain stability for the nuclear family.

Netto et al. (2019) analyse that the conjunction between neoliberalism and social conservatism results in an opposition to the notion of social solidarity promoted by the State. In other words, one of the arguments will be that, now, social solidarity would be known through family relations, which are interpreted as based on "love or duty". Friedman and Friedman (1980, p. 5) will say it is a pretension of the State to want "to promote the welfare of the 'general public', [and claim to know] better than anyone what the public interest is, and how to achieve it". They further state:

> The difference between social security and earlier arrangements is that it is impersonal and compulsory—while the older agreements were voluntary and personal. Moral responsibility is a personal matter, not a social one. Children helped parents out of love or duty. Now they contribute to the support of someone else's parents, and this out of obligation or fear. The old transfers strengthened family ties; the compulsory ones weaken them. (Friedman & Friedman, 1980, p. 113)

Cooper's reinterpretation follows this interpretation and corroborates the detachment of the individual as the centre of neoconservatism, positioning the family as the core of neoconservative political agendas. It is interpreted that such a conjunction operates as a normativity related to the requirement of the individual's self-sufficiency towards the family, with moral responsibility often focused on the individual's ability to cover the costs of constituting a family. This is a logic of competition, especially in a scenario where such a circumstance becomes increasingly difficult and, in this sense, the emphasis on the subject as an entrepreneur of oneself is understood. As an important image of such a requirement, I highlight the narrative of Nissin (23 years old, Germany) when he says:

> I drew my own plan on when I should start a marriage and when I should start dating. Although I have options to meet women and meet them often, I am planning to marry or really get to know someone for a long-term relationship later. As I have already said, after **realizing that men are considered objects of success, I wanted to focus more on success and improve myself.** I am not saying it is a good thing to be just an object of success, but it really **makes a difference in how people see us, if we are successful people. That is why I am trying to improve myself in this area of life.**

Nissin invests in his self-improvement and career success as necessities for family formation.

Cooper (2017) also analysed the emergence and centrality of a "moral crisis of inflation"[5] in the American context, which strengthened and "solidified" the

[5] Cooper (2017) will further discuss how, within this crisis, a programme named Aid to Families with Dependent Children (AFDC)—which has many similarities to what became Bolsa Família Programme in the Brazilian context—gained central prominence in economic debates about inflation in the 1970s. The researcher wondered what would explain the obsessive focus of neoliberals

neoconservative alliance in public discourse. Crises, here, represent experiences in which social and economic anxieties and uncertainties are "shared and unequally distributed" but, above all, are moments when individuals continuously reinterpret and "reevaluate their realities" (Albino et al., 2021, p. 9). In the case of Brazil, we can observe the strengthening of a moral family agenda in the face of moments that were interpreted as "crises".[6] Thus, the "crisis" surrounding Dilma Rousseff's second government is highlighted, which was predominantly read as a "spending crisis" and quickly directed towards the PT government (centrally with the Bolsa Família Program).

The moralization of the crisis in Brazil involved the issue of the attack on the Bolsa Família[7] Programme, which was interpreted as "excessive spending". Similar to the American case with the Aid to Families with Dependent Children (AFDC)

---

and neoconservatives on such a marginal programme that involved minimal federal budget spending. She will say that the AFDC was constructed as a moral embodiment of inflation, representing a welfare programme for poor populations who did not contribute to pension funds (unlike social insurance programmes intended for stable families who paid taxes). At the time when neoliberals and neoconservatives turned inflation into a "political crisis", the AFDC programme had more African American mothers than white women, as well as many divorced mothers or mothers that had never been married. Quickly, it became the symbol of "a general crisis of the American family" (Cooper, 2017, p. 29). Conceived by neoliberals and neoconservatives as a symptom of inflation and the disintegration of the traditional family, this programme became, according to Cooper, the foundation for the formulation of "a new non-distributive political philosophy of family values" (ibid., p. 46) under the Carter and Reagan administrations. However, this family philosophy would have to wait until the Clinton administration to culminate in the transformation of the social security system and in a massive federal system that allowed for the surveillance and regulation of the private family responsibilities of the poor.

[6]Albino et al. (2021), in the introduction to the book *Neoliberalism, Neoconservatism, and Crisis in Dark Times*, state that neoconservatism governs populations and subjects through the management of a state of crisis. Inspired by Foucault and interpreting neoliberalism as a mode of governmentality, they emphasize that "precarity, vulnerability, and unequally distributed dispossession politically challenge subjects, while also leading them to question the emerging meaning of crisis and critique" (Albino et al., 2021, p. 20). Athanasiou (2011/2021) will also say that states of crisis are a form of governmentality and that neoliberal governments "utilize the ever-present emergency crises, along with an entire affective apparatus of fear and insecurity that accompany them, to legitimize the need to take actions towards managing uncertainties and establishing a new and secure normality" (Athanasiou, 2011/2021, p. 157), which requires urgency and radicality of action, as will be discussed in Sect. 5.1.6.

[7]The Bolsa Família Programme (BF) was implemented in 2003 by the federal government under Luiz Inácio Lula da Silva. It represented an effort to unify a set of pre-existing income transfer programmes focused on poor families, which had been created since the 1990s. The program gained international visibility, as its centralized registry enabled the distribution of 11 million monthly benefits, covering 19.4% of Brazilian households by 2007. This programme achieved measurable results, lifting millions of Brazilians out of extreme poverty and hunger. In fact, the programme had a modest budgetary expenditure (less than 1% of GDP) (Rocha, 2011), yet it became a central target for critics. Opposition arguments often involved moral considerations, alongside a growing discourse on the need for fiscal austerity. Its similarity to the Aid to Families with Dependent Children (AFDC) in the United States stands out, particularly in the designation of women as the primary recipients of the benefits. This reflected not an incentive but a clear assessment of the realities faced by low-income families in Brazil.

programme, I highlight that the Bolsa Família programme included families composed only of women, broadly benefiting poor and Afro-descendant families. In other words, the programme also promoted survival in the face of diverse family configurations, which were not always "choices", but reflected a reality of abandonment and parental neglect in the country. Along with the attack on this programme, the discussion about the attack on the traditional family emerged, with the controversy of the "mamadeira de piroca" and the supposed distribution of "*gay kits*".[8] In Nuria (19 years old, Brazil), we find a direct mention of this.

> **But he [Bolsonaro] was saying that a *gay kit* was being distributed in schools, saying that sexual education was being taught incorrectly, and he wasn't wrong about that.** Because a child of 6 to 8 years old, they won't know if they want to be gay or lesbian, you know? **Like he said, I let the homosexual be homosexual.** The person being this or that. The problem is that you can't influence a person to be something they have no notion of yet. For example, when I was 7 or 8 years old, I didn't know if I wanted to be homosexual or heterosexual. I just wanted to play with Barbie. So what he said was, "it's too early to talk about sexuality with children, because it's something they have no notion of". Should parents explain this? They should. But often, due to **the lack of family structure, they already delegate this to the State.**

Corroborating the argument that families delegate their functions to the State, the presence of the metaphor of the State as a "father" was also identified. On one hand, there is the construction of criticism towards people who would expect the "father-State" to be the one providing sustenance without work. On the other hand, there is also the "father-State" as the one seeking to establish law and order without legitimacy. Letícia (32 years old, Brazil) will say:

> The daddy-State. Oh, the daddy-State made a law there because there are many hypertensive people, so let's remove salt from the table. No! The person has to have the right. If they want, the State can't say no, you can't, I think... I am really against this, really against it!

The use of the metaphor seems especially intertwined with what was presented here about the fact that the "family", and not the "individual", is placed at the centre of the neoconservative discursive strategy. The State is not compared to a boss, but to a father. Safatle also states that the "overlap between the social body and the family structure" involves a fantasy that the family would be a nucleus of "naturalized, non-problematic hierarchical relations, of authority based on love and devotion" (Safatle, 2020, p. 22). In this space, places of authority and submission would be natural places; therefore, the "father" of the family, who should not be replaced by the State, gains legitimacy to act as a producer of law and control, based on love and duty.

In the German case, we have two moments that are interpreted as crises: the "refugee crisis" back in 2015, and the recent "gas crisis", which is frequently

---

[8]The controversy of the "mamadeira de piroca" began with material distributed during Dilma Rousseff's presidency in the project to combat homophobia. The material was attacked and attributed, already through the figure of Jair Bolsonaro, the name *gay kit*. The *fake news* related to it was that baby bottles with rubber nipples in the shape of a penis were distributed in daycare centers to combat homophobia (Maranhão et al., 2018).

mentioned in conjunction with the issue of the Russia-Ukraine War. However, in the face of both crises, there is a fundamental difference in the narratives of young people compared to Brazil, because in Germany, the Welfare State is called upon and placed as responsible for creating and implementing policies that will "solve the crises". However, the solution and call are centrally to redirect these expenses to "German families", presented as "the people themselves" (*Völk* or *Bevölkerung*).

To understand this particularity, it is essential to address the German ordoliberalism, which is presented by Foucault (2008a, 2008b) as the neoliberal European solution, and is mainly distinguished by not being opposed to the existence of the State but rather for seeing it as the producer of the legal framework that guarantees free competition in the market (Dardot & Laval, 2016). The State:

> should carry out actions to break monopolies and, simultaneously, articulate an international security relationship, in which freedom and political economy are interconnected by security mechanisms (...). The problem of neoliberalism is, contrary [to liberalism], to know how the global exercise of political power can be regulated based on the principles of a market economy. It is not, therefore, about freeing up an empty space, but about relating, referring, projecting in a general art of governing the formal principles of a market economy. (Foucault, 2008a, 2008b, p. 181)

Havertz (2019) will say that German populist right-wing groups adopt ordoliberalism to perpetuate authoritarianism. He will say that the European solution prescribes a regulatory structure for the economy centred on creating a competitive order with the aim of producing and justifying social differences. Thus, radical right-wing groups would propose a connection between the economic differentiation system and systems of differentiation of nation, race, religion, and culture.

Meiering et al. (2020) mention that the "familism"[9] in German radical right-wing groups also originates from a *völkisch* (racial nationalist) discourse, which defends the German family against a gradual "elimination" of the supposed original European Christian white population through migration—based on the "great replacement"[10] conspiracy. In this way, it becomes evident that, to understand the same set of narratives related to the family, we can explore a series of "systems of representations". These systems, in the cases of Brazil and Germany, have

[9] Kemper (2014, p. 61) defines familism as a restricted, biological-populational, national, and normative image of the family, which seeks to marginalize or combat families that do not correspond to these models, such as single parents, non-Germans, financially disadvantaged families, and the so-called "*patchwork*" or "rainbow" families (referring to LGBTQIA+ families).

[10] Leconte (2019) points out that the "*grand remplacement*" was a theory coined by the French writer Renaud Camus, which was integrated into the party networks of the AfD from 2017. She explains that Alexander Gauland, in that year, began a campaign based on "preventing the replacement of the population due to the current migration policy". The researcher states that this was an appropriation of a foreign reference for the rehabilitation of racist discourse—related to Nazism—with a reactivation and mark of the penetration of two groups within the party structure (the traditional new German right of the 1980s and the identitarian movement). The circulation of such discourse represents, therefore, an attempt to establish a "brand" of identitarian strength of the AfD, defining a differentiation in relation to the external party environment, as well as defining the "winners" of a normative definition struggle within the organization.

particularities but end up uniting in establishing the family as a threatened entity. Therefore, and beyond the differences, it is understood that the moments that are interpreted and enunciated as "crises" are fundamental for strengthening the discourse of the "moral economy", which immediately relates the events to a "spending crisis" that threatens the "traditional family". The main difference is that in the narratives of young Brazilians, a defence of austerity emerges, while in the German context, young people suggest a "redirection" of spending, using, as pointed out above, criteria such as race and religion, which will be translated by the signifier "culture".

Still within this theme, it is important to highlight that, by observing the narratives of young people, it was possible to identify an openness to "preservation through transformation". In other words, new legal structures are taking shape and seeking to "accommodate" what could previously be a "deviation" within the movements of radical right-wing groups. Now, gays also identify and have a place in radical right-wing groups—as is the case of Simon (22 years old, Germany). Similarly, LGB[11] families are legitimized by Nuria (19 years old, Brazil). Thus, in a movement here interpreted as an "accommodation", there is an expansion of minority participation within the movements of radical right-wing groups. The big question is under what conditions these minorities can participate, that is, what remains as an unshakable axis in a constant expansion.

Cruz's (2021) research on right-wing LGBT activism contributes to this reflection, pointing out that gay activists found acceptance in the political field of the right. He indicates that the right-wing groups do not constitute an impermeable opposition to gender and sexuality issues, but that entry is conditioned on the diffusion of the discourse that LGBTQIA+ movements no longer represent or have become incapable of politically representing people who identify as lesbian, gay, bisexual, transgender, queer, intersex, and others. This conception gives rise to a dispute around LGBTQIA+ political identities, opposing "moderate" activists, who do not intend to confront capitalism or the status quo, to an LGBTQIA+ movement systematically accused of being "radical", "leftist", "victimizing", and, finally, "enemy of the family".

Cruz (2021) will say that two styles of activism have emerged from this process: The first is identified with the conservative and nationalist discourse, focusing the discussion on moral, anti-corruption, and pro-armament agendas; the other has a liberal profile focused on defending individual freedoms, minimal state, and free market. The latter would claim a position of neutrality in an attempt to escape the right/left dichotomy, although many of its members are linked to movements, parties, and organizations with a tradition in the political field of the right. Despite the differences, these two styles of activism would also have their affinities, uniting on themes such as the defence of capitalism, anti-communism, and sympathy for

[11] Here, I do not include trans, *queer* non-binary, and intersex individuals because they did not emerge in the narratives and are groups that suffer direct attacks. In this sense, it is possible to identify that the integration of LGB families may be conditioned to the reproduction of traditional gender roles and the adoption of a nuclear family format.

various aspects of the so-called anti-gender discourse. Seeking to highlight the issue of the place of "minorities" within the groups, I analyse how this anti-gender discourse opened a place for women within radical right-wing groups.

5.1.2 Female Anti-Feminism: Gender-Defined Political Spaces

In the interviews conducted, it was possible to observe a majority of young Brazilian women who adhere to the anti-feminism agenda, presenting it as the centre of their activism. Aline (20 years old, Brazil) and Catarina (20 years old, Brazil) were the examples provided in the thesis, but, in general, a vast majority of women were identified in Brazil and Germany who act as influencers and activists of the anti-feminist and anti-gender agenda. Catarina (20 years old, Brazil) states:

> Today, yes, mainly because of feminism. I identify a lot with anti-feminism because I am a woman and, to be honest, **feminism does not represent me**. In my opinion, **it only takes the woman out of the role of a woman**. It makes the woman no longer a woman. It takes away her identity as a woman. So that's my opinion. And that's how it happened in high school. Anyway, it still happens a little. There are people who don't want to have children, but, anyway, because this ends up having an influence from feminism, because feminism, it was born, it has an Enlightenment cradle. And the Enlightenment is all formed by men, even feminist ideas. Feminists think this way because they were influenced by men and by lovers.

Aline (20 years old, Brazil) shares her journey and impact on social media:

> Since then, in 2020, the pandemic came. And it was in 2020 that I started to study much more about social issues, which, like it or not, is what is voted on, too. Before that, I was very much like: "Why is feminism so bad, people?" I'm going to study feminism to be able to refute you who are saying that feminism is bad. **Then I studied and turned against feminism, right? I ended up falling into their trap (laughs). But, studying, I saw that feminism is not really all those things they say, that it conquered everything** (...). The first videos went quite viral here in the city. I received a lot of attacks from people who already didn't like me very much, I don't know why. I never talked to them, but they spoke badly of me on Twitter. Then it passed here. Then I started to grow outside, right? In the State of São Paulo, in Brazil. Today, on TikTok, I have about... more than 30,000 followers; on Instagram, I hit 8000 followers; today, much less. I'm there, making content, right? Doing what I like, I really like debating too. On TikTok, on Instagram. I'm out there, doing this work.

It is noticeable that the two young women found a space for identification, but also for recognition and impact through direct opposition to feminism and, consequently, to an anti-gender agenda. Although the theme is present in the narrative of some young people who identified as men, I propose a reflection on anti-feminism as an agenda led and represented by a majority of young women. By this, I mean that, in the expansion of radical rights, there is an active search for the incorporation of more women (Campion, 2020). However, such entry seems to maintain gender as a definer of positions and agendas within the movements and the very online universe of radical rights. The interviews allow us to see that this has an even greater weight when we deal with young women, who are still feeling their way in an environment that is predominantly led by adult men.

Roy (2022) researched the activism of women within the AfD and FPÖ, and hence, her research helps to cover a gap in my research. The absence of interviews with young women in Germany makes it difficult to construct a comparison involving the gender issue. However, many of Roy's research results reinforce the reflections presented here. The researcher comments that, in meeting with the interviewees, she began to consider that the decision of such women to participate in these parties is not illogical but part of the success of radical rights. Furthermore, she states that such women do not act against their interests because there is no far-right agenda that goes directly against what these women understand as their condition as women.

Roy refers to Puwar's research, which is based on feminist, racial critique, and post-colonial studies, and addresses the "paradox of the arrival of women and racialized minorities in spaces from which they have historically or conceptually been excluded" (Puwar, 2004. p. 181). In this case, the focused environment was, broadly, politics—a space where white men are still the majority. Puwar's research involved semi-structured interviews with white women and black men who act as parliamentarians in Westminster. She sought to encompass representatives of various political orientations.

Puwar offers a precise critique of the entry of these minorities, which have been interpreted as diversity, but these bodies still position themselves as foreigners. In a predominantly male and white environment, the author points out that such subjects become disembodied, with a "gender-free" and "race-free" facade. However, in the case of women and blacks, their bodies enter marked and identified by gender and race, which delineates space and circulation. Puwar uses the concept of "space invaders", which Roy also adopts for the context of women's participation in the AfD and FPÖ. This concept highlights the ambiguity of the present in which the message is given: "There is room for everyone, but everyone must stay 'in their place'". In this sense, it is interesting when Simon and Thomas, in relation to different parties, declare their opposition to quotas for women in politics. Simon (22 years old, Germany) will say:

> In fact, there aren't that many [women in politics], unfortunately. Of course, I would like to see a few more. **But we don't want quotas in any case. It's probably more because, unfortunately, many women are less to the right than to the left. But we definitely try to win over women.** I know some young women from my circle who are members. **But it's difficult to reach the top when you're still young and unknown.** I'm almost certain that in one or two years, there will be a few more women there.

Thomas (22 years old, Germany) states that:

> However, especially in a male-dominated world, it has been shown that a woman can still reach the highest office, like Angela Merkel, and can establish herself in it, without the need for a female quota. Why need a quota to get a position? **So if a woman or a man needs a quota to obtain a position, then she or he has no place in politics, has no place in the position. It should just be a matter of being able to assert oneself.** Our party is also becoming increasingly male-dominated over time, but still, women are able to assert

> themselves. And the real participation is that women assert themselves before us, men, and sometimes show where the issue lies. And I believe that a quota for women is not necessary. **Women have their skills, everyone knows that. Women have certain tools to assert themselves before men. And female intuition can also be a decisive advantage on many occasions.** And these advantages should simply be taken advantage of, and thus, women can assert themselves.

By opposing quotas, Thomas states that there is still no place for women in politics, while Simon declares that there are no women "there", referring to the highest positions. Both young men attribute specific "tools" or "political orientations" to women. Vinicius (25 years old, Brazil) states that:

> (...) **women have their essence, their nature, the fact of being very detail-oriented.** Different from us, men, who are sometimes stubborn. Sometimes, we are very impulsive. No! **Women are more cautious; women are more detail-oriented.** So this is very important so that we do not fall into certain political traps. **Because women are very attentive, very detail-oriented**. They are very... They are very cautious, right? Grounded. So I see that women in politics are very important indeed, especially in these aspects of details, of analysing things more, more in-depth, anyway. And women help us a lot with this. If it depended only on men, we would be in trouble for being too impulsive.

In terms of "natural" feminine characteristics, another element that emerges in the interviews and has been explored in the literature (Campion, 2020), especially after the emergence of the *Tradwives*, is the consideration of women with the fundamental role of procreation, care, and motherhood. Nuria (19 years old, Brazil) and Aline (20 years old, Brazil) highlight the desire to be mothers and position the fight against abortion as a central element of their political agenda. In Greece, the emergence of the Golden Dawn Party (GD) further incited research on women in radical right-wing movements, highlighting that the portrayal of these women has been condensed into the position of "mothers of the nation". However, in the European case, the element of "reproductive purity" is added.

Zuquete (2018) states that the entry of women into European identity movements was also a calculated effort to distinguish these movements from those of the past. Mattheis (2018) states that three discourses stand out for women's activism: gender complementarity between men and women, an *alt*-maternalism, and the idea of Western civilization as a gift from white men to white women. In this sense, Simon's (22 years old, Germany) discourse about his party "trying to win over women" is highlighted. The idea of conquest is particularly interesting and indeed refers to the possibility that something is offered to them; however, this something will be limited and come with distinct demands.

When it comes to Brazil, the racial issue does not emerge as fundamental in anti-feminism, but the limitations given in terms of the participation of young women within radical right-wing movements seem to be similar. There is an interest and guidance from men and leaders for young women to become public figures of the groups and movements. However, it is noticeable that the places offered to these young women are not as broad as those offered to young male activists. Even Letícia (32 years old, Brazil), who does not relate her activism to the anti-feminist agenda, is invited to assume the Women's Directory of a party.

It is not ignored that anti-gender and anti-feminism are agendas that permeate all radical right-wing movements, being identified by Meiering et al. (2020) as "bridging narratives"[12] for radicalization within the groups. However, the term "anti-feminism" itself did not emerge in the narratives of any of the interviewees who identified as men. In the case of the interviewees, Carlos (19 years old, Brazil) stands out, who makes a direct attack on feminists, saying that:

> I have already seen an interview with Italo Marsili, who is a psychologist, right? He says...—and I very much agree with his statement—that "a true militant feminist, really, I don't know any [who is] happy'. I don't know any either. So it has a lot to do with internal problems. She doesn't resolve the internal [problems] and gets involved with feminism. Feminism manages to capture, like every ideology, all ideologies. It manages to capture the passion of...people lost in the world and bring them to its cause, right? It's that useful idiot, right? It's the guy who understands nothing, but he is useful for the cause. What I see is that feminism is composed of women resentful of their relationships or the lack of relationships. I don't know.... They are very resentful women and, then, everything to them is machismo, everything to them is rape, that kind of thing. The result of this is that society does not adhere to their movement, really, no.

Investigating anti-feminism among right-wing groups in Germany, Kemper (2014) argued that the classic anti-feminism of the 1960s underwent fundamental changes. Men do not identify themselves nor are they considered perpetrators (natural and, therefore, legitimate), but, conversely, are declared as victims of "feminism", a line of reasoning that Kemper designates as "masculism" (2014). Igor (23 years old, Brazil) says, regarding his mother, that:

> she identifies with a more leftist, more progressive discourse, at certain points even a bit revolutionary, and, even because she is my mother, she has a certain moral influence over me, but I didn't agree with that, and then we debated a lot about it. Sometimes, eventually, she would evoke this issue of moral authority, her superiority in relation to experience, life experience, since she is 34 years older than me. And that only kind of increased my impetus to contest, to think that I shouldn't agree with what she was saying just because she is my mother or because she is older, I should seek for myself what I thought was right. For example, maybe even because I am a man and all, feminism was never an agenda that attracted me, maybe due to a certain gender consciousness, of being a man and wanting in a way to defend my gender. I'm just giving a more obvious example.

The idea of defending one's gender refers to the same pattern of identification as a victim. The same happens with Carlos (19 years old, Brazil), when he shifts the idea of the perpetuation of violence by women, who would have a "hatred of men".

> So, like a feminist girl, right, you will see that she is a more sexually libertine girl, you know? That she normally has a greater hatred towards men. She is very angry when it comes to these issues about men and women. She reacts very violently, you know?

[12] Meiering et al. (2020) investigate anti-feminism along with gender constructions—such as masculinism, heroic and toxic masculinity, and femininity as a reproductive function—as fundamental linking narratives, which produce internal cohesion and external connections between radical right-wing groups and movements. They state that such narratives are "customized in specific ways for the respective area, but they remain part of the same set of narratives and perform similar functions, structuring patterns of perception, attributions of belonging, and options for action, while also serving as conveyor belts for radicalization processes" (Meiering et al., 2020, p. 8).

In other words, violence now appears as a characteristic of feminists, who would force men to "defend their gender". Most interviewees recognize or even mention the existence of violence against women. However, like Carlos (19 years old, Brazil), this is not associated with a structure of oppression, but with individual cases that should be punished.

Regarding violence against women, Farris (2017) states that one of the central arguments mobilized by nationalist right-wing groups is the profound danger that Muslim men would represent for Western societies, due to their oppressive behaviour towards women. In the case of the young people interviewed in this research, the attack against immigrants happened mainly due to a lack of integration and labour disputes. However, there were moments when they were referred to as antisocial and uncontrolled, which seems to corroborate what Roy found in interviews with activists. Her German interviewees presented a series of accounts about personal experiences, or those of others, related to abusive or inappropriate behaviour by Muslim men.

Berg (2018), in "Between Anti-feminism and Ethnic Sexism", discusses the mobilization of such an agenda in Germany. She recalls December 2017 when a young woman was murdered by her ex-boyfriend in Kandel. There were mobilizations on Facebook, Twitter, and YouTube, and, in addition to being organized in the form of demonstrations, radical right-wing groups joined the extreme right to launch the slogan "Kandel is everywhere"[13] (Kandel ist überall). The murder was transformed into a political symbol of the failure of the German government's migration and refugee policy as the perpetrator was from Afghanistan. The author points out that, on one hand, radical right-wing groups defend the anti-feminist agenda, with direct opposition to gender studies. On the other hand, they emphasize, even amid demonstrations, the rights of women and minorities, declaring that "gender equality" would be part of "German values".

Both in Brazil and Germany, the issue of the fight against violence against women is incorporated as an agenda of radical right-wing groups but disconnected from its structural and gender dimension. Thus, the discussion promoted by feminists regarding inequalities between men and women and the existence of gender violence are treated as fallacious and as a tool to mobilize a "supposed debt" of women. It is Aline (20 years old, Brazil) who recounts that her first post that gained traction was one saying that she "owed nothing to feminism". She says:

> I discovered like this. I was seeing all the fallacy that they told me being destroyed. I was seeing that I didn't need feminism for these things. That a person, to be against aggression, right?... they say a lot that feminism is against aggression towards women and everything else. For a person to be against aggression, they don't need to be a feminist. They just need

[13] In the case of Kandel's demonstrations, the groups shared images of brass plaques under the title "Merkel's Stumbling Stones" (*Merkels Stolpersteine*). They refer to the "stumbling stones" scattered throughout Germany to honour the victims of the Nazi regime, seeking to equate the crimes. In the list of demands, they included closing the borders to all types of immigration, deportation of illegal immigrants, and even assimilation to *jus sanguinis* (a principle of descent for acquiring German citizenship).

> to have two neurons to be a human being. It's having logic. I don't need to be part of a movement to be against aggression. Whether against women, against children, against the elderly, against men. It doesn't matter! So I don't need to be part of feminism to be a decent human being, right?

She explains in detail that anti-feminism does not have an agenda of its own, being able to be connected to liberalism or conservatism. The core discourse of the body of authors who have become references for anti-feminism in Brazil is the proof that feminism would have constructed a fallacy regarding its importance in the achievement of women's rights. Sparemberger et al. (2021) particularly analysed the posts of Ana Campagnolo, who served a term as a state deputy in Santa Catarina (elected in 2018) and published one of the most impactful books on anti-feminism, "Feminismo: perversão e subversão" (Feminism: Perversion and Subversion, which is mentioned by Aline). The researchers analyse the Brazilian scenario through the concept of "cultural war", coined by Hunter (1991), and declare that the former deputy figures as an important "soldier". They identify that, in the case of the deputy, a central signifier is Christianity. The idea that there is an attack by a "minority" group is forged by constructing a general scenario in which 90% of the Brazilian population is grouped as "Christian"—among Catholic and Evangelical denominations. Ana Campagnolo extends to communism and global leftists a persecution of Christianity, emphasizing news about attacks on temples and a supposed "loss of religious freedom".[14] In this sense, we analyse, in the next section, religion and its incidence in the narratives of young people.

5.1.3 God and Religion: Between Cultural Christianity and the Neo-Pentecostal Spiritual Battle

Dantas (2013) conducted an investigation on neo-Pentecostalism[15]—focusing on the case of the Universal Church of the Kingdom of God (UCKG)—and its strategies and articulation with the political sphere. The author explains that the discourse

[14] Regarding these discourses, it is interesting to point out that Brazil participated, with the mediation of representatives from Baptist and neo-Pentecostal churches, in the signing of the Religious Freedom Alliance. This alliance, organized in 2020—and ironically signed by representatives from Poland, Hungary, the United States (still under Donald Trump's administration), and Brazil (at the time governed by Jair Bolsonaro)—involved only countries with a Christian majority. Despite presenting religious freedom as their main banner, there were mentions of the threat faced by Christian groups worldwide. In the Brazilian context, organizations such as the National Association of Evangelical Jurists (ANAJURE), in addition to the former Minister of Women, Family, and Human Rights, Damares Alves, were prominent figures. Ana Campagnolo's posts seem to follow the same discursive construction, where "religious freedom" is coined as an agenda, but contents are propagated that alarm about a direct opposition to the Christian universe, with an attack on its symbols and representatives.

[15] It was the sociologist Ricardo Mariano (1995) who popularized the designation of "neo-Pentecostalism" in Brazil to define the movement that emerged from the late 1970s, bringing transfor-

about the "demonization" of politics is a strategy used to legitimize the church's political participation and encourage the faithful to participate in elections. By stating that Brazilian politics is dominated by Satan, the Universal Church reinforces its religious mission to liberate politics from evil and moralize it. The election of evangelical candidates is seen as a strategy to occupy institutions that are considered "totally controlled" by the devil, aiming to promote the exorcism of politics, the "redemption" of society, and the victory over evil. The faithful are encouraged to vote for "men of God" capable of confronting evil spirits and purifying politics. The vote, besides being an exercise of citizenship, also acquires a religious connotation, inserting itself into the logic of the spiritual battle.

Dantas further explains that, in the particular universe of the UCKG—one of the largest Brazilian denominations—religion and politics come close to one another and mix, making it difficult to identify the boundaries that separate both phenomena. Religious ideologies invade the political field, attributing new meanings to it, while political symbols cross the religious sphere, modifying their meanings. Religious conversion would have a political character as each converted individual becomes electoral capital, increasing the chances of electing new political representatives and strengthening the opportunity to build an ambitious power project based on religious ideologies and practices (Dantas, 2013). In the case of Catarina (20 years old, Brazil), we see an account of her conversion process.

> And there I did it. And I was converted by the Gospel. From that moment on, my conversion took place. And I became a Christian. Although I was born in the church, I was not yet converted. I was not yet a Christian with Christian attitudes. I still didn't live. My lifestyle was not a Christian lifestyle, despite going to church. But I didn't have the mindset of a Christian person, only after being converted (...) Because the heart of man is evil, since his childhood, since his infancy, basically. So, what separated me from God, so that I didn't live as a Christian, was my heart. Which, distant from Him, evil, let's say, as the Bible says, did not approach Him by its own will. So, it was necessary for God to seek me. (...) I didn't have... and without knowing it... I didn't have God in my heart.

It is interesting to highlight the discourse about the natural evil of man because it is in this Manichaeism that ideals about evangelization and conversion are sustained fundamental elements of some neo-Pentecostal branches, which understand that those who have not had contact with the Gospel remain in the field of the "diabolical". In this sense, Catarina (20 years old, Brazil) presents a discourse distinct from Aline (20 years old, Brazil)—who does not identify as evangelical—about what feminism would be.

---

mations and diversification to national evangelicalism: rejection of the sectarian withdrawal from the world, of ascetic practices, and of the old "believer" stereotype; dissemination of prosperity theology linked to a capitalist ideology (promises of "abundant life" and prosperity in exchange for tithes and offerings); emphasis on doctrines of spiritual warfare; and a reduction in apocalyptic expectations. Today, there are critiques of the distinction between traditional Pentecostalism and neo-Pentecostalism. In this book, however, the focus is on the issue of spiritual warfare, which gains greater prominence in these designations. This book highlights, first and foremost, that evangelicalism in Brazil is diverse, and other movements also shape trajectories related to radical right-wing groups, as well as agendas described in this chapter.

> Thus, anti-feminism—as the name itself says, right?—is against feminism. For me, in my view, as I say on my page, **for me, it is a diabolical religion. Because feminism itself encompasses, influences attitudes of various religions, in which they precisely sacrifice babies and also sacrifice the lives of women.** Now I don't remember the names of these religions, but there is even a woman I follow, who talks about this kind of thing that happens. Her name is Regiane, by the way. For me, anti-feminism is just, like, a position of being anti-feminist. But for me, it is to really stand up and defend that. "No. I am against feminism and I consider myself, Isabela, I consider myself an even radical anti-feminist" (laughs).

Calling feminism a "diabolical religion" demonstrates a mixture of political and religious aspects within the Brazilian radical right. Regarding the position of women in neo-Pentecostal churches, Gabatz (2018) states that these have been spaces that offer women alternatives for community insertion and re-elaboration of their identities, occupying, in the hierarchies, prominent and strategic positions, besides being recognized as heads of families. However, the Bible and biology are used to produce a discursive practice that attributes essential characteristics to men and women, determined by sexual division. The main element has been the positioning of women as formed by nature and by God for motherhood. In accordance with Teixeira (2019), the researcher states that the neo-Pentecostal religious universe is marked by adhesions and re-significations, not confining women to a submissive position.

Evangelical churches, not only in the neo-Pentecostal form but also Presbyterian and Baptist, are, therefore, a particularity of the Brazilian conservative scenario compared to the German one. They became partners of the State[16] even during the Workers' Party administrations and, with that, took on an important part of the management of social assistance equipment in the peripheries, encouraging the training of many young psychologists and social workers—as is the case of Catarina (20 years old, Brazil). These young people act by reproducing the church's guidelines regarding life. This issue has been a challenge for the federal councils[17] of the categories, which observe the growth of the conservative discourse perpetuated by their professionals. Teixeira (2019) points out that one of the pillars of the introduction of neo-Pentecostal churches is also the dispute regarding the human rights agenda, which has been weakened as the agenda is taken over by the discourse on the preservation of the traditional family.

---

[16] The process of evangelical churches entering social assistance practices is explored in Scheliga's thesis (2012), *Educating Senses, Guiding a Praxis: Ethnography of Assistance Practices among Brazilian Evangelicals*. The author outlines the process in which RENAS (National Evangelical Network of Social Action) becomes close to the National Council of Social Assistance and the National Youth Council, still under Lula's government, in 2007.

[17] The Psychologists in Action slate is running for the presidency of the Federal Council of Psychology. The group has, in the presidency and vice presidency, leaders from Baptist and neo-Pentecostal churches. The psychologists in the presidency have publicly defended conversion therapy. In 2017, the vice president of the slate obtained an injunction from the first-instance judge of the 14th Civil Special Court of Brasília, Waldemar Claudio de Carvalho, which authorized the treatment of LGBTQI+ individuals, but this injunction was overturned in 2019 by Minister Cármen Lúcia of the Supreme Federal Court (STF).

Despite the emphasis on neo-Pentecostalism, a branch followed by Catarina (20 years old, Brazil) and Nuria (19 years old, Brazil), I emphasize that, in the universe of the interviewees, religion did not stand out as a central aspect of the trajectories, involving a minority of young people who attend religious spaces. In the case of Aline (20 years old, Brazil), for example, Judaism was brought as a new religious experience, and, in the case of the other interviewees, the religion mentioned was Catholic. In this sense, Stockemer et al. (2020) suggest that there is a complicated relationship between the movements of the new right, religion, and secularization. The researchers argue that the movements and parties employ Christianity, mainly, as a marker of cultural identity to mobilize voters around a new cleavage of post-religious identity. However, the radical right generally remains distant from Christian doctrine, beliefs, and institutions. Instead, they combine cultural references to Christianity with secular policies, indicating a secularization of Christian symbols rather than a resurgence of religion in Western politics. Instead of a real relationship with religion, there would be an instrumentalization of it, with the strategic use of symbols, rhetoric, and religious values to mobilize support and create a sense of cultural identity among their followers.

Religion would serve as a powerful tool to rally a base and appeal to a shared heritage and values, referring to an ethnic myth of a common Nordic origin. In the face of this use, the groups would minimize or ignore aspects of religious doctrine or ethics that do not fit into their agendas and practices. Some movements, especially in countries with a Christian majority, would adopt, therefore, a form of "cultural Christianity" (Stockemer et al., 2020). This refers to the emphasis on Christian symbols, traditions, and values as markers of national or cultural identity rather than a strict adherence to religious doctrine or institutionalized faith. Here, I highlight what Thomas (22 years old, Germany) says about this:

> Religion is a fundamental part of our values, norms, and standards, [which are] almost religious. This is what we live today even among the non-religious. Like loving, loving your neighbour. That's what it demands. Actually, this came from Christianity, but it's something that everyone loves nowadays. Even people who call themselves atheists, that is, who want our values to come from their values. From what is open... **And the religious and the secular are one. It is important to separate religion. But, in doing so, not all those who influenced and shaped our way of life, so to speak, and our senses, should be disregarded and forgotten. Therefore, we should remember them, yes. But, in a general sense, politics and religion should not work together.**

Simon (22 years old, Germany) says:

> Well, when I was little, we were those typical hypocritical Christians who went to church at Christmas. But, after a while, it stopped. But I still call myself a Christian. I am and I maintain that. And I think it's better, to be honest. It's better if you are a Christian and don't want to go to church, don't pretend that you're not so hypocritical and then just go to church at Christmas, because it's "appropriate", even if you don't really want to go. You can also be a Christian without going to church.

Other investigations (Saunders, 2019) have pointed to a complex mosaic where nationalist arguments connect to pagan and pre-Christian mythologies that relate specific lands to peoples and their cultural heritages. Movements of the radical right are "mythologizing" the pagan place in their struggles to establish or resist spatial legitimacy in different regions of Europe. The resulting discourses focus on the notion of "authenticity" in the modern/postmodern era, where myths become "true" both for pagans and nationalists. Thus, to justify common identity, one looks back to the past. Seeking to deepen the analysis regarding the positioning of young people in relation to the past, the next section explores narratives related to local and global historical memories.

5.1.4 The (Ab)Uses of Memory: Positioning Oneself in Relation to the Past

Throughout the set of narratives, it was possible to identify that most young people seek to position themselves in relation to the historical past, both in terms of a reference to memories of violations—which shape the local and global collective memory—and through a positioning of their groups in relation to past political regimes. Cultural and decolonial studies on memory have highlighted its influence on the dynamics and power relations in a society, pointing to memory as a collective construction, which requires discursive efficacy and institutional recognition. For this reason, issues such as the tensions between history and memory (Martín-Baró, 1989; Gaborit, 2011), the disputes over the meaning of the recent past and its different interpretations (Shafir, 2005; Gagnebin, 2010), and the controversies surrounding official and unofficial memory policies (Ansara, 2012; Canabarro, 2014) are central in memory studies today.

Regarding the radical right, some authors have delved into the theme of the (ab) uses of memory, presenting distinct perspectives on the mechanisms involved. Couto Neto (2019) and Pereira (2015) highlight that we face the construction of a "revisionist" and even "denialist" history, based on rhetoric that idealizes, justifies, and militates for the self-absolution of past violations. Anderson (2019), on the other hand, develops the hypothesis that contemporary far-right parties and movements do not rely on historical revisionism but rather on a variety of collective memory construction in which negative connotations of events are re-evaluated for the proclamation of a national "identity" and "pride". Finally, Levi and Rothberg (2018) emphasize the use of a dual memory framework, blending ambivalent memories of the defeated and the conquerors, which allows them to position themselves as a victimized group that, at the same time, embraces past projects of domination. The confluence among the authors lies in the recognition of the power of memories in legitimizing claims and political projects in the present.

In the case of the analysis of young people's narratives, the hypothesis of a dual memory presented by Levi and Rothberg (2018) is particularly interesting. Regarding the Brazilian military dictatorship (1964–1985), Carlos says:

> So, man, the movie showed everything. Man, it showed everything about the guy's body, showed the trajectory, then he started talking about the military dictatorship. **It showed his**

> **view there, the political view, right?** That I don't agree with the guy. **I don't agree that the guerrillas were always the good guys. There were excesses on both sides, but the story has to be told with the truth, right? There is no such thing, the military were not just the good guys and the guerrillas were not just the good guys either, both were wrong.** So I see that the truth you analyse with... you know? Taking it apart piece by piece, you analyse it through very small things, you go deeper, deeper, deeper and then you reach the truth, you understand? Like, sometimes there's that general truth. Like, they say, every guerrilla defended democracy, and so on, blah, blah. It wasn't quite like that, you understand?

In the narrative, ambivalent memories are presented, favouring a relativization of the acts committed by the dictatorial government, against an assumption that the abuses were proportional and committed by "both sides". Kehl (2010)[18] states that such memory is based on the presentation of the guerrillas as an opposition group, composed of "terrorist communists" who kidnapped, robbed banks, and murdered. Faced with a binary morality, the guerrillas would have been positioned as villains, which demanded the dictatorial government to take extreme measures. The psychoanalyst emphasizes that, through the construction of such memory, the dictatorial government is positioned as the protector of families, and it is assumed that there were two forces, of equal proportion, competing on the social stage.

The historian Couto Neto (2019) analysed the construction and sharing of such memories through social networks, especially YouTube. He explains that the success of YouTube is related to the idea of decentralization of knowledge production, as the network is identified with a participatory culture, in which viewers actively request content, sharing it on other social networks. Neto identified a video with enormous repercussion and sharing among the radical right, titled "Dictatorship? My father describes how it was". The video is based on an interview with the father of a "vlogger", who shares his memories of the period, justifying the practices of violence as necessary to ensure security and stability. In the video, the vlogger eGuinorante (YouTube, 2021) states:

> You cannot trust anyone who talks about "dictatorship" without having lived through that period. Generally, if you were beaten, and everything else, it's because you weren't doing something right, because of something wrong you were doing. Now, everyone is a saint. Now everyone is a saint, after it's over, everyone is a saint.

The statement supports a perverse equation in which the violation of some people's rights is indispensable for the preservation of the majority's rights. That is, despite not denying the existence of torture, in order to "preserve" the memory promoted by the victims, they reinforce a logic of punishment and legitimation of the dictatorial government's abuses. Dantas and Ansara (2020) analyse that the process of producing policies of forgetting (Ansara, 2012) after the Brazilian military dictatorship

---

[18] Kehl (2010) highlights that torture practiced by the State is always defined as a crime against humanity, meaning that those who suffer torture by the State must always be positioned as victims. For Kehl, it is not possible to identify two sides in this scenario, only a disproportionate force coming from the State, capable of producing deep social traumas, generated by the movements of suspecting, torturing, murdering, and even making one forget.

made it possible to make "natural, invisible, and even unconscious the power relations" (Dantas & Ansara, 2020, pp. 32–3), in such a way that the dictatorship could be presented as necessary for maintaining social order. Festa (2017) identifies such discourse as part of a "cultural war", which benefits from the rhetoric of hate and the construction of binaries. The researcher references the book "Orvil: tentativas de tomar o poder" (Orvil: Attempts to Seize Power, Maciel & Nascimento, 1979/2012), which was published in opposition to the book and report "Brasil: Nunca Mais" (Brasil: never again, Arquidiocese de São Paulo, 1985), enumerating various crimes attributed to the left, questioning the character of the "guerrillas", and sustaining the existence of a permanent enemy: "the communist threat".

The book is related to the construction of a new theoretical model on public security policy and the police in Brazil during the military dictatorship. The model was theoretically based on the National Security Doctrine (NSD) and was characterized by submission to the precepts of war and the division of the world into two opposing blocs—communist and capitalist—considering each dissident as an "internal enemy". The dissemination of different "sources of memory" that present the Military Coup as a counter-revolution would allow its reactivation. Many leaders of the radical right identify human rights activists, academics, social movements, and LGBTQIA+ and feminist groups as internal enemies, all of whom are again called "communists" (Cruz et al., 2017).

Similarly, the identification of such groups as an internal threat has been made by representatives of the "monarchist cause" in Brazil. As a particularity of the Brazilian radical right, the existence of young activism related to monarchist movements was identified. Quadros (2017) analyses it as a "crowned conservatism", which would have expanded in the face of an articulation between the Brazilian Imperial House and the government bases of former President Jair Bolsonaro. Igor describes his path of identification with the monarchist movement, which is based on questioning how the period of the empire is presented in schools:

> In 2018, the year of one of the most controversial elections here, as I have never identified with the more progressive discourse of the PT and everything, I joined the campaign of the candidate who was victorious. (...) And this, whether I wanted it or not, presented me with something... it presented me with views that until recently were not discussed much, like more liberal economic issues, privatization, or more conservative authors (...) And then, in these debates and everything, a friend of mine introduced me to the monarchist cause, that Brazil indeed adopted this system between 1822 and 1889 and, in high school, we learned something like this. I think this topic was presented in a very watered-down manner, we didn't study it in depth. And then, indeed, beginning to study this and comparing it with other countries like England or Denmark, the northern European countries that are indeed parliamentary monarchies, I started wondering if this wouldn't be good for Brazil. Then, in 2020, when there was a rupture with former minister Sérgio Moro, who until then was the symbol of the fight against corruption—I'm not saying he indeed is, but, whether I wanted it or not, it was the image that was established with the current president, whom I then supported—and I was left somewhat hopeless that the republic could work here and even that I agreed or approved the current manager. And then I went back to studying this monarchy agenda more, which, whether I wanted it or not, is a reform. It's a structural change in the system, much deeper, as it would presuppose changing from presidentialism to parliamentarism, from republic to monarchy, reforms in the electoral system, in the party system. In society itself. And I was idealizing, right?

As we see, the young man is introduced in 2018 to the "monarchist cause", which gains strength in light of a "disbelief in the republic". His journey is related to the support for former President Jair Bolsonaro, as well as identification with the "fight against corruption", which also begins to be led by members of the Brazilian Imperial House. The period of monarchist-parliamentarianism is presented as a period of stability, while the present is presented as a "state of crisis".

Quadros (2017) explains that the Brazilian Imperial House, whose main figure is Dom Bertrand,[19] and its supporters are active and are "now the target of media reports, promote monarchist meetings, support movements, draft official statements on topics of great national repercussion, maintain websites on the internet, and lecture at events" (Quadros, 2017, p. 22). Olavo de Carvalho, a self-proclaimed "philosopher" of the new right—and frequently mentioned by young Brazilians—was also a defender of the monarchy and a promoter of the term "counter-revolution" to describe the Brazilian military dictatorship. Foresti (2013) analyses that the term was recovered from the ideas of Plínio Corrêa de Oliveira, founder of the TFP. The researcher states that the founding discourse of the TFP—actively disseminated by Plínio during the years of greatest repression of the dictatorship—has a direct influence on the configuration of the projects and agendas of the radical right of the present. The attack on the "red clergy"—referring to the branch of the Catholic Church that adheres to Liberation Theology—and the activation of the discourse of the "threat and the communist ghost" are pillars of Plínio's discourses, which constantly mention the dangers of a moral crisis. It is understood, therefore, that the memory of the dictatorship promoted by the radical right is directly linked to the (re)activation of the discourse about the "communist danger", which would always remain "lurking" and justify the need for radical actions and changes.

In the German case, it is interesting to note that no young person mentions historical memories related to Nazism, only highlighting that the correlation of their groups with the regime is unfair and inappropriate. Alexander (18 years old, Germany) emphasizes that the topic is covered for too long in school:

---

[19] The Imperial House represents the main organization of a series of movements, which have been growing since 2015, whose desire is the restoration of the monarchy in Brazil. The most radical group of this spectrum is Pró-Monarquia, but it also includes the Monarchical Restoration, the Order of Young Monarchists, Orleanism, as well as the Brazilian Monarchical Circle and a series of local circles. They advocate for the implementation of a parliamentary monarchy in Brazil, with elections for the parliament and the return of the Orleans and Bragança family to the throne. The main figure is the self-proclaimed prince Dom Bertrand, the current heir following the recent death of Dom Luiz. Currently, representatives of the pro-monarchy agenda have managed to pave the way in governmental positions and have received support from radical right-wing deputies, such as Paulo Martins (PSC-PR) and Carla Zambelli (PSL-SP). The Pro-Monarchy and the Imperial House are strongly connected and represent a return of the strength of the Brazilian Society for the Defense of Tradition, Family, and Property (TFP), as well as the legacy of Plínio Corrêa de Oliveira. Dom Bertrand was a member of the TFP and is now the director of institutional relations at the Plínio Corrêa de Oliveira Institute (IPCO), an organization known for its ultraconservative Catholic character.

> And the history up to National Socialism is actually the typical thing that everyone should learn. It is the typical thing that everyone must learn and that should be the main part of history lessons. (...) this is much reported about National Socialism. Of course, you should be informed about it, but not to the point of covering 200 years in half a year, and the other 12 [years of Nazi Germany] also in half a year.

It is understood that the extended amount of time spent studying Nazism in schools is related to a global and local consensus that established the rejection of Nazi terror and its positioning as an atrocity. Huhle (2016) explains that, in the case of German history teaching, this consensus and approach to the memory of Nazism only happened after reunification,[20] constituting National Socialism as a topic extensively covered in schools, from the perspective of the "victims". Alexander's discourse, however, represents the questioning of such a choice, positioning the period as just an episode—comparable and, indeed, less important—compared to the "200 previous years". In this sense, it can be highlighted that the German radical right positions itself squarely against the German "guilt", often characterizing the country's memorial culture as a "culture of shame" for society.

The memory of the country's division, as well as reunification in 1989, gains prominence in some activism trajectories. Thomas (22 years old, Germany) presents himself as a typical East German, and although he does not refer to the communist regime (1949–1990) at any time, he recounts that the differences in his family are marked by the former regional divisions. The young man explains:

> Well, my father is different from me and my mother. My stepfather is also different. My father is originally from the opposite side, which could be considered a "class enemy" according to the German division. My mother, my stepfather, and I are all from the eastern side, but he is from the western side of Germany, more precisely from North Rhine-Westphalia. Unlike his brother, who refused to do military service, my father served in the *Bundeswehr*, as did my grandfather. Approximately at the same time my stepfather was serving in the National People's Army of the GDR.

He describes that such origin defines different political positions and is a mark that still divides Germans today. Regarding German memory culture, Binder (2021) states that, after the Second World War, West Germany would have maintained itself through a "*völkisch*" memory culture, which lamented Germany's defeat in the

[20] Huhle (2016) analyses and compares the construction of an education for human rights and historical learning in Latin America and Germany. He critically positions himself against the German system, which would not have articulated such historical learning to education for human rights, whereas in the case of Latin America, the memory of the dictatorships would have been directly incorporated into an international grammar of human rights. He points out that this difference may be related to the temporal distance from the atrocities, as well as the division of Germany, which delayed its approach to the UN and other international organizations. However, the reflection that stands out in his research concerns the fact that the grammar of human rights directly influences the way historical memory is transformed into historical learning. Thus, we can understand that, in the Brazilian case, the memory of the dictatorship in Brazil as an atrocity is directly articulated to the promotion and construction of human rights policies. Considering this fact, it becomes more understandable the equivalence established in the discourses of the radical right between the "protection" or "sacralization" of the "guerrillas" during the dictatorship to the protection of "criminals" in the present, both attributed to the left.

Second World War, while quickly aligning with the position of the "West", which rose against the "communist threat". In the 1950s and 1960s, the memory would have been replaced by the heroic identity of the "*Wirtschaftwunder*" (Economic Miracle or Miracle of the Rhine). Hilmar (2023) explains that this heroic discourse also gains effectiveness in East Germany by establishing an "economic legacy of pride in the industrial society and in the 'productive work'" (Hilmar, 2023, p. 301). Referencing hyperinflation and the economic crisis of the 1920s as a cultural trauma, the capacity for reconstruction and the development of the post-World War II economy would be interpreted as a heroic act. Binder states that it was only in the 1970s and 1980s that the country experienced the emergence of an identity related to the Holocaust, accompanied by a collective guilt sustained in the aspect of fundamental trauma of Germany's action in World War II.

After reunification, the researcher states that German identity once again becomes a territory of dispute, even though the identity related to the Holocaust became more deeply institutionalized during the 1990s and early 2000s. In the eastern part, the discourse that saw reunification as a process leading to the demoralization and frustration of the potential of this region of the country would become stronger. The memory of a group that fought and worked hard for the country, which would be deserving of "social recognition", is legitimized. Thomas is emphatic in saying that his city, that is a part of East Germany, presents itself as an "unfulfilled promise", that is, a historic city that, due to reunification, becomes impoverished and forgotten. He says that:

> Because I am really proud of my city, but I have been experiencing the deterioration of my city for years, and it makes me sad. And I want to change that. My city [is] the city of the great composer Georg Friedrich Händel (...). He is the greatest composer in the world, but today no one cares about his city. A city that lost its economic relevance, I don't know if he would approve of that. I don't believe he would approve. I believe his city should be an important cultural and artistic metropolis.

Hilmar (2023) explains that, in the case of the German radical right, there is a promotion of "economic narratives" that reference the economic change that occurred during the transition from the communist regime to the market society after 1989. According to the researcher, interpretations are offered that suggest the structure of social recognition contains very serious problems, which could be repaired through privilege projects for German citizens who have the real desire to work but not the opportunities. Similar to the Brazilian context, the discourse of the existence of corruption would be used to justify the need for changes, which are based on a reconstruction of an "economic pride," which seems well portrayed in Thomas's narrative. Economic change is placed at the centre of the young activist's concerns, who states that:

> But capitalism works. It just doesn't work in Germany because what we are experiencing here is no longer capitalism. It's a mix of capitalism and socialism, where the masses are discouraged and give up, leading to increased unemployment, loss of tax revenues, like the commercial tax. And what does the federal government do about it? Nothing. The government always has enough money to spend. But we face all these issues.

Hilmar (2023) further analyses that the need to restore native economic pride is a unifying reference source for the identity politics promoted by the German radical right. Such identity is related to the shared discredit of the communist regime, remembered as a system that distributed rewards for economic performance based on political criteria. The communist threat and danger are also (re)activated and directed at the left and minority movements—as well as the Greens. Such groups are associated with an idea of coercive social justice—as we will revisit later—since they reinforce the reward of unworthy individuals, considered so for not being native or not being willing to work. Thus, a unified German identity is proposed by the values of hard work and the ability to rise economically. The instrumentalization of memories seems, therefore, to also relate to the establishment of the figure of the "Others", that is, those who threaten the full realization of this potentiality. In the next section, I will seek to explore how two agendas that differ in the German and Brazilian contexts may be based on a similar representation system, which also relies on the described (ab)uses of memory within the radical right.

5.1.5 The Threatening Other: The Encounter Between the "Normal" and the "Law-Abiding Citizen"

Two agendas stood out for marking a difference between the groups of Brazilian and German interviewees: on one hand, the defence of immigration control—mentioned only in the context of the German radical right interviewees—on the other, the defence of civil armament, brought only by the Brazilians. I unify the two agendas for analysis, discussing the possibility of interpreting them from a common normative origin: the establishment of a threatening "Other" subject to exclusion and/or elimination. In the German case, the majority of interviewees mentioned the "immigration problem", addressing the need for greater restrictions by the State. In Brazil, practically all interviewees mentioned the defence of civilian gun ownership, demanding a relaxation of the Disarmament Statute.

The memory of Nazism was invoked by some of the young Brazilians as a force to legitimize the civil gun ownership agenda.[21] They expressed that authoritarian

[21] The issue of public security has a significant impact on political campaigns in Brazil, driven by the perception of increased violence and the demand for punitive measures. At the beginning of the twenty-first century, there was an intensification of punitive legislative proposals in response to the growing media coverage of violence. In parallel, civil and non-governmental organizations, aligned with the federal government, highlighted the relationship between easy access to firearms and the growth of violence and crime. In 2005, the Disarmament Statute was discussed and submitted to a popular referendum, in which the population rejected the total ban on weapons. During the campaigns and debates, political leaders emerged who advocated agendas focused on harder punitive measures, reduction of the age of criminal responsibility, and the right to self-defence, including the relaxation of access to weapons for the protection of family and property. The Statute was, however, approved, imposing restrictions on civilian acquisition of weapons. In the following years, pro-gun deputies organized themselves, forming the so-called "bullet caucus". Despite this,

leaders, like Hitler, disarmed the population to impose a dictatorship. Translating the idea of the State as a potential tyrant, the defence of civil gun ownership was presented as a fundamental individual right. Carlos (19 years old, Brazil) says that:

> Hitler promoted disarmament. I mean, it wasn't Hitler, it was the Republic before Hitler. I forgot the name... The Weimar Republic started the disarmament and Hitler just followed the herd. Which was very interesting for him. There was even an operation that Hitler promoted against Albert Einstein, right? He believed that Albert Einstein was armed, right? They conducted a search and seizure at his house and found a bread knife. **To show the disarmament paranoia of a Nazi leader. So, [just] to show how it was a Nazi agenda... Nazi and also communist, right?** The Soviets did this, in China they did this, now our brothers there, in Venezuela this happened too, so there is a very important stage for a dictatorship to happen. And, secondly, that **I (...) with a weapon have much less chance of dying at the hands of a criminal, I have a chance of defence. It has to do with these two issues: freedom and self-defence. Which is stipulated in the Constitution and also stipulated in the Human Rights there at the UN and everything else... which is personal defence.**

It is observed that civil gun ownership is positioned as a right based on freedom against the State and self-defence against criminals. In opposition to the criminal, the narratives found the category of the "law-abiding citizen", who presents a morally superior character and is under constant threat, having to assume their own protection and, often, "take justice into their own hands". Illustrating such an image, we see Vinicius (25 years old, Brazil) say:

> To deal with this problem, we have to end this Disarmament Statute and arm the civilian, you know? **Because the State, it is omnipresent, it is flawed, so we have to give the right of legitimate defence to the people.** For me, in my conception, it's not that it will end violence, but **at least an innocent, a family man, can survive, can face it, can take care of his family and try at least to mitigate the violence**. Because I know that this is difficult, it's something that happens quickly. (...) And if... How do you say it? And if you self-identify as a person who will protect both himself and the people around him. **So, for me, to at least mitigate this problem of violence, besides public policies like stricter laws for criminals and offenders, also civil gun possession, which for me is important for the protection of the law-abiding citizen.**

The young man lists the complexity of the issue but presents gun ownership as a mechanism of protection. It is observed that the figure of the family man is that of the innocent and threatened, who faces crime to take care of his family. He sums up the figure of the "law-abiding citizen", who also demands and calls for more punitive legislation. Teles (2018) reflects on the militarization of politics and life and on the dynamics of producing this duality "internal enemy" versus "law-abiding citizen" from a state architecture in a racist, patriarchal, and genocidal society. He understands that, in this society, fear takes the form of a technology of control. Costa (2021) positions the "law-abiding" as a discursive representation that aims to "confer legitimacy to certain social practices and, therefore, with which different

until 2019, Brazil sought to regulate civilian access to firearms in various ways (Santos, 2024). The election of Jair Bolsonaro represented a profound change in the country's gun policy, by easing access to weapons and strengthening Hunters, Shooters, and Collectors (CACs) as political figures equivalent to the "law-abiding citizen".

subjects can identify" (Costa, 2021, p. 8). He points out that this figure replaces, from the 2000s, the "honest worker," through a new category that dilutes the distance between exploited workers, privileged middle class, and employers. For this reason, the new category would present itself as "homogenizing and enigmatic" (Costa, 2021, p. 4), excluding only those classified as "bums" or "criminals."

Costa understands that the strength of such representation lies in its ability to "hide the power relations involved, as well as act as a moral delimiter of objective relations of social segregation and police violence" (Costa, 2021, p. 4). The "law-abiding citizen" would reveal the limits of the idea of "citizenship" in Brazil, also warning about the conditions of criminalizing poverty. Regarding the criminalization of poverty, it is also important to highlight the formation of "walled cities" (Caldeira, 2000) from the 1990s and the transformation in the format and experience of organized crime. Investigative and police journalism programmes multiplied on Brazilian broadcast television since that decade and became the main space where persecutions and accusations against faces, mostly of young and black people, are portrayed (Oliveira, 2011; Romão, 2013).

In *Precarious Life*, Judith Butler (2011) reflects on what ethically connects us to alterity, to the Other identified with people marked by precarious lives. In Butler's argument, the representation of alterity constitutes a means of humanization/dehumanization, of recognition of the ethical-moral bond with the Other, or of justification of its elimination. She argues that the media, by personifying and representing war through faces printed in newspapers and magazines, for example, ends up eliminating, in the image of these faces, both the notion of loss and the precariousness of life lived by these young people. In other words, this face masks human suffering and the proximity to the precariousness of life, erasing the perception of loss that exists in war. For Butler (2011), this annulment of the perception of loss—the human insensitivity to pain and suffering—is the mechanism by which dehumanization is consummated.

In Brazil, people from the periphery, the poor, and black people are stigmatized and portrayed as "dangerous" and "criminals" daily by police journalism programmes. Caldeira (2000) points out that Brazilian society, with its legitimization of revenge and punitivism, created the motto "a good criminal is a dead criminal", which implies that, when it comes to criminals, death would be justified. The murders in the outskirts are justified by the same association: "They die because they are criminals". In the trajectory of Catarina (20 years old, Brazil), for example, this issue was brought up by a teacher and is described as one of the gateways to reflections on politics. Letícia (32 years old, Brazil) also provides elements to understand the discourses that connect female armament with a defence against violence identified in the figure of criminals:

> There are many studies in the United States, from states, about women, they carry guns, know how to shoot, know how to handle weapons. They have greater security. (...) If one day I am attacked by someone bigger than me, a man who has a much larger muscle mass, my only chance is with a firearm, right? **But I am a person who knows how to handle a weapon, I go to the shooting range, I am in training, but still, my only chance is this.** (...) Even more so because the rate of aggression against women, especially regarding rape,

> sexual violence crime, is with unarmed people, usually with a knife. In most statistics. But I talked to many people who said that, **in Brazil, in the past, and I myself remember that there wasn't so much gun control, and people would say "wow, but it was much safer back then".** (...) **And I believe and there is even jurisprudence with this justification, that the State cannot protect people. The State cannot be everywhere at the same time.**

The young woman is emphatic in pointing out that weapons are necessary in the face of a flawed and incapable State[22] and highlights a supposed "past" in which there was more security. Thus, it is understood that this discourse also refers to the reactivation of the memory of the dictatorship as a time of greater security and greater state "effectiveness" in the pursuit of internal enemies.

In the German case, most interviewees pointed out that the State should be responsible for acting in the restriction of immigration processes.[23] Although both agendas point to state "errors" or "failures", the solution is seen as arising from different actions. Alexander (18 years old, Germany) will say that his political group "wants everything to be regulated with them—regulated immigration and no uncontrolled flow of refugees". This particularity can be reflected in light of the—already conducted—analysis of the German ordoliberal tradition.

At the core of Simon's (22 years old, Germany) and Thomas's (22 years old, Germany) arguments against immigration is the need for the country's economic development and the emphasis on the fact that immigrants do not provide a qualified "workforce" for Germany. This aligns with Havertz's (2019) hypothesis about the establishment of a competitive system among individuals, where the inequalities produced within the system are converted into hierarchies between social groups, guided by "social Darwinism". Following this hypothesis, it is not surprising that we find narratives in which Muslims are presented as not integrated and part of a culture that clashes with the German "normal". I find particularly interesting the experience of Alexander (18 years old, Germany), who begins to revisit and reinterpret the changes in his surroundings from the construction of a refugee centre in his city.

---

[22] It is essential to consider that, in terms of discourses related to public security in Brazil, beyond the pro-gun agenda, there is punitivism. Pinto Neto and Cipriani (2021) locate this as a discursive and subjective engagement in the Brazilian radical right. In the case of punitivism, there would also be a call for the State to regulate, either through demands for the reduction of the age of criminal responsibility or for increased and more severe penalties. However, in the case of the analysis of the interviews with young people, this element was not predominant, revealing a greater emphasis on the defence of the pro-gun agenda articulated to the positioning of the State as incapable of "solving the problem".

[23] In Germany, migration flows are not recent, but they gained prominence as a political issue in the 2017 elections. In the 1990s, there was a large influx of migrants due to the end of the Cold War and civil wars in the former Yugoslavia, Africa, and Asia, peaking in 1992. After a decline in immigration at the end of the decade, a new wave began in 2009, following the global economic crisis, intensifying in 2014 with the conflicts in Syria, Iraq, and Afghanistan. In 2017, the AfD party adopted the slogan "*Wir holen unser Land zurück!*" ("We are going to take back our country!") and, by placing the anti-immigration agenda at the center of the campaign, won seats in parliament.

> As I said, during the refugee crisis, we also had a refugee centre built here in our area. And since then, we also had strange incidents, like somehow at ten o'clock at night the music was still playing on the loudspeakers and you could hear it a little or something like that. You can't say if it was them, but there was a lot more trash scattered around. Or that they ran outside and shouted. It was nothing that moved me at that moment. **But then, when I thought about it again a few years later, I realized that all the incidents that had just happened like the stabbings or the terrorist attacks. That's how I realized that somehow this was linked to what we were also living at home, that something like this could happen, that they couldn't behave.** And that's what got me. In this sense, at least regarding migration and refugees, it put me in tune with the party.

Thus, it is noted that the encounter with the party led the young man to revisit the past and establish a generalization, positioning immigrants as those who "cannot behave". Wahl (2020) emphasizes that it is essential to consider that radical right-wing groups use references to real experiences. For the researcher, the danger of discourses that appeal to young people is the generalization and mobilization of a "politics of fear" (Wodak, 2015). He points out that the far-right evokes the fear of foreigners, accusing immigrants of being frightening and uncontrolled people who must be fought. Additionally, it mobilizes anxieties about economic and social changes, globalization, articulating them to the establishment of a common enemy. We could associate that the defence of civilian gun ownership in Brazil would come as a result of the same type of fear mobilization, which concerns the threat of the "internal enemy", whose violence is also understood by the label of "out of control". In both contexts, two sets of common characteristics are attributed: the idea that this Other breaks norms and is uncontrollable and the idea that they abuse or are defended and protected by the welfare state (Sakki & Pettersson, 2016).

Nussbaum (2013) has been one of the leading figures in the analysis of emotions and their fundamental relationship with politics. She understands that various emotions can support political principles and projects but that natural emotions can be directed towards exclusion and stigmatization, as would be the case with the mobilization of fear. However, even if we consider that fear is a possible common origin, the challenge of understanding why the weapon emerges as a solution in the Brazilian context still prevails. For this, one reflects on the function of social coercion by the State and how it is organized and legitimized in the country. Muniz and Proença Júnior (2013), in "Armamento é Direitos Humanos: nossos fins, os meios e seus modos", point out that, in the context of different countries, the way of establishing police power and making it a coercive agent will also define how society will interpret defence and public security. The association between guns and security in Brazil would have emerged in light of the idea that coercive power is a fundamental part of politics, that is, in light of a militarization of life and a constant legitimization of coercive actions through weapons and violence. Thus, Carlos's (19 years old, Brazil) statement provides a key understanding of the discursive construction[24] of

[24] It is important to mention that several works have also explored and revealed economic interests related to the implementation and expansion of the arms industry. To read more about the dimension of American militarism and the *lobby* that also affects Brazil, see Panetta (2017). The construction of the agenda in Brazil is also a reflection of the American context; however, in the

such an agenda: "That's how it is, a weapon is power! Mao Tse Tung himself says that the greatest political power is the barrel of a gun, and he is right".

In Germany, however, the construction of social coercion through armed means does not seem to be as present, with the State still being understood as the mediator and responsible for regulating the entry of immigrants. Urban violence in the country is not armed, but it is still attributed to the Other. Simon's (22 years old, Germany) narrative is especially interesting because it combines two fundamental components for analysis. He says:

> We all want this country. Basically, to save it from... the people... who are leading us to an energy crisis caused by us. From... I don't want to use the word, especially from a flood of culturally strange people (einer Überflutung von kulturfremden Menschen), which leads us to believe that they could solve our shortage of skilled workers when they themselves cannot easily write and speak their own language. We want to build a strong argument. We want to campaign for an immigration system like those of Switzerland, Canada, New Zealand, and Australia. We need qualified people.

Firstly, there is the idea of salvation and then the use of "culturally strange people" (kulturfremden Menschen). Such vocabulary is established within the movements of the European radical right, which have treated identity, nationality, and culture as rigid, innate, and immutable instances. Thus, by labelling immigrants as culturally strange, the idea of a "normal" is established, and a system of representation is constructed that opposes the "normals" to the "culturally strange".

A fundamental image of the construction of this system is found in the recent slogan of the AfD, which says "*Deutschland, aber normal!*" (Germany, but normal!). The slogan is launched amid the pandemic and is well illustrated by a political campaign in which the AfD begins with a voice-off: "normal—what is that nowadays?" This question is then seen being typed into an online search engine. Next, scenes of family life are aesthetically portrayed in the style of a Super-8 amateur film from the 1960s or 1970s, in which a heterosexual and white family is sat at table and laughs happily. Then you hear: "In the past, it used to be said that being normal was somewhat boring. Completely normal and square". Then there is a visual shift to the present, when we see images of warning signs with coronavirus hygiene measures in public spaces and closed restaurant outdoor areas. "But today? Isn't it that now 'normality' might be what we are missing? What we really want!" The background music becomes more dramatic, followed by images of a young woman with make-up and masked holding a megaphone, an "Antifa" flag waving in the wind, and in front of the Brandenburg Gate, a protest banner in front of the G20 and burning barricades: "Why has the world around us become so crazy". Another shift leads to emotionally charged scenes of a white family, "and suddenly we realize that 'normal' is something very special... Normal is a home"; a woman paints the garden fence with her daughter, "...are safe borders"; a man is handcuffed, without showing his face, "...are clean streets". The view of a village church in an idyllic

theoretical context of this investigation, the analytical effort undertaken here is to unravel what are the discourses that address young people in such a way that, in their process of identification, this becomes an agenda of extreme urgency.

landscape of forests and fields, "normal is simply beautiful", and finally Berlin at sunset, "*Deutschland. Aber normal*".[25]

This propaganda provides a very clear view of the mechanisms used to construct the elements that place the "normal" under attack. Families once again appear as a central element of "normality",[26] which is threatened by the government's restrictive measures during the pandemic, by protest movements (which focus on Antifas and the Greens), and finally, by the "faceless", those who are not contained by the fence, in a clear reference to immigrants. Roy (2022) found the same discourse in her interviews with women members of the AfD and the FPÖ. She will highlight that the women describe themselves as "normal", emphasizing that one of the interviewees will say, "I am a completely normal person, a completely normal woman".

On one hand, Roy identifies that such a narrative reflects a field of argumentation that seeks to sustain that the party would not be "so bad", since women like her, completely "normal", would also have a place. However, in a broader field, the idea of "normal" is extended to what Wodak and Reisigl (2015) will define as cultural(ist) racism. Racism is defined by Anthias and Yuval-Davis (1992, p. 2) as "modes of exclusion, inferiorization, subordination, and exploitation" that will vary according to social and historical contexts. For the authors, "otherness" would be constituted from elements such as skin colour, ethnic categories, culture, and religion, producing the idea of an "immutable and deviant" Other. Anthias and Yuval-Davis (1992) align with Achille Mbembe (2020) when this author says that "culture" becomes the new central element of racism, now understood as a result of genealogical differences. Wodak (2015) says that this is constituted from a process of ascription, in which characteristics and stereotypes are attributed to a specific group based on their cultural, ethnic, or religious origins. Through this process, the idea of the group's inferiority is perpetuated, justifying their exclusion, marginalization, or discrimination.

Mulinari and Neergaard (2015) define cultural(ist) racism as based on "two key assumptions: first, that culture (or religion) is a characteristic essentially similar to biology, an essence; second, that there is a 'natural' connection between place (nation) and culture, allowing the claim of a culture as superior" (Mulinari & Neergaard, 2015, p. 508). Fekete (2009) also argues that, in current racism, cultural justifications have replaced racial justifications and that, for example, "Muslim culture"—despite its diversity—is presented as monolithic and constructed as "foreign' and incompatible with European values. A dominant racist narrative is, for

[25] For the full video, see https://www.youtube.com/watch?v=XHNlw2tuuDk

[26] Safatle (2020) provides an analysis of the "overlap between the social body and family structure" that seems to occur in the case of the cited advertisement. He will say that such overlap has a clear function. "Everything happens as if the family were the model of 'harmonious relations' that would have the power to eliminate the often seemingly insurmountable nature of social conflicts. Familism in politics presupposes the social fantasy of the family as a nucleus of naturalized, non-problematic hierarchical relations, of authority based on love and devotion. A nucleus in which the social places of authority and submission are natural places. Something very distant from the Freudian explanation of the family as a nucleus producing neuroses" (Safatle, 2020, p. 22).

example, that European Muslims cling to their culture, thus being unable to "integrate" (Fekete, 2009, p. 85). This narrative manifests when Simon labels migrants as "antisocial".

To reflect on this issue and the demands for integration, I consider the trajectory of Nissin (23 years old, Germany) important and illustrative. Coming from a Muslim family, he decides to convert to Christianity. He identifies as someone with a migratory background but seeks to differentiate himself from other immigrants by identifying as a conservative Christian German. His transformation process is marked by baptism, which symbolizes a broader process of integration. The young man comments that, previously, he felt that people did not take him seriously. By undergoing a process described as "self-improvement", he begins to be treated with more respect and to be truly noticed. Thus, it is observed that integration is conditioned to the abandonment of original references and adherence to a new system of representation, within which the demarcation of new style and appearance also differentiates him from the "culture" of other immigrants.

As illustrated throughout this chapter, the signifier "culture"[27] appears as central to the radical right, which is also reflected in the recurrence of the term according to the word cloud. Hall (2000) already predicted that the struggles for power and meanings would become increasingly symbolic and discursive, consequently taking the form of cultural politics. However, I consider that readings about the current scenario as a "cultural war"[28] (Quadros, 2014; Santos, 2020) bring risks regarding the reinforcement of a binary and the identification of an internal enemy, which are intrinsic parts of the radical right's systems of representation. The radical right has reinforced its position as a countermovement by declaring to operate a "cultural counter-revolution". Thus, by stating that we are facing a cultural war, the idea of

[27] Igreja (2021) develops an anthropological study focused on the analysis of the relationship of Bolsonarism with ethnic-racial identities, primarily indigenous. In the case of the interviews in this research, the indigenous issue did not gain prominence; however, there are elements of the research that corroborate the understanding of the construction of the Other and the position of alterity in radical rights. The researcher highlights that "multiculturalism" gains strength in the 1990s in the global North and South but acquires new meanings under the influence of global neoliberalism and the rise of far-right governments. Such groups would bring debates about "identity", "culture", and "cultural essentialisms" to the core of politics, giving them new meanings. Identities, in this context, would be radicalized and instrumentalized, constructed at the borders, and in interaction with the discourse about the Other. Thus, the study also highlights that it is in the construction of the Other that global radical rights seek to provide elements for a cohesive identification among their supporters and activists.

[28] The concept of "culture wars" was retrieved from the 1990s and the book *Culture Wars* by James Davison Hunter, in 1991. In the book, the opposition between two antagonistic worldviews is presented, one related to conservatism and the right and the other related to progressivism, associated with groups on the political spectrum of the left. The phenomenon is described with a focus on interpretations of dilemmas considered moral. I understand that, when we think about the field of differences, there is an attempt to emphasize that there is a conflict in our times around the definitions of culture; however, the concept of "war" seems to reinforce a view of continuity of the Cold War and, with that, a reductionist polarity, which can serve, more directly, the systems of representation operated by radical rights.

the existence of internal enemies—who need to be identified and pursued—is reactivated, and the discourse that positions the problems as located in "culture" is also reinforced. Nuria (19 years old, Brazil) will say:

> Because we have that famous Brazilian way of getting ahead of others. So this moral problem that Brazil has is what generates other problems. Because Brazil likes to get ahead because of culture. So it is both cultural and moral that Brazil has problems that, unfortunately, will take a while to fix. Because it's not just every four years, electing a president that will fix this. But rather gradually, because it's a cultural issue, so Brazil's problem is indeed in culture and morality, which generates other problems.

It is understood that the signifier "culture" has been appropriated and revisited in a way to emphasize elements of "human nature", which will be interpreted through moral and binary paths. In the German case, there is a deepening of the problem, as immigrants are pointed out as a problem in the face of an issue conceived as "cultural". When speaking of the "culturally strange", culture is not only understood as something static; a valuation path is established in which deviant behaviours are linked to a "culture". Thus, it is also understood that the meanings and contexts of use of the signifiers—listed from the recurrence analysis done through the NVivo software—are important to understand the grammar of the new right-wing movements. In the following sections, I proceed, therefore, to the analysis of some of these signifiers, seeking to understand processes of emptying or dispute that allow a strategic use, which becomes fundamental in the implementation of the political projects of such groups and movements.

5.1.6 *The People and the Populace (*der Volk*): Concealment of Power and Oppression Relations*

At the centre of the word cloud generated and illustrated at the beginning of the chapter (Table 5.1 and Fig. 5.1), we find the signifiers "people"[29] which make up 3% of recurrence within the 100 most used terms. During the transcription and the analysis itself, this was not a noted element, but, in light of the result, I returned to the interviews and sought to understand how the terms were used by the young people. Going back through the interviews allowed me to observe that the terms were used for "generalizations", that is, when constituting their observations and explanations in terms of their political projects, the young people intensely addressed what a "general set"—of which they see themselves as a part of —desired, did, needed, or experienced. "We" and "the people" referred to an apparently homogeneous group that shared the same anxieties and projects with them. This dimension can be observed when Nuria (19 years old, Brazil) says:

[29] The term "people" was directly used in the interviews in English, but it is also used as a translation for the terms "pessoas" in Portuguese and "Volk" and "Menschen" in German. The different uses will be discussed.

> But I will not represent only my community but all the people. Because it doesn't matter if the person is just Christian, I care if they are a human being. Because people like to make this segregation, right? Oh, separate the white from the black, these things, but I don't like this separation of people because of that. I like to know the following, that the law says "we are equal before the law". Obviously, we have different social and economic expectations, but the law makes things fairer for the people. So I seek justice for all the people and not just for what suits me, but for the people.

This element draws attention and aligns with some analyses made in previous sections (Costa, 2021) that point out that, in the discourse of radical right-wing groups, power relations are concealed. Berg (2018) also states that, in the discourse of German radical right-wing groups, processes of attribution, homogenization, and generalization are used. It is noticeable that the recurrence of terms related to class and inequality is practically null. "Oppression", "poverty", "wealth", and "precariousness" do not seem to conform to the grammar of the political struggle of young activists; in contrast, terms like "economy", "freedom", "culture", and "money" gain centrality.

The frequent use of "people" also raised questions about its specific meanings in the original languages. As a result, it was necessary to address translation-related issues. In German and Portuguese, the terms "Volk" and "povo" (populace) and "Menschen" or "pessoas" (people) have distinct meanings. However, in the English interviews (2 out of 12), "people" can be translated as either "populace" or "people", depending on the context. The approach to this issue involved performing a translation that was informed by the discursive context.

An example where "people" could be equivalent to populace is found when Nissin (23 years old, Germany) says:

> I would never consider myself an extremist. I have no hatred against any minority or anything like that. I'm just saying that, for example, when it comes to migration, I'm just saying that it's getting out of control and that the policy is no longer focused on our own populace, for the people who live in Germany, who have lived here for many years. Even the migrants who have lived here for many years are just making policy for other countries. For example, we had a big flood last year in Germany, in the western part of Germany. And the government decided to give only 300 euros to each person living in that area at first. And, at the same time, they sent 300 million euros to Afghanistan. And everyone was thinking: "Well, this is our own **populace",** the people are suffering from the floods and no longer have a home. But the government still has 300 million for Afghanistan.

To have a better understanding of the difference, it is essential to understand the development around the idea of "German populace" (Deutsche Volk). A rather important name is Erich Keyser. The historian and ethnologist, influenced by the folklorist Adolf Helbok, defined the *Volk* (people) as a "historically developed community life, in which people, due to their family descent, form a blood community and a functional community and, in this way, differentiate themselves from other peoples" (Keyser, 1935, p. 3). Keyser became known for his collaboration with National Socialism, developing research that reinforced ideas about the existence of a German ethnicity, which was explored through racial research (*Rassenforchung*). Keyser also claimed that the composition of the people would be related to the region inhabited by the population (*Bevölkesraum*), which would constitute a "living space" of specific human communities. His approach, therefore, pointed to the existence of an essence and a value of contemporary "Germanism", based on the identification of a racial-biological "core" of the German people, as well as "foreign" elements in its ethnic body (*Volkskörper*) (Pinwinkler, 2004).

Santos (2018) explains that National Socialism, based on such theories, employs the discourse about the need for expansion and preservation of the *Volk*, which would be an "organic entity" that "had to be secured by any means" (Santos, 2018, p. 41). In other words, there would be a need for policies that promoted the preservation of the numbers of this racially pure people. Thus, the concepts of "*Volk*", "*Rasse*", and "*Bevölkesraum*" are considered intrinsically connected to the Nazi past, being avoided by various political groups. The turning point occurs with the rise of radical right-wing movements in the last decade, which reclaim the concept[30] through a new theory centred on the *Bevölksraum* (people's space) and centred on the concept of "culture". In ethnopluralism—positioned as an alternative to multiculturalism—it is understood that peoples "belong" to specific regions of the planet and should remain there.

Considering such a connection with the National Socialist past, I sought to understand when such terms were used and in what contexts they emerged. Simon (22 years old, Germany) says that:

> However, we do none of that, **because our state spends money all over the world, but has nothing for its own population (*die eigene Bevölkerung*).** This is causing extreme discontent. Especially because we are advised to take cold showers or use only a cloth to clean ourselves, to save energy. And, thus, this cannot continue. **It is terrible. These are not future prospects, because this year will not be the last year we have shortages.**

Similarly to Nissin, *Bevölkerung*[31] is used to argue regarding government spending, which should be directed only to "the German people". Considering the fact that such discourses are mobilized in direct association with the anti-immigration agenda, the idea that the ethnic-racial connotations of the past are reinstated is strengthened.

Regarding the terms *Volk* and *Bevölkerung*, the case of Thomas (22 years old, Germany) is noteworthy, as he does not use the term at any time to refer to Germany

---

[30] The slogan of the PEGIDA group, "*Wir sind das Volk*" (We are the people), is a reference to racial theories about the composition of the people, within a movement whose main banner is the fight against the Islamization of the West (Volk, 2020).

[31] On the AfD website, for example, there is a section for news and texts related to the family, where there is a news article titled "*Familienförderung und Bevölkerungsentwicklung*" (Family support and population development). There, the ethnic connotation of the term is evident: "The dramatic increase in the number of people without marriage and without children and the disappearance of normal medium-sized families—which the main political parties have already accepted as inevitable—are leading to a reduction of our native population (*angestammten Bevölkerung*) by more than 250 thousand people per year, with a trend of significant increase. The AfD (Alternative for Germany) opposes this trend of self-denial and wishes to make German society fundamentally more family and child-friendly. Germany, given the current demographic conditions, needs a paradigm shift towards a population policy (*Bevölkerungspolitik*) in the form of an activating family policy" (Alternative für Deutschland, n.d.).

but allows himself to use "*brasilianische Volk*", highlighting the need for this "people" to become a strong nation:

> It is an important aspect for **the Brazilian people to become strong, a strong nation. If the people continue to divide themselves**, Brazil will never be able to become the leading power, the great economic and diplomatic power in the South American continent. (...) **The Brazilian people need to become part of politics,** take responsibility for the entire South American continent, if politicians can no longer do this.

In a complex manner, it is perceived that the generalizations provided through the use of people are inverted when the arguments become the state's priority systems. The generalization that seeks to appear as an "inclusive" dimension of radical right-wing movements is nullified by the presence of various normativities that define distinct values for people based on gender, nationality, ethnicity, religion, and sexual orientation. In this sense, I return to Butler (2000), when reflecting on the weight of bodies, highlighting that categorization systems that seek to present themselves as general, inclusive, and natural are precisely those that prioritize the construction of a deviant Other. In the German case, the *völkisch* discourses seem to function as biopolitical instruments whose function is to regulate the people according to a biological-national and racial conception. In the Brazilian case, the discourses about the law-abiding citizens also seem to perform the same function, highlighting the limitations of the guarantee of rights, clearly translated by the idea that "human rights" should be directed at "righteous humans".

5.1.7 The Calculations of Freedom: Social Justice as Coercion

"Freedom" also appeared as a central signifier in the discourses of the young people, emerging as a term of high recurrence. The theme has already been widely explored through research that seeks to highlight the new conceptions of freedom established in the face of neoliberal normativity (Dardot & Laval, 2016; da Silva Junior, 2020; Franco et al., 2020). Here, I aim to reflect on how such normativities are reflected in the narratives of the young interviewees, selecting some excerpts in which freedom is presented as an agenda:

> But I also have some people from the past who hate me now because I voted for the AfD, which I can't understand at all, because I used to get along very well with them and I wouldn't hate them now if they went to *Fridays for Future*. Even if I... even if I don't like it, go ahead, **that's democracy, that's freedom. Everyone should do what they want.** But you still have to be able to talk about it. And not immediately demonize someone. **(Simon, 22 years old, Germany)**
>
> Now, what we need to be against is dictatorship. Because the dictatorship censored people, left a lot of people imprisoned, and I already know many people who have testimonies, who came from a dictatorship. So **I have to be against that which goes against individual freedom, regardless of whether it is right or left. I know that so many ideologies are flawed in themselves, I have to see; therefore, if it takes away the individual's freedom, if it is something extreme, I have to be against it.** Because I am in favour of individual freedom, so why would I be in favour of something that takes away my

> freedom and that of my neighbour? **That's what I am, my concept is freedom. Property, family, patriotism! (Nuria, 19 years old, Brazil)**
>
> Freedom has always been a very high point. It is the central point. **I think we always have to fight for our freedom. Nothing, nothing, nothing is more precious than our freedom.** Nothing. So this philosophy that I already have inside me began, to go against this issue of dictatorship, against governments, tyranny, against the State. What I have a lot, like, is that I don't like the State. The daddy-State. **Oh, the daddy-State made a law because there are a lot of hypertensive people, so let's take the salt off the table. No! The person has to have the right. If they want it, the State cannot say no. (Letícia, 32 years old, Brazil)**
>
> **The freedom to undertake is something that the conservative also defends, because economic liberalism, while socialism defends everything unified, but it didn't work.** (...) **And inflation, health problems, infrastructure problems, and several other problems** that existed at the time of the Soviet Union with Stalin's socialist government. And, in the course of this, I went to see the other side of the coin. I identified and saw that this works. So, for me, it was this trajectory, **of studying both sides and identifying with what is really the most correct when it comes to the human being, you know? Which are the principles, economic freedom. And the Judeo-Christian moral that is our Western base for our democracy and for our development. (Vinicius, 25 years old, Brazil)**

As we see, in the set of discourses, freedom starts to be defined from what denies it. In other words, there is a prevalence of negative notions of freedom, through which the State is positioned as a potential tyrant, responsible for the implementation of dictatorships. The only one who defines it more directly is Simon (22 years old, Germany) when he says that "everyone should do what they want". Avoiding an analysis of the intrinsic contradiction of such a statement in light of the proposed political project, I emphasize that the narrative reveals that submission to the law starts to be presented as a matter of choice, in terms of cost-benefit.

da Silva Junior (2020) points out that the new social contract[32] in force can be understood from the concept of freedom proposed in the discourses of some of the main theorists of neoliberalism. Thus, there would be new psychic dynamics sustained by administrative rationality, which would be the formal principle of the policy proposed by the neoliberal discourse. These new dynamics, in the social dimension, would be sustained by a moral discourse, which defines that, for the free subject, "submission to the law is a rational choice, based on a cost-benefit calculation" (da Silva Junior, 2020, p. 276). Both Friedman and Hayek emphasize that freedom is always based on the notion of choice that will occur in the face of a natural and reflective calculation, whose bases are the laws of the market. It is no wonder that, often, freedom is presented as associated with economic issues, which are also positioned as reproducers of something "natural and correct" to man, as expressed by Vinicius (25 years old, Brazil).

Letícia (32 years old, Brazil) is the one who directly points to the State as a "constrainer" and "limiter" of freedoms. This notion prevails more in narratives coming from Brazil but is also present in the German case when referring to the pandemic

[32] The notion of social contract can be taken as "correlate to Foucault's concept of modes of subjectivation (1994), because it deals with the discursive formations and social devices in which the subjects constitute themselves as such" (da Silva Junior, 2020, p. 259).

period, during which isolation measures were understood as part of state tyranny. Brown (2018) analyses that freedom has become an abstract principle of ensuring personal freedom against the presumed coerciveness of political life. This principle is widely mobilized by radical right-wing groups to challenge norms of equality, tolerance, and inclusion in the name of freedom and choice. One of the consequences is the expansion of hate speech[33] and exclusion, which are also ways to mobilize reactions and provoke discussion about "freedom of expression". Some identified examples are:

> Thus, I really watched many, many speeches in the *Bundestag* by our members of parliament and found them all excellent. I really followed some of the *Bundestag* sessions live. Always on television. That's right. **And I was really excited that somehow all the leftists would be eliminated by us.** And then I also got kind of excited with them. (Alexander, 18 years old, Germany)
>
> **I mean in the sense of, like, the "gender ideology" being buried, never entering the educational institution. And the same for the issue of LGBT agendas, right?** The criminalization of homophobia, it seems very nice to say that you are in favour of the criminalization of homophobia... but at the core of this issue, there is malice. It's that thing, not everything you see is what it is. Not everything you hear is what it is. (Carlos, 19 years old, Brazil)
>
> To me, it means to try to change this country for the better. Sometimes, I would even say not to change it for the better, but to save it**. We have to save this country and we can only do it together**. I as a right-wing activist. We are in favour of the rule of law (*Rechtsstaatlichkeit*). **We are in favour of finally helping the citizens of this country again, giving them a helping hand, and not some antisocial migrants who come here because they immediately get Hartz4.** (Simon, 22 years old, Germany)

Hate speech emerged in the interviews as disaffected affects,[34] that is, they appeared as arguments occupying a place similar to the entire set of the radical right-wing political agenda, with a weak connection to personal trajectories. Strategically, hate speech has expanded the "protected personal sphere", especially within social networks that, when intertwined with the universe of large corporations, reinforce the discourse that "state regulation" is coercive and similar to dictatorial power. As this "protected personal sphere" gains more space, rights that were originally claimed for the individual are extended to corporations, families, and churches. Privatization, for Brown (2018), also operates in confronting and positioning "social justice" as

---

[33] "Hate speeches" are those that tend to insult, intimidate, or harass people due to their race, colour, ethnicity, nationality, sex, gender, religion, or political stance or are still connected to their potential or capacity to incite violence, hatred, or discrimination against groups or individuals. The legal definition is widely discussed and debated, but here we use a broad definition to discuss, in a more in-depth manner, its effect in the public sphere.

[34] Brown (2018) proposes understanding this manifestation as an exercise of unrestricted power, stemming from a "desublimation of the will to power". It traces back to the works of Nietzsche and Freud and states that, to align with life in society, it would be necessary to sublimate impulses and instincts, for Freud, and the will to power, for Nietzsche. The philosopher will say that, in the face of a recent nihilism, there is a retreat to a will to power in its elemental form, with the attachment to religion and moral values as cynical instruments for the use of power. I find it "appealing" to think this way, but the limit of such consideration would be to trace back to the idea of an inherently evil or uncontrolled human nature.

tyrannical. The position assumed by radical right-wing actors and movements is that their actions are reactions to a system of promoting social justice positioned as dictatorial and repressive. Thus, an attempt is made to broaden the limits of the private, with the expansion of hate speech in the public arena and the consequent argument about "freedom of expression".

Butler (2021), in her book *Excitable Speech: A Politivs of the Performative*, incites a fruitful discussion regarding the dynamics of expansion in recent years. The author emphasizes that hate speech has the aim to offend, but in this discursive act, the one who is addressed immediately becomes a subject to whom one speaks. This means that groups that have been constantly attacked through discourse have also emerged on the public scene, becoming increasingly visible. Butler always refers to spaces of appearance, that is, the public sphere as composed of those who "embody" the possibility of being spoken of. I use this reference not to position myself regarding what should be done "legally" in relation to such speeches but to raise the alert that the public sphere (of appearance) in recent years has been strongly "conformed" and "discursively" led by radical right-wing groups. Noting this alerts us to the conformation of a logic of "attack and counterattack", which favours the loss of dimensions that were once fundamental in politics—that is, both in theoretical constructions about politics and democracy and in procedural dimensions that promoted spaces for negotiation and deliberation for project construction. In relation to this, I highlight the discourse about madness, which emerged in interviews in both countries and plays a similar role, positioning individuals as incapable of making "rational choices".

5.1.8 The Discourse of Madness: Urgency and Radicality of Action

In the interviews, an element identified and still little explored was the reference by young people to a state of madness or degradation of society. Such madness, associated with a lack of control, seems to function as important calls for the urgency (and radicality) of the necessary action. Normally, these discourses are composed of generalizations, not being something circumscribed to a group or minority, which could be framed as hate speech. In the case of these narratives, it is society and youth that are interpreted through the lens of pathologization and, consequently, the inability to make rational choices.

The use of madness to incarcerate and discipline bodies is an element that has been widely explored (Foucault, 1961, 1971; Corbanezi, 2009); however, researchers (Safatle et al., 2020) have been investigating its meaning in terms of the pathologization of the social. The authors state that the transformations of politics are today related to the mobilization of a moral psychology that justifies "economic actions and the paralysis of criticism through the massive mobilization of psychological and moral discourses" (p. 20). For them, when criticisms within the political field are displaced to pathological descriptions, the dimension of negotiation, deliberation, and decision is eliminated from the public sphere. Carlos (19 years old, Brazil) states that:

> then only very strong and very fierce civil disobedience, as happened in Ukraine, can change something in Brazil. But I see that Brazilians don't want to do that. They complain, complain, but instead of helping each other, they go and report the merchant who is opening their business. Merchant reporting merchant, so Brazil is in total madness. We are crazier than March of last year.

In other words, saying that Brazil is in madness legitimizes the need to change the courses of action. In line with this, Nuria (20 years old, Brazil) also turns madness into a realization that there are no longer conditions for dialogue and understanding:

> And it is also thanks to the fact that the Brazilian people have always been very innocent, very lazy to study, that they elected certain presidents, who, I'm sorry, but harmed the economy. Harmed everything here in Brazil. So, many times, when I try to say this to young people, they curse me! Even when I'm stating the obvious, it's the same thing I had seen in a book, which says the following, "that the world is so crazy that one day you will have to explain to people why the grass is green". The world is already at that level. I have to explain the obvious to people, the same as explaining why 2 plus 2 is 4.

Finally, Moritz (23 years old, Germany) will say that there is a decadence in society, which causes wealth to be lost:

> Ah, I think there is also a kind of decadence in society in general, because maybe you can see that younger people now are getting dumber and more degenerate and... Hmm. There was, like, after World War II, the generation that created a great amount of wealth. And that's why people in other countries say: "Ah, Germany is such a rich country" and so on. But I think the current generation is doing everything to obtain these conditions and this state. I hope you understand what I mean.

In the case of these last two narratives, it is essential to indicate that the evidence of madness and degeneration is seen in the economy and the country's wealth. The "neoliberal social pact" would centralize the "protection" of the market from any threat, which could even come from the population that, with their poor choices, could harm it. In other words, the correlation between the economy and the moral and individual behaviour of people is sustained, nullifying dimensions of power relations based on exploitation and expropriation. By saying that society is crazy or degenerate, behaviours are deemed irrational, and coercive and violent actions gain greater legitimacy. In other words, if people are no longer acting "rationally", some external power may be called upon to act to put things "in place".

Safatle (2020) will say that one of the important contemporary facts is also the redescribing of the motivational logic of political action to a grammar of emotions. He will say that political struggles are no longer described in political terms, such as "justice", "equity", "exploitation", and "inequality", but through emotional terms. In relation to this, I highlight that one of the signifiers that was excluded from the cloud due to its grammatical classification, but which was discussed in the field of youth trajectories, deserving attention, is "against". When inserted into the universe of the 100 most recurrent terms, it stands out with a 0.33%. Often, the radical right positioning of being "against" was read as destructive, as well as evidence of the absence of a political project. However, through the analysis of trajectories and narratives, it is perceived that being "against" promotes a subjective position and an important identification for young activists, not constituting a barrier or impediment to the expansion of a political project. Igor (23 years old, Brazil) mentions that:

> I have never been the type who likes everything to lead to the same conclusion. I even like to be a bit against, with some things, to hear what the other side has to say. If it makes sense, if it doesn't make sense, because if everyone agreed with everyone, I think life wouldn't have much emotion.

He is not the only one who states that being "against" something and being able to position oneself this way provides a life with "more emotion". However, it is understood that when Igor says "what the other side has to say", he revisits binary divisions between me/them, what I am, and what I am against. Such identity polarities reinforce a homogenization of groups and a call for young people to immediately position themselves within this duality. The challenge seems to lie in showing what is beyond, that is, giving space to what is outside the dual polarity in the public sphere. It is in this place that I locate the search for bonds and the fragments of resistance found in the narratives, as "loose ends" and spaces of action that do not cater to the maintenance of the orders of domination and social polarization promoted by the radical right.

5.1.9 The Search for Bonds and the Fissures of Resistance

Returning to the "systems of representation" and the analysis of neoliberalism, it is important to consider that, in the last decade, many analyses of neoliberalism pointed to a fetishization of individuals, producing fragmentation and narcissism, with a progressive destruction/weakening of social ties (Boltanski & Chiapello, 1999; Bauman, 1999). This critique can even be found at the end of Dardot and Laval's (2016) analysis, when they point out that collective action would be weakened in the face of a growth of social selfishness and the denial of solidarity.

In analysing the narratives and reconstructing the trajectories, I did not find elements that directly corroborate this interpretation. Quite the opposite, I observed that there is still an active search for social ties, as well as a concern with elements of collectivity. A fundamental issue seems to be that the young people interviewed identify within a common political spectrum, yet they admit to sharing political spaces with peers who align with different strands. They emphasize that, in these spaces, they find dialogue and exchange. Letícia (32 years old, Brazil) describes this process:

> And this whole issue of politics, of being exposed to this issue, **I ended up meeting people with whom I would never think of having a friendship**, with whom I would have a conversation, with whom I would have so many points in common… and that is very cool. That is what is bringing very relevant positive points. In this whole issue of text, of the internet, I ended up in a project. Which is a group that does live streams practically every day to talk

> about everything. Economy, politics, philosophy, everything, everything that is on the agenda of the day, **we each start to speak from our own perspective.**

In academia, this has already been interpreted as an exchange "among equals"; however, the reconstruction of trajectories carried out in the context of this research allows questioning such a perspective. The homogenization of the radical right also seems to be operated from the outside, through the construction of the image of a "cohesive" set. In Brazil, this translates into the expansion and adherence to the term and stigma of "bolsonarista". In the narratives, it is noticeable that the groups organized by these young people do not focus solely on supporting the candidate, but multiply, gaining names related to patriotism and conservatism. Nuria (19 years old, Brazil) says that:

> And then, if I say that I am a patriot, everyone will refer me to Bolsonaro. Because Bolsonaro raises the Brazilian flag, but I don't need to be a *bolsonarista* to support Brazil. I am a normal person who wants individual freedom! I am a patriot, yes, but that doesn't mean I am in favour of Bolsonaro. That's just what people need to realize.

The groups seem to present themselves as sufficiently "open" to accept and engage in dialogue with people with different levels of engagement and alignment with the agendas. This trait seems fundamental to understanding the expansion experienced in the spaces of the radical right in recent years—especially in the digital environment.

In the German case, the analysis of the radical right has also focused on the AfD. The party has occupied a place similar to "bolsonarism", as it has been widely discussed in academic and media discourse. Even in the present research, when referencing the literature discussing the theme in Germany, it is noted that the party is the main focus. The role of Jair Bolsonaro and the AfD in configuring a discourse and political grammar of the radical right is not denied. However, not treating the young people as bolsonaristas or as "AfD supporters" was a theoretical choice, which sought to give visibility to the variety of trajectories and identifications found in the interviews. Although most interviewees indicated voting for Bolsonaro, in Brazil, and the AfD, in Germany, the narratives reveal dissatisfactions and the presentation of elements that "remain" and seem to be "adjusted" in the search for representation in the institutional political sphere. Aline (20 years old, Brazil) says that:

> Because people **place a lot of expectation on the president, but don't see that there are senators, federal deputies. Then in the state sphere, there is the governor, state deputy.** People don't think about that either. **That these people also have great importance and power!** It's not just the president. So it ended up that many people were disappointed, many people didn't understand, many people realized only later. I was a bit like that too, because I didn't understand very well. So I came to understand in these four years, right? **So, that's more or less it, that's my criticism, that's my point. It's not that blind view of Bolsonaro, the blind view of a *bolsonarista*, right?**

Thomas (22 years old, Germany) says that:

> In **a city like mine, politics is dealt with in clubs, and in an independent city, laws are enacted.** Do you really understand what this means for you? At least at a certain age, you

> might not even realize the consequences of a decision. But, no matter, when it comes to decisions in the municipal parliament, in this case, the city council, the decisions made by the city administration affect you directly, they affect your living environment. And so I decided to get involved with other spaces as well. More and more, I participated in discussions, but I began to realize that perhaps it would be better not just to talk but also to get actively involved.

The narratives of Aline and Thomas also indicate an important phenomenon: the learning processes involved in engagement. The young activists interviewed demonstrate a concern with various instances of participation and deliberation, considering it essential that their groups are represented at different levels. Moreover, they gain knowledge about the functioning of power instances. The narratives reveal that—in the very process of participation—from various demands and identifications, young people develop interest and expand their knowledge about such instances and their functioning. Many admit wanting to act at local level, which, in some cases, seems to be "the possible order", but in others, it also seems to represent a realization that local politics have a significant influence on daily life.

Regarding daily life, it is important to indicate that the experience of many young people ends up reflecting an "empirical" perception of the mechanisms of power and their effects in terms of "abuses" and "oppressions". Thus, some narratives highlight fissures and the emergence of discourses that break the articulation of the "signifying chain" of the radical right. Carlos (19 years old, Brazil), for example, talks about the military police:

> And today we observe that it is quite different, you cannot give power. Brazilians have a syndrome of the oppressed who want to be oppressors, right? This is especially true in the military police, because they don't understand that they are proletarians just like us. They understand that they are something different, that they are participating in the power game, but no, the military police is an instrument of those in power.

It is noted that Carlos lists power as influential in the way institutions operate. Beyond that, the fact of speaking about "the oppressed who want to become oppressors" and the condition of "proletarian" shows that there are intersections of other political projects in the construction of his grammar. Still regarding Carlos's narratives, it is noteworthy that he was the only young person who mentioned being black and living in the periphery, addressing racism in terms of a personal experience:

> What really exists is class prejudice in Brazil. There is no structural prejudice as they say in all areas, but there is class prejudice. Let's suppose... if you are from a certain economic class, another economic class above you will have prejudice against you. This is clear, completely clear. This happens with white, Japanese, black, everything... If you are not well behaved in a shopping mall, everyone will look at you in a strange way, right? They will think you... will do something. Of course, there is also the connotation of colour, the bourgeois class is somewhat racist, yes. Now the middle class, the lower middle class, lower... is not racist! Now what really needs to be done, in my view, far from being a guy to formulate public policy, is to end this thing, like Milton Friedman—a Brazilian author, not Brazilian, I mean American—he says, right: "treat the other by name, not say the black man, the white man". Foster this type of division and also be tougher in the case of real racism. What happens that I see in colleges today? Formulate what racism is. Everything, nowadays, can be considered racism, not by what the person does, but by what the person is. I see a lot in college, if the person, the people are more right-wing, more Bolsonaro,

> everything else... everything they do will be considered racism, now if a left-wing guy says "you monkey and everything else"... Then no, then no, it's a different interpretation of the law, everything else... and there is no punishment, there is not even any process, so this hypocrisy has to end and... really want to solve it.

The young man begins by admitting the difference in classes and the existence of racism; however, in seeking to (re)align himself with what has been interpellating him, he mentions the need to annul these traits to treat the "other by name". Finally, he ends up leading his own reflection to a critique of the left, resuming a frequently brought-up theme, which concerns the existence of a "distinct treatment" for the left and the right in educational spaces and universities. Such a narrative is yet another portrait that his life experience brings perceptions about power relations; however, such experiences end up being reversed into reiterations of the binary between left and right.

Regarding the reinterpretation of experiences, it is also highlighted that most of the Brazilian interviewees presented arguments about an expansion of interest in politics after 2018, associated with the electoral process. These elections were pointed out as a moment of access to the public sphere, never before reached. Igor (23 years old, Brazil) comments:

> I think that anywhere I go, there will be one or another person interested in this, because, as I said, after 2018, I think Brazilian society as a whole is becoming more interested in politics, whether it is to agree with the current government, or to disagree. (...) Then I think the 2018 elections reflected, like, **a desire for change,** which I'm not saying happened. I think it didn't happen, because in my current view, in the Brazilian system, the president is just the tip of the *iceberg*. So it's no use changing, so to speak, the major symbol of the executive. **If the representatives themselves are not changed or if society itself is not more conscious of its vote, of who it is voting for, if it doesn't know how to oversee its politicians. So the 2018 election reflected a movement that I don't know if it will continue, but I think it was important that it happened.**

This aligns with Rocha's (2019) analysis of the organization of "counterpublics" that emerge in the public sphere. She draws on Warner (2002) to assert that counterpublics are imbued with a disruptive performativity, consisting of groups that share identities, interests, and discourses so conflicting with the cultural horizon that they risk facing hostile reactions when expressed to dominant public. In this direction, I point out the hostile reactions described by Aline in the face of her anti-feminist activism on the networks:

> Usually, when one of my videos goes viral, right?—on TikTok, usually—it ends up receiving a lot of this, right? Or threats like "kill yourself!" "jump off a bridge!" It's not really a threat, it's harassment? I don't know, I think it would be that. Here in my city, at the beginning, I also received threats. They said they would cancel my CPF and throw a bag of faeces at me. But when they see me on the street, they turn their face (laughs). But on the internet, it's more about harassment, saying **"kill yourself", "jump off a bridge", "hang yourself". Or like "marry a 60-year-old man and have 40 children!" Because since you're against feminism, you have to do that. "Go wash dishes", "wash dishes and take care of your old man", things like that.** But I ignore it, if that's the person's argument, it doesn't matter.

In other words, there is a need to consider that the emergence of counterpublics also brought and brings reactions. It is not necessary to position them as victims in these scenarios but to observe that part of the radicalization processes is also connected to the hostility found in external environments. In other words, the more hostile the outside world seems, the greater the chances of closure and identification with more radical agendas.

Still on the assertion that there would have been greater access to the public sphere from 2018, a question arises about the reverberation of this access in terms of reducing inequality in the field of political participation. I bring this up because Fuks, in 2011, concluded that economic inequality had a considerable impact on inequality in youth political participation: Young people with more educated parents and more elite professional occupations were the ones who participated most in civil society organizations, student activities, and specific political actions. It would be very difficult to measure this change solely in terms of the emergence of radical right movements because we are talking about a period of multiplication of movements based on differences, as well as massive expansion of access to higher education. However, it seems essential to highlight that youth have gained space in these new groups, also including a series of collectives that have promoted and directed the formation of young leaders. On one hand, we can revisit discussions about the need for young people for the legitimation of political projects, and on the other, it is also an indication that young people have been interested and have approached power structures, seeking to do so without the constant and direct mediation of adults.

Finally, regarding this interest and the engagement of young people, it is noteworthy that all interviewees expressed the desire to be actors of social change. Nuria (19 years old, Brazil) comments that:

> So I do research related to these elected councillors who are from my party. I am affiliated with the party and they always ask me to do these things. Not just my party but also the people who are there in the City Council. So I do this with great pleasure **because I believe in change. That change has to come from within all of us.**

Simon (22 years old, Germany) says that:

> We have many problems here: inflation, high taxes, high gas prices. **And for that, we need the youth. Young people are the politicians of today. Of tomorrow. We need them very much. Definitely, we still have very few of them. That also led me to participate. Yes!**

In this sense, the research aligns with Krasteva (2017) when she creates the category of "contestation citizenship", highlighting that her interviewees also expressed the desire to be actors of social change. The *pathos* of contestation of the far-right youth and the ambition for political innovation are translated by this concept (Krasteva, 2013, 2016), which considers the formation of a new type of citizenship where belonging and participation interfere, but where above all activity and mobilization play a fundamental role. She states that disillusionment with politics, as "usual", has led the youth of the right to engage with the streets and now accumulate protest experience. This is confirmed by narratives that show a majority of young people who participated or participate in protests and mobilizations. The idea of an "expansion of conflict" surpasses the dimension of radical right-wing groups, and the very concept of contestatory citizenship is used by the researcher to bring together, in the German context, the Greens, and the radical right. She points out that, similarly, these groups represent anti-system sentiments, coming into conflict with the socioeconomic analyses prioritized by the left.

This analysis brings to light one of the greatest controversies in constructing the analysis of youth participation in radical right-wing groups. Could it be equated with the political participation of other political spectrums and orientations that align with the promotion of equality? I consider that by interpreting this activism as political participation, it was possible to relate it to other experiences of political participation, which are also driven by the desire for social change and involve learning processes. However, having common origins and sharing similar strategies does not transform their contents.

Thus, I conclude this chapter by highlighting that discursive interpellations—fruits of neoliberal normativities—have an impact and resonance on the participation of young people from various political spectrums. Both "protagonism" and "youth empowerment" have become a "regulatory norm" constantly reiterated in the two countries studied. The great difference—explored during this last chapter—lies in the grammar of the social transformation projects of the radical right. And, considering that, within the scope of the present research, grammar is considered as the articulation of the chain of signifiers—which represents the set of discourses and, consequently, the constitution of reality—we can understand that this project seeks to erase other systems of representation, legitimizing and naturalizing oppressive power relations.

Through the deconstruction of narratives, systems of representation and normativities that sustain the political agendas of the radical right were evidenced. Contrary to what might be expected, a large part of the agendas and issues are not justified through personal experiences but are brought as a reproduction of reiterated discourses in the public sphere. This is an indication that the movements and networks of the radical right are gaining increasing discursive efficacy and need to be combated not at an individual level but at an institutional level, in order to repopulate the public sphere and ensure it as an environment for dialogue and negotiation. For this reason, I seek, in the final considerations, to also highlight how the fissures of resistance identified in this section can guide the construction of democratic alternatives to confront the processes of radicalization.

References

Albino, C., Oliveira, J., & Melo, M. (2021). *Neoliberalismo, neoconservadorismo e crise em tempos sombrios*. Editora Seriguela.

Almeida, E. (2009). Os estudos sobre grupos juvenis: presenças e ausências. In *O Estado da Arte sobre juventude na pós-graduação brasileira: Educação, Ciências Sociais e Serviço Social (1999-2006)* (Vol. 2). Argvmentvm.

Alternative für Deutschland. (n.d.). Home. Retrieved January, 2023, from https://www.afd.de/

Anderson, L. L. L. (2019). *Reframing remembrance: A case study on collective memory in far-right party discourse* (Doctoral dissertation, Carleton University).

Ansara, S. (2012). Políticas de memória X políticas do esquecimento: possibilidades de desconstrução da matriz colonial. *Revista Psicologia Política, 12*(24), 297–311.

Anthias, F., & Yuval-Davis, N. (1992). *Racialised boundaries: Race, nation, colour and class and the anti-racist struggle*. Routledge.
Arquidiocese de São Paulo. (1985). *Brasil: nunca mais*. Vozes.
Athanasiou, A. (2021). Estados de emergência, modos de emersão: atuações críticas de "o povo" em tempos de crise. In C. Albino, J. Oliveira, & M. Melo (Eds.), *Neoliberalismo, neoconservadorismo e crise em tempos sombrios*. Editora Seriguela. (Original work published in 2011).
Bauman, Z. (1999). *O mal-estar da pós-modernidade*. Companhia das Letras.
Becker, G. (1981). *Treatise on the family*. University of Chicago Press.
Berg, L. (2018). Between anti-feminism and ethnicized sexism. In M. Fielitz & N. Thurston (Eds.), *Post-digital cultures of the far right: Online actions and offline consequences in Europe and the US*. Transcript.
Binder, W. (2021). Memory culture, the civil sphere, and right-wing populism in Germany. In J. Alexander, P. Kivisto, & G. Sciortino (Eds.), *Populism in the civil sphere* (pp. 178–204). Polity Press.
Boltanski, L., & Chiapello, E. (1999). *Le nouvel esprit du capitalisme* (Vol. 10). Gallimard.
Brown, W. (2018). Neoliberalism's Frankenstein: Authoritarian freedom in twenty-first century "democracies". *Critical Times, 1*(1), 60–79.
Brown, W. (2019). *In the ruins of neoliberalism: The rise of antidemocratic politics in the west*. Columbia University Press. https://doi.org/10.7312/brow19384
Browning, D. (2003). Critical familism, civil society, and the law. *Hofstra Law Review, 32*(1), 313.
Butler, J. (2000). Corpos que pesam: sobre os limites discursivos do "sexo". In G. L. Louro et al. (Eds.), *O corpo educado: pedagogias da sexualidade*. Autêntica.
Butler, J. (2011). Vida precária. *Contemporânea-Revista de Sociologia da UFSCar, 1*(1), 13–33.
Butler, J. (2021). *Excitable speech: A politics of the performative*. Routledge.
Caldeira, T. P. R. (2000). *Cidade de muros: crime, segregação e cidadania em São Paulo*. Editora 34.
Campion, K. (2020). Women in the extreme and radical right: Forms of participation and their implications. *Social Sciences, 9*(9), 149.
Canabarro, I. S. (2014). Caminhos da comissão nacional da verdade (CNV): memórias em construção. *Sequência, 35*(69), 215–234. https://doi.org/10.5007/2177-7055.2014V35N69P215
Cooper, M. (2017). *Family values: Between neoliberalism and the new social conservatism*. MIT Press.
Corbanezi, E. R. (2009). *Sobre a razão do Mesmo que enuncia a não-razão do Outro: às voltas com a História da Loucura e O Alienista*. [Master's thesis, Universidade Estadual de Campinas]. Biblioteca Digital UNICAMP. Retrieved from http://www.bibliotecadigital.unicamp.br/document/?code=000470712
Costa, J. F. A. (2021). Quem é o "cidadão de bem"? *Psicologia USP, 32*.
Couto Neto, G. H. (2019). A "nova direita" no YouTube: conservadorismo e negacionismo histórico sobre a Ditadura Militar brasileira. *Revista Ágora, 29*. Retrieved from https://periodicos.ufes.br/agora/article/view/26411
Cruz, R. (2021). "Sou gay e o movimento LGBTQI+ não me representa": mapeando a emergência de um ativismo gay à direita no Brasil. *Cahiers des Amériques latines, 98*, 43–66.
Cruz, A. V. H., Minchoni, T., Matsumoto, A. E., & Andrade, S. S. (2017). A Ditadura que se Perpetua: Direitos Humanos e a Militarização da Questão Social. *Psicologia: Ciência e Profissão, 37*(spe), 239–252. https://doi.org/10.1590/1982-3703180002017
da Silva Junior, N. (2020). O Brasil da barbárie à desumanização neoliberal: do "Pacto edípico, pacto social", de Hélio Pellegrino, ao "E daí?", de Jair Bolsonaro. In V. Safatle, N. da Silva Junior, & C. Dunker (Eds.), *Neoliberalismo como gestão do sofrimento psíquico*. Autêntica.
Dantas, B. S. D. A. (2013). Psicologia política das religiões: uma análise dos símbolos e ideologias da Igreja Universal do Reino de Deus. *Revista Psicologia Política, 13*(28), 489–506.
Dantas, B. S. A., & Ansara, S. (2020). Articulações entre Memória, Poder e Ideologia: Notas sobre a Conjuntura Política Brasileira. In A. R. Hernandez et al. (Eds.), *Psicologia Política e Memória* (pp. 31–44). Apris.
Dardot, P. & Laval, C. (2016). *A nova razão de mundo: ensaio sobre a sociedade neoliberal*. Boitempo.

eGuinorante. (2021, February 5). *Ditadura: Meu pai te conta como foi* [Video]. YouTube. Retrieved from https://www.youtube.com/watch?v=N1wtmoWkwvk

Farris, S. R. (2017). *In the name of women's rights: The rise of femonationalism*. Duke University Press.

Fekete, L. (2009). *Suitable enemy: Racism, migration and islamophobia in Europe*. Pluto Press.

Festa, M. V. P. (2017). O Projeto Orvil e a introdução da guerra cultural no contexto brasileiro. *Educação Contemporânea - Reflexões, 17*(36).

Foresti, L. F. L. (2013). *O Arauto da Contra-Revolução: O pensamento conservador de Plínio Corrêa de Oliveira (1968-1976)* [Master's thesis, Pontifícia Universidade Católica de São Paulo]. Repositório PUC-SP. Retrieved from https://sapientia.pucsp.br/handle/handle/12775

Foucault, M. (1961). *A História da Loucura na Idade Clássica* (5th ed.). Perspectiva.

Foucault, M. (1971). *A arqueologia do saber*. Vozes.

Foucault, M. (2008a). Nascimento da Biopolítica. In M. Foucault (Ed.), *Curso no Collège de France (1978-1979)*. Martins Fontes.

Foucault, M. (2008b). Segurança, Território, População. In M. Foucault (Ed.), *Curso no Collège de France (1977-1978)*. Martins Fontes.

Franco, F., Castro, J. C. L., Manzi, R., Safatle, V., & Afshar, Y. (2020). O sujeito e a ordem do mercado: gênese teórica do neoliberalismo. In V. Saflatle, N. da Silva Junior, & C. Dunker (Eds.), *Neoliberalismo como gestão do sofrimento psíquico* (pp. 47–76). Autêntica.

Friedman, M., & Friedman, R. (1980). *Liberdade de escolher*. Record.

Fuks, M. (2011). Efeitos diretos, indiretos e tardios: trajetórias da transmissão intergeracional da participação política. *Lua Nova: Revista de Cultura e Política, 83*, 145–178.

Gabatz, C. (2018). Idiossincrasias religiosas contemporâneas: Qual o lugar das mulheres nas Igrejas Neopentecostais? *Revista Pistis Praxis, 10*(1).

Gaborit, M. (2011). Memória histórica: reverter a história a partir das vítimas. In R. S. Guzzo & F. Lacerna Júnior (Eds.), *Psicologia Social para América Latina: o resgate da Psicologia da Libertação*. Alínea.

Gagnebin, J. M. (2010). O preço de uma reconciliação extorquida. In E. Telles & V. Safatle (Eds.), *O que resta da ditadura*. Boitempo.

Hall, S. (2000). Quem precisa da identidade? In T. T. Silva (Ed.), *Identidade e diferença: a perspectiva dos estudos culturais* (pp. 103–133). Vozes.

Havertz, R. (2019). Right-wing populism and neoliberalism in Germany: The AfD's embrace of ordoliberalism. *New Political Economy, 24*(3), 385–403.

Hilmar, T. (2023). Restoring economic pride? How right-wing populists moralize economic change. *Journal of Contemporary European Studies, 31*(2), 291–305.

Huhle, R. (2016). Human rights education and historical learning. In C. Lenz, S. Brattland, & L. Kvande (Eds.), *Crossing borders. Combining human rights education and history education* (pp. 209–225). LIT.

Hunter, J. D. (1991). *Culture wars: The struggle to define America*. Basic Books.

Igreja, R. L. (2021). Populism, inequality, and the construction of the "other": An anthropological approach to the far right in Brazil. *Vibrant: Virtual Brazilian Anthropology, 18*, e18802.

Kehl, M. R. (2010). Tortura e Sintoma Social. In E. Telles & V. Safatle (Eds.), *O que resta da ditadura*. Boitempo.

Kemper, A. (2014). *Keimzelle der Nation – Teil 2. Wie sich in Europa Parteien und Bewegungen für konservative Familienwerte, gegen Toleranz und Vielfalt und gegen eine progressive Geschlechterpolitik radikalisieren*. Frieedrich-Ebert-Stiftung. Forum Politik und Gesellschaft. Retrieved from http://library.fes.de/pdf-files/dialog/11163.pdf

Keyser, E. (1935). Bevölkerungswissenschaft und Geschichtsforschung. *Archiv für Bevölkerungswissenschaft und Bevölkerungspolitik, 5*, 1–8.

Krasteva, A. (2013). L'e-citoyenneté – le projet politique de la révolution numérique. In A. Krasteva (Ed.), *E-citoyennetés* (pp. 11–22). Harmattan.

Krasteva, A. (2016). Occupy Bulgaria or the emergence of post-communist contestatory citizenship. *Southeastern Europe, 40*(2), 158–187.

Krasteva, A. (2017). Re/De/constructing far-right youth. In G. Lazaridis & G. Campani (Eds.), *Understanding the populist shift: Othering in a Europe in crisis* (pp. 150–178). Routledge.
Leconte, C. (2019). La carrière militante du «grand remplacement» au sein du milieu partisan de l'Alternative pour l'Allemagne (AfD). *Politix, 2*, 111–134.
Levi, N., & Rothberg, M. (2018). Memory studies in a moment of danger: Fascism, postfascism, and the contemporary political imaginary. *Memory Studies, 11*(3), 355–367. https://doi.org/10.1177/1750698018771868
Maranhão, E., Coelho, F., & Dias, T. (2018). "Fake news acima de tudo, fake news acima de todos": Bolsonaro e o "kit gay", "ideologia de gênero" e fim da "família tradicional". *Revista Eletrônica Correlatio, 17*(2), 65–90.
Mariano, R. (1995). *Neopentecostalismo: os pentecostais estao mudando* (Master's thesis, Universidade de São Paulo). Repositório USP. Retrieved from https://repositorio.usp.br/item/000744189
Markowitz, A. J., & Ryan, R. M. (2016). Father absence and adolescent depression and delinquency: A comparison of siblings approach. *Journal of Marriage and Family, 78*(5), 1300–1314.
Martín-Baró, I. (1989). La violencia política y la guerra como causas del trauma psicosocial. *Revista de Psicología de El Salvador, 9*(35), 89–108.
Mattheis, A. (2018). Shieldmaidens of whiteness: (Alt) Maternalism and women recruiting for the far/alt-right. *Journal for Deradicalization, 17*, 128–162.
Mbembe, A. (2020). *Necropolítica*. Melusina.
Meiering, D., Dziri, A., & Foroutan, N. (2020). Connecting structures: Resistance, heroic masculinity and anti-feminism as bridging narratives within group radicalization. *International Journal of Conflict and Violence (IJCV), 14*(2), 1–19. https://doi.org/10.4119/IJCV-3805
Moraes, P. M., Nunes, R., Horst, C. H. M., & Mioto, R. C. T. (2020). Familismo e política social: aproximações com as bases da formação sócio-histórica brasileira. *Revista de Políticas Públicas da UFMA, 24*, 802–818.
Mulinari, D., & Neergaard, A. (2015). Racist dreams and municipal budgets: Women representing a culturally racist party in local politics. *Social Identities, 21*(5), 506–523.
Muniz, J. D. O., & Proença Júnior, D. (2013). Armamento é Direitos Humanos: nossos fins, os meios e seus modos. *Sociedade e Estado, 28*, 119–141.
Netto, M. N., Cavalcante, S. M., & Chaguri, M. M. (2019). O homem médio e o conservadorismo liberal no Brasil contemporâneo: o lugar da família. *Anais do 43° Encontro Anual da ANPOCS*.
Nussbaum, M. C. (2013). *Political emotions*. Harvard University Press.
Oliveira, D. D. (2011). Cidade Alerta: jornalismo policial, vigilância e violência. In I. M. M. Gomes (Ed.), *Gêneros Televisivos e Modos de Endereçamento no Telejornalismo* (Vol. 1). EDUFBA.
Panetta, V. J. (2017). O mercado de armas de fogo no Brasil: Legislação, características da indústria e lobby armamentista. [Undergraduate thesis, Universidade Estadual de Campinas]. Biblioteca Digital Unicamp. Retrieved from https://repositorio.unicamp.br/Busca/Download?codigoArquivo=513732
Pereira, M. H. F. (2015). Nova direita? Guerras de memória em tempos de Comissão da Verdade (2012-2014). *Varia Historia, 31*(57), 863–902. https://doi.org/10.1590/0104-87752015000300008
Pinto Neto, M., & Cipriani, M. (2021). Populismo Autoritário e Bolsonarismo Popular: caminhos comparados do punitivismo a partir de Stuart Hall. *Revista de criminologias contemporâneas, 1*(1), 41–56.
Pinwinkler, A. (2004). Volk, Bevölkerung, Rasse, and Raum: Erich Keyser's ambiguous concept of a German history of population, ca. 1918-1955. In I. Haar & M. Fahlbusch (Eds.), *German scholars and ethnic cleansing 1920-1945* (pp. 86–99). Berghahn Books.
Puwar, N. (2004). *Space invaders: Race, gender and bodies out of place*. Berg.
Quadros, M. P. R. (2014). Neoconservadorismo e direita religiosa nos Estados Unidos: Formação ideológica, "guerra cultural" e política externa. *Espaço Plural, 15*(31), 43–61.
Quadros, M. P. R. (2017). Conservadorismo coroado: movimentos monarquistas no Brasil atual. *Estudos de sociologia, 22*(42).
Rocha, S. (2011). O programa Bolsa Família: evolução e efeitos sobre a pobreza. *Economia e Sociedade, 20*, 113–139.

Rocha, C. (2019). *"Menos Marx, mais Mises": uma gênese da nova direita brasileira (2006-2018).* [Doctoral dissertation, Universidade de São Paulo]. Biblioteca Digital USP. Retrieved from https://www.teses.usp.br/teses/disponiveis/8/8131/tde-19092019-174426/pt-br.php

Rogers, E. M., & Sebald, H. (1962). A distinction between familism, family integration, and kinship orientation. *Marriage and Family Living, 24*(1), 25–30.

Romão, D. M. M. (2013). *Jornalismo policial: indústria cultural e violência* [Dissertação de Mestrado, Instituto de Psicologia, Universidade de São Paulo].

Roy, N. (2022). *"We are just normal women": Narratives of far-right women members of the AfD and FPÖ.* [Doctoral dissertation, University of York]. White Rose eTheses. Retrieved from https://etheses.whiterose.ac.uk/33153/1/Roy_FinalThesis_CentreforWomensStudies.pdf

Sabogal, F., Marín, G., Otero-Sabogal, R., Marín, B. V., & Perez-Stable, E. J. (1987). Hispanic familism and acculturation: What changes and what doesn't? *Hispanic Journal of Behavioral Sciences, 9*(4), 397–412.

Safatle, V. (2020). A economia é a continuação da psicologia por outros meios: sofrimento psíquico e o neoliberalismo como economia moral. In V. Safatle, N. da Silva Junior, & C. Dunker (Eds.), *Neoliberalismo como gestão do sofrimento psíquico* (Vol. 1). Autêntica.

Safatle, W., da Silva Junior, N., & Dunker, C. (2020). *Neoliberalismo como gestão do sofrimento psíquico.* Autêntica.

Sakki, I., & Pettersson, K. (2016). Discursive constructions of otherness in populist radical right political blogs. *European Journal of Social Psychology, 46*(2), 156–170.

Santos, C. A. M. (2018). *O Sonho Colonial do III Reich: A Influência Nacional-Socialista na América Latina.* [Master's thesis, Universidade Nova de Lisboa]. Repositório RUN. Retrieved from https://run.unl.pt/handle/10362/60855

Santos, F. R. C. (2020). O que se entende por Retórica da Guerra Cultural. *Domínios de Lingu@gem.* https://doi.org/10.14393/DL45-v15n1a2021-6

Santos, V. O. A. (2024). *"Mais bala pela vida": O discurso punitivo da bancada da bala sobre o controle do crime e a resolução dos problemas criminais no Brasil* [Doctoral dissertation, Universidade de São Paulo]. Repositório USP. Retrieved from https://repositorio.usp.br/item/003198048

Saunders, R. A. (2019). Of gods and men: Uses and abuses of neo-paganism by nationalist movements in the "north". In S. Halink (Ed.), *Northern myths, modern identities.* Brill. https://doi.org/10.1163/9789004398436_009

Scheliga, E. L. (2012). *Educando sentidos, orientando uma práxis - etnografia das práticas assistenciais de evangélicos brasileiros.* [Doctoral dissertation, Universidade de São Paulo]. Biblioteca Digital USP. Retrieved from https://doi.org/10.11606/T.8.2011.TDE-10052012-084930

Shafir, I. P. (2005). *Obstinaciones de La Memoria: La dictadura militar chilena en las tramas del recuerdo.* [Doctoral dissertation, Universidad Autónoma de Barcelona]. CORA. Retrieved from https://www.tesisenred.net/handle/10803/5444

Sparemberger, C., Lobo, I. E., & da Silva, I. C. (2021). A nova direita e as guerras culturais: um estudo de caso da atuação de Ana Campagnolo no Facebook. *Em Tese, 18*(2), 196–213.

Stockemer, D., Niemann, A., Unger, D., & Speyer, J. (2020). The "refugee crisis," immigration attitudes, and euroscepticism. *International Migration Review, 54*(3), 883–912.

Teixeira, J. M. (2019). *A conduta universal: governo de si e políticas de gênero na Igreja Universal do Reino de Deus.* [Doctoral dissertation, Universidade de São Paulo]. Biblioteca Digital USP. Retrieved from https://doi.org/10.11606/T.8.2019.TDE-30052019-103135

Teles, E. (2018). A produção do inimigo e a insistência do Brasil violento e de exceção. In E. Solano (Ed.), *Ódio como política.* Boitempo.

Volk, S. (2020). "Wir sind das Volk!" Representative claim-making and populist style in the PEGIDA movement's discourse. *German Politics, 29*(4), 599–616.

Wahl, K. (2020). *The radical right: Biopsychosocial roots and international variations.* Palgrave Macmillan.

Warner, M. (2002). Publics and counterpublics. *Public Culture, 14*(1), 49–90.

Wodak, R. (2015). *The politics of fear: What right-wing populist discourses mean.* Sage.

Wodak, R., & Reisigl, M. (2015). Discourse and racism. In D. Tannen, H. E. Hamilton, & D. Schiffrin (Eds.), *The handbook of discourse analysis* (pp. 576–596). Wiley.

Zuquete, J. P. (2018). *The Identitarians.* University of Notre Dame Press.

Chapter 6
Final Considerations

The research presented in this book was developed during the period from 2019 to 2023, in which the two countries studied—Brazil and Germany—experienced elections and changes in the composition of the Executive and Legislative powers. The changes may have represented transformations in the experience of those living in these countries; however, at a macro and global level, the news about radicalization and the emergence of new "extremist" groups and movements does not stop. The tone remains pessimistic, given the victory of leaders associated with the radical right in other countries around the world. By highlighting this fact, I seek only to emphasize that the choice to research an ongoing phenomenon—which perhaps makes the investigation more relevant—also means a huge challenge.

Given the objective of analysing and comparing the discourses, identities, and meanings of the political participation of young people in the radical right of Brazil and Germany, I needed to accept the limits and potentials of my choices. I was accompanied by the constant doubt about whether I would be able to get the interviews, if they were sufficient, if they were representative, if they met ethical demands, as well as if I would be able to write something that respected the time and the "stories" provided by my interviewees. Upon reaching the end, I can admire the path and understand that the process of constructing and executing the research involved courage and curiosity. Not only that, it also required dedication to maintain methodological rigor and promote dialogue and interdisciplinary articulation. Consequently, this book also constituted an invitation to traverse and visualize such a path.

In the first chapter, I was able to reference those who came before me and paved the way for research like this. In a movement of critical literature review, I revisited the tortuous paths of the (in)definition about the phenomenon of the expansion of groups, actors, movements, parties, and leaders that present as common characteristics the attack on the guarantee of minority rights, as well as the State as a regulator of social inequalities. Unlike the past, such groups have invested in integrating into democratic processes and changing them "from within", presenting themselves

B. Besen, *Youth Activism in the Radical Right of Brazil and Germany*,
https://doi.org/10.1007/978-3-031-87635-6_6

with agendas that are not recognized as democratic by the entire universe of those who are "outside". Such groups, in their position—whether as a counterpublic, as Rocha (2019) identified, or as a countermovement, as the interviewees themselves presented—have been able to discursively conform the public sphere, so that, in recent years, they have gained a permanent place in the media and academia, as well as in everyday conversations.

Anchored in the body of Latin American and European research, I also justified the theoretical decision to designate these groups as "direitas radicais", translated here as "radical right", highlighting their plurality and the processes of radicalization. This choice, during the preparation of this book, gained even more consistency. It was also in this chapter that I discussed the particularity of using the biographical narratives of young activists as a lens for the phenomenon. In the face of a broad tradition of quantitative studies that scrutinized electoral behaviour, activism studies have employed a new tradition that—with the leadership of researchers like Anna Krasteva, Cynthia Miller-Idriss, Agnieszka Pasieka, and Rosana Pinheiro-Machado—indicated a greater sensitivity to the nuances of the phenomenon through the adoption of qualitative methods. Furthermore, a universe of ethnographic studies—conducted both in the Brazilian and European contexts—already pointed to a complex constellation of subjectivities that reflected hope and despair (Jarrín et al., 2022) as coexisting affects.

Thus, theoretically based on post-structuralism and Foucaultian power analytics, I focused on the trajectories and narratives of young activists from the radical right in Brazil and Germany, seeking to identify the processes of political subjectivation and discursive interpellation. The reconstructions (Rosenthal, 2004) were a methodological choice, but the fact of recording them in the book was also an invitation to get close to them. This was important because, during the research and in dialogue with peers, I noticed that many had formed a shell, through which they shielded themselves from any contact with what seemed irreconcilable with their worldviews. In other words, with the help of algorithms, many began to listen to and interpret the radical right only through what arrived in terms of news about the leaders or comments from those positioned in their political spectrum, or at least outside what was recognized as a "far-right field".

Thus, the reconstruction of the trajectories of young activists was done with the care of anonymization, but with the concern of being faithful to the complexity of participation trajectories, which revealed diverse constellations of conflicts, levels of engagement, and identities. Through the trajectories, different meanings of political participation also manifested, which emerged as a source of upward social mobility, a form of social integration, a strong family bond, the denial of a predetermined future, a proof of nobility, an act of rebellion, an attempt to order the world, a validation of knowledge, a (re)elaboration of the marks of a country's division, and a search for security and a religious mission. Differentiating them had an analytical function, but the immersion and reading of the reconstructions allow us to see that this universe of meanings also mixes and interpenetrates in individual experiences and trajectories.

Among the trajectories, "marks" of the differences between the systems of education in the countries were noted, also stemming from the different welfare regimes. These particularities were identified in the practices of political participation. While in Brazil, the young interviewees showed themselves to be extremely concerned with presenting themselves as dedicated students and avid readers, whose career choice could also reflect the political trajectory; in Germany, the young people expressed their desire to pursue private careers, finding in the institutional spaces of organizations linked to parties a practice of everyday political participation.

Overall, the biographies articulated with the literature indicated that many of the practices identified and highlighted by the young people in their trajectories are part of a normativity that defines conditions for formal participation in the twenty-first century. Centred on the discourse about "youth protagonism", political groups began to need young people "on board" to legitimize their projects. By submitting to such an order, these young people achieve the necessary recognition to present their agendas—even those attacking minorities—in the public sphere, interpreted in this book as both physical and digital spaces of appearance (Butler, 2015).

With this background and considering that young people constantly move between practices recognized and not recognized as democratic participation, I proposed to understand this participation as "liminal". The *liminality* also refers to post-structuralist studies that emphasize the movement and instability of the subject, who, in the face of the interpellation of a set of discourses, will be able to perform particular and effective "identity collages". In other words, the *liminality* is also based on the recognition of the practical efficacy of identities, which—at this historical moment—can ensure greater proximity to the spaces of power and deliberation in society.

Advancing in the book, we enter the fifth chapter, which centred on the grammar of projects and political participation in the radical right. On one hand, it sought to list what the signifiers were, that, together, formed the regimes of representation and truth. On the other hand, it sought to understand what the "discursive positions" were and, consequently, the "places" offered to such young people within the movements. Thus, the categories were presented, based on the (de)construction of narratives, coding, and research of term recurrence in the transcriptions. The choice for this perspective leads to some fundamental differences compared to the universe of research already conducted on the phenomenon. By adopting a discursive approach, I chose not to operate with the concept of ideology as a falsification of reality, that is, I worked with the concept of "systems of representation". Avoiding relativism, the proposed analysis adopted a critical dimension, seeking to recognize power relations and reveal the archaeology of perspectives taken as truth, also revealing how unjust and oppressive social conditions become reified as "historical data".

Firstly, the recurrence and intensity of the theme of "family" within the narratives of young people in both countries were identified. Through the analysis of the narratives, it was understood that there was a variety of approaches to the theme, which found a common ground in the discourse about the attack on the centrality and ordering of the family in societies, promoted by the left and LGBTQIA+ and feminist movements. Taking as reference the works of Dardot and Laval (2016),

Cooper (2017), and Brown (2019), I conducted an analysis of the normativities related to the formation of such discourse. By revisiting a genealogy of conservative social and neoliberal discourse, I arrived at the interpretation that the synthesis of this encounter occurs primarily in the promotion of the family preservation agenda. Positioning it as a referential space, its relationships are read as not based on power but on love and duty.

This understanding required an inversion, in which neoliberal normativity is understood as a response to the destabilization operated by the movements fighting for minority rights, which propose and support new family structures, destabilizing the existing power relations. The family becomes protected because—for neoliberals—it will be the space for the transfer of state responsibilities. In contrast—and as a demand of social conservatives—the state must ensure the "moral order" necessary for the construction and preservation of traditional families.

In this chapter, I also explained how moments of "crisis" were and continue to be fundamental for reinforcing this alliance between conservatives and neoliberals, through a moralization and pathologization of experiences. In the Brazilian case, descriptions of the "gay kit" episode were identified in the narratives of young people, as well as attacks on state redistribution programmes. As a discursive strategy, it is said that the state cannot act as a "father": It is not the one who can give orders or provide sustenance for those who do not work. However, this patriarchal order can and should be established and reiterated within the family sphere.

In the German case, "familism" emerged in the narratives of young people through the discourse on political projects to "save", "protect", and "prioritize" the German people. I highlighted the rise of the "great replacement" theory, which is based on a *völkisch* (racial nationalist) discourse, defending the German family against a gradual "elimination" of the supposed original white Christian European population (Meiering et al., 2020). Also, as a particularity of the German context, ordoliberalism was analysed—as a neoliberal European solution—which prescribes a regulatory structure for the economy centred on creating a competitive order—based on the preservation of the "law of the market", with the aim of producing and justifying social differences (Havertz, 2019). In the discourse of the radical right, the economic differentiation system establishes itself as a system of differentiation of nation, ethnicity, and religion, synthesized in the term "culture". It is through this regime of representation that the young interviewees present immigrants and refugees as "competition", emphasizing that they are not the adequate solution for the lack of qualified labour in the country.

Bringing together the narratives of the two countries, I also discussed the existence of movements of "preservation through transformation", that is, the creation of new structures that "accommodate" what could previously be a "deviation" within the radical right. Now, homosexuals and women also identify and have a place in the groups, just as families formed by gays and lesbians can be legitimized. In a movement interpreted as an "accommodation", the participation of minorities within the movements, groups, and parties has expanded, with an order given by a simple discursive formation: "there is a place for everyone, but everyone must stay in their place". An active search is made by the radical right to "conquer" minorities; however, their entry entails the task of being spokespersons for specific agendas and issues. Through the narratives accessed in the research and anchored in a universe of research on the entry of women and LGBT people into politics, I highlighted that defined places and agendas are offered to these groups. As a main feature of the interviews and the observation of social networks, I identified the anti-feminist and anti-gender agenda being delegated and assumed by young women.

In the case of the Brazilian radical right, I also highlighted that the trajectories—mainly of young women—can be influenced by neo-Pentecostal evangelical churches. Dantas (2013) contributes to the identification of a political project of church expansion through conversion, in which the faithful gain a religious mission, consisting of the fight against "demonization", identified in the left and feminist movements. In a complex manner, church spaces provide protagonism to women; however, they define motherhood and care as especially feminine functions and "gifts". Following this logic, women are also assigned careers in the field of psychology and social assistance, which, inserted in the context of institutions now managed by religious groups, provide a privileged place for the dissemination of disciplinary prescriptions for subjects in situations of social vulnerability. Within the neo-Pentecostal logic, the mission of evangelization and conversion seems to translate—in the trajectory of these young women—into the commitment to "spread the word" even further, using social networks as a platform for the dissemination of anti-feminism and the pro-life agenda.

In the German context, I evidenced that religion did not have the same prominence, being presented as a "source of references". For the analysis of this discursive positioning, I used the concept of cultural Christianity (Stockemer et al., 2020), which refers to the emphasis on Christian symbols, traditions, and values as markers of national or cultural identity rather than a strict adherence to religious doctrine or institutionalized faith. This demonstrates a practical effectiveness of such discourse that constructs a direct opposition between Christianity and Islam as parts of a "natural and national culture".

Reflecting on the ways of constituting the national, I also addressed the (ab)uses of local and global memory for the legitimation of the radical right-wing political projects. In the Brazilian case, the memory of the Brazilian military dictatorship is formed by the recognition of the existence of torture, accompanied by the legitimation of such violations through the construction of the "internal enemy" that needs to be contained. Still in the Brazilian case, I discussed the particularity of monarchism, which also sustains itself on the discourse about the communist threat but seeks to evoke the idealization of the Brazilian parliamentary-monarchical period. In both cases, it is asserted that, in the face of the present moral crisis, there is a past to be referenced.

In the German case, however, a well-established glorious past is not identified, but a native identity, which is unified by the discourse of accusation about the maintenance of an unjust social recognition structure, which could be repaired through projects of privilege for German citizens who have the real desire to work but not the opportunities. In light of the marks left by the reunification in 1989, resentment is built—mainly in former East Germany—due to the "denied recognition". Through the (ab)uses of memory, there is, as a similarity between Brazil and Germany, the construction of the Others, those who are positioned as impediments to the realization or threats to the promised "economic pride" (Hilmar, 2023).

Moving towards a deeper analysis of the construction of the Other, narratives about the anti-immigration agenda, defended by all the young people interviewed in the German context, were explored. Such construction has been interpreted in the literature, centrally, as a product of a politics of fear (Wahl, 2020); however, in this book, other complementary analytical keys were presented, which concern discursive articulations. The set of discourses was interpreted as attribution (Wodak, 2015), understood as a mechanism that is part of a cultural(ist) racism, in which characteristics and stereotypes are attributed to a specific group based on their ethnic and/or religious origins. Through this process, the idea of the group's inferiority is perpetuated, justifying their exclusion, marginalization, or discrimination. Unlike the Brazilians, the young people interviewed in Germany still direct their demands to the State, pointing out the need for the government to control and restrict immigration and refugee policy.

Through the identification of the "cultural strangers" (*kulturfremden*) vs. "normals" duality presented in Germany, I was also able to discuss the "criminals" vs. "law-abiding citizens" duality used in the Brazilian context. The category "law-abiding citizen" appeared in the narratives of young Brazilian activists as a way to support the civil gun ownership agenda. Such discursive representation presents itself as "homogenizing and enigmatic" (Costa, 2021), highlighting the limited conditions of access to citizenship in the country. Regarding the civil gun ownership agenda, it was also evidenced that the positioning of the weapon as a symbol of power and social coercion is connected to the process of militarization of life in Brazil (Safatle & Teles, 2019), which reflects a public security doctrine whose origin dates back to the military regime (1964–1985). Supported by the diagnosis of the State's failures in providing public security, the idea that the weapon enables "taking justice into one's own hands" is legitimized.

Through the analysis of the recurrent use of the signifier "people" as well as the use of the term *Völk* and *Bevölkerung* in the German context, I analysed that the formation of the threatening Other is only possible with a frequent use of generalizations and an absence of reference to power relations. In the universe of the most recurrent signifiers, terms such as justice, inequality, oppression, and poverty, among others that were central in the formation of the grammar of politics, even within traditional right-wing circles, were not identified. The grammar of the radical right also seems to include madness as a—not new but revisited—category of social pathologization. The discourse about the madness and degeneration of society seems to function as an important call for the urgency and radicality of action. In the case of the analysed narratives, it is society and youth that are interpreted through the lens of pathologization and, consequently, the inability to make rational choices. In such a scenario, the call for coercive forces and violent actions, which would override the inability of "decision-making" by people, becomes more legitimate.

Both in the dimension of trajectories and narratives, that is, both at the level of subjectivation processes and interpellation, an element emerged as crucial: defining oneself through opposition or by being "against" something. The individual experiences of injustice and the collective discourses of antagonism—from which activists and the collective movement have acquired an identity—proved to be key pieces for the organization of society in a binary logic. The "law-abiding citizens" vs. "criminals" and the "cultural strangers" vs. "normals" are immediately located in a political polarity that has been translated as right vs. left (and Greens in Germany). In this sense, the last section of the book sought to highlight that the fissure of resistance may reside in identifying the limit of such "totalizing" representations and identities, accounting for subjects in their multiplicity. I sought to demonstrate that young people experience, in their daily lives, the intersections of power relations, oppression, and marginalization. In both societies and contexts studied, they are still the most victimized by socioeconomic contradictions. It is still within the age group of the interviewees that the worst unemployment rates are found, and young people are still the major victims of violence. I do not intend to portray them as victims now but rather to highlight that, in many of the trajectories and narratives, there are experiences that cannot be "articulated" within the chain of signification offered by radical right-wing groups. Moreover, the desire to live "a good life" in such circumstances also produces anxiety and fear. The conditions of precariousness and violence produced structurally—which promote the sensation of an empty future (Albino et al., 2021)—are denounced through the description of injustices in the distribution of power and the emphasis given by young people to the need to be actors of social change.

It is for this reason that I point out that the gap is particularly located in what "remains" and "escapes" from totalizing representation networks. As the post-structuralist tradition has reinforced, signs have inexhaustible possibilities of signification and can only gain a particular—provisional and incomplete—meaning in a determined significant context. The analysis revealed that the context provided these young people with contingent meanings for their conflicts, with identification also involving negotiation with their particular trajectories. When we consider that these identifications are not closed, a place of action emerges, which can only occur in an intersubjective process, which produces the destabilization of discursive chains through the presentation and constitution of multiple political projects. Hall states that subjects find themselves "in a constant and agonistic process of struggling against, resisting, negotiating, and accommodating to the regulatory or normative orders with which they are confronted and which regulate them" (Hall, 1996, p. 13).

I still believe, as Bhabha (1996) points out, that resistance emerges in the field of intersubjectivity, that is, in the field of relationship and language. The theorist states that rarely does a real intervention occur through the presentation of a competing system of representation. He points out that there are border places—thresholds and edges—that allow subjects to move outside totalizing systems, occupying, even if momentarily, positions where it is possible to visualize the fragmentary and incomplete nature of the adopted representation systems. As much as Bhabha goes to the limit, saying that there is no control in this process, I believe that his observation is an important inspiration for understanding that we do not have to "teach" a competing system of representation. It is necessary to invest in what remains, what exceeds, and what does not fit, something that emerges in the field of exchange, which needs to have space in the public sphere.

Currently, the need to identify and position oneself has been called upon by both radical right-wing and left-wing groups, in a threat that "not taking a position is being complicit". However, more than positioning, this book calls for and questions the conditions of dialogue that have been promoted for and by young people outside a binary political identification logic. Admitting the risk of such a statement, I argue that the public sphere should be less conformed and constituted by the recognition of identities, allowing those who have not yet positioned themselves to be brought into dialogue. This means providing space and openness for new places to be inaugurated and explored. This does not dismiss the importance and advances that have been achieved by movements guaranteeing minority rights and based on differences; the defence is for the public sphere to also provide recognition and space for those who are exploring and learning—especially when we refer to young people.

The reconstruction of trajectories allowed for the visualization of engagement as a process, in which the discursive interpellation of radical right-wing groups occurs gradually and is always based on antagonism. I could observe, through narratives and social networks themselves, that radical right-wing groups have created and provided spaces for dialogue, which start from greater diversity but tend to "narrow" and consequently radicalize. I consider that, even at the level of public policies, it is possible to act throughout these processes. This requires, first and foremost, conducting research that explores the socialization spaces of these young people, whether digital or in person, and investigates the formation of dialogue and exchange groups. Furthermore, it seems fundamental to expand the field of qualitative, mixed, and comparative investigations on the phenomenon. I know that, at the digital level, exploration is more advanced, but, as presented here, the in-person space—including the streets—has gained importance in engagement.

I also highlight that a presupposition for such research should be that these young people are subjects to whom one should and can speak, as well as should and can listen. I quoted Galeano at the beginning of this book because I believe we share admiration and respect for the contradiction that is in others, as well as in ourselves. Thus, I hope that those who reach the end of this reading have also found something different and unexpected along the way and that this converts into greater curiosity about what "escapes" or is beyond their convictions. I do not ignore that this path also involves encountering dimensions of the uncanny, but I emphasize that this uncanny should not be interpreted as an individual disposition. Here, it revealed itself as part and effect of reiterated and strengthened normativities, which rely on discourses and representation systems that conceal and sustain oppressive power relations.

It is up to us—researchers, militants, and activists—to continue fighting to highlight and denounce these inequalities, sustaining social justice as a fundamental horizon of politics, and negotiation and dialogue as conditions of political action. I understand that there is breath and interest in continuing to investigate radical right-wing groups, in order to constitute a body of knowledge that allows the construction of democratic solutions. The formations of local and global knowledge are important tools, which also depend on the articulation of transnational alliance networks aimed at the exchange of knowledge and strategies in terms of tools against radicalization.

When we think about youth, it seems fundamental to consider the learning and transformation processes experienced in recent years. I do not believe there is a place to return to, that is, the transformations and impacts of the emergence and expansion of radical right-wing movements will not be annulled, nor will we return to a state similar to that shaped by the democratic pact experienced in the post-war period, in the German case, or in the post-military dictatorship period, in the Brazilian case. We will continue to need to (re/de)construct from contradictions, seeking breath for creative proposition and for the recovery of utopia. In the face of widespread pessimism—also deepened among leftist youth—I would like to conclude this book with notes of hope, a hope based on the belief that paths are never closed, but it is not enough to wait, it is necessary to act and walk. However, on this journey, we will not only need those who are like us. We need to rebuild dialogue and bridges even with those whom, at some point, we considered to be our radical opposites.

References

Albino, C., Oliveira, J., & Melo, M. (2021). *Neoliberalismo, neoconservadorismo e crise em tempos sombrios*. Editora Seriguela.

Bhabha, H. (1996). Culture's in-between. In S. Hall & P. du Gay (Eds.), *Questions of cultural identity* (pp. 53–60). Sage.

Brown, W. (2019). *In the ruins of neoliberalism: The rise of antidemocratic politics in the west*. Columbia University Press. https://doi.org/10.7312/brow19384

Butler, J. (2015). *Notes toward a performative theory of assembly*. Harvard University Press.

Cooper, M. (2017). *Family values: Between neoliberalism and the new social conservatism*. MIT Press.

Costa, J. F. A. (2021). Quem é o 'cidadão de bem'? *Psicologia USP, 32*, e190106.

Dantas, B. S. D. A. (2013). Psicologia política das religiões: uma análise dos símbolos e ideologias da Igreja Universal do Reino de Deus. *Revista Psicologia Política, 13*(28), 489–506.

Dardot, P., & Laval, C. (2016). *A nova razão de mundo: ensaio sobre a sociedade neoliberal*. Boitempo.

Hall, S. (1996). The west and the rest: Discourse and power. *Revista Brasileira de Ciências Sociais, 21*(60).

Havertz, R. (2019). Right-wing populism and neoliberalism in Germany: The AfD's embrace of ordoliberalism. *New Political Economy, 24*(3), 385–403.

Hilmar, T. (2023). Restoring economic pride? How right-wing populists moralize economic change. *Journal of Contemporary European Studies, 31*(2), 291–305.

Jarrín, A., Junge, B., Mitchell, S., Cantero, L., & Biondi, K. (Eds.). (2022). *Democracia Precária: etnografias de esperança, desespero e resistência no Brasil*. Zouk.

Meiering, D., Dziri, A., & Foroutan, N. (2020). Connecting structures: Resistance, heroic masculinity and anti-feminism as bridging narratives within group radicalization. *International Journal of Conflict and Violence (IJCV), 14*(2), 1–19. https://doi.org/10.4119/IJCV-3805

Rocha, C. (2019). "Menos Marx, mais Mises": uma gênese da nova direita brasileira. [Doctoral dissertation, Universidade de São Paulo]. Biblioteca Digital USP. Retrieved from https://www.teses.usp.br/teses/disponiveis/8/8131/tde-19092019-174426

Rosenthal, G. (2004). Biographical research. In C. Seale et al. (Eds.), *Qualitative research practice* (pp. 48–64). Sage.

Safatle, V., & Teles, E. (2019). *O que resta da ditadura: a exceção brasileira*. Boitempo Editorial.

Stockemer, D., Niemann, A., Unger, D., & Speyer, J. (2020). The 'refugee crisis,' immigration attitudes, and euroscepticism. *International Migration Review, 54*(3), 883–912.

Wahl, K. (2020). *The radical right: Biopsychosocial roots and international variations*. Palgrave Macmillan.

Wodak, R. (2015). *The politics of fear: What right-wing populist discourses mean*. Sage.

Index

B. Besen, *Youth Activism in the Radical Right of Brazil and Germany*,
https://doi.org/10.1007/978-3-031-87635-6

The manufacturer's authorised representative in the EU is Springer Nature Customer Service Centre GmbH, Europaplatz 3, 69115 Heidelberg, Germany. If you have any concerns regarding our products, please contact ProductSafety@springernature.com

Printed and bound by CPI Group (UK) Ltd, Croydon, CR0 4YY
01/10/2026
02225956-0002